The Tide
is Turning
Toward Catholicism

David J. Hartline

CATHOLIC
REPORT

Scripture verses contained herein are from the St. Joseph Edition of the New American Bible, New York, 1970; Revised 1992

Catholic Report
P.O. Box 775
Worthington, OH 43085
Orders: (800) 932-3826
www.CatholicReport.org

Cover design: Ted Schluenderfritz

Printed in the United States of America

ISBN-10: 0-9790732-0-0
ISBN-13: 978-0-9790732-0-5

TABLE OF CONTENTS

DEDICATION

This book is dedicated to:

My treasure (cf., Lk. 12:34), my precious wife Theresa, without whose support you would not be holding this book in your hands. Her love, guidance, humor, and attention to detail – not to mention her prodigious editing skills – were heaven sent. God has graced me with many gifts and blessings in my life, but she is the greatest I have ever received.

My parents David and Hilde Hartline, who taught me to love God and follow His ways.

My sister Renate, who tragically left this world at age 16. In her short life, she taught us all many lessons, especially ones on faith.

Finally, this book is dedicated to all the men and women who labor in the vineyards for the Church and faithfully do her work.

ACKNOWLEDGMENTS

As I wrote in my dedication, I owe a profound debt to my wife Theresa and my parents David and Hilde Hartline, each of whom has taught me to love God more perfectly and follow His ways more closely.

A special thanks to my friends Drs. Peter and Suzanne Schuler and Rick Schuler, who provided invaluable feedback on the manuscript. Former colleagues and friends Mark Butler, Jeri Rod, and Ed Zettler all viewed portions of the manuscript and provided their insight, as well. Tom Nash of Catholics United for the Faith and Protestants Rich Rojas and author Jedd Medefind helped fill in the blanks on several issues.

Amy Welborn and Michael Dubruiel helped me get the ball rolling with their initial support of the article that inspired this book. They also helped encourage me in my belief that a book expanding on the article was needed. Carolyn Klika at Catholic Word did yeoman's work in helping to pull the book together, and I want to especially thank her colleague Brian O'Neel for his excellent editing and research and keeping me on point. Authors Tom Craughwell and Tim Drake gave advice that was very useful. Ted Schluenderfritz's artistic skills deserve a special thanks (see for yourself; he did the front cover and his other works are at www.5sparrows.com), as does Tom Weiland of StarWorks Marketing who did such an excellent job with the book's layout. Also deserving of mention is the wise Bill Koshelnyk, who generously steered me to many knowledgeable people.

Catholic bloggers Mark Shea and Gerald Augustinus have both linked to so many of my CatholicReport.org articles that they are probably a large part of the reason you are reading this book. Then there were the many people who kindly granted me interviews and provided me with their guidance: Bishops Frederick Campbell, Robert Carlson, Robert Kurtz, CR, and Fathers Bill Hahn and Jeff Rimmelspach. Additionally, sports personalities Gerry Faust, Lou Holtz, Rudy Ruettiger, and Dick Vitale provided countless insights. The following people also helped: Patrick Madrid, Msgr. Francis Maniscalco, Dan Mulhall, Candis LaPrade, Patrick Egbuchunam, Julie Nickell, Ramon Tancinco, Rob Schuler, Joel Torczon, Charles Flagherty, George Marlin, and Karl Keating, whose Catholic Answers site (http://www.catholic.com) gave me a wealth of insight and inspiration for my faith and this book. My gratitude also goes to Ken Collura, as well as Matt Dopkis and Bobby Whitman of dynamIt Technologies for their technical expertise. And where would this endeavor be if not for the loyal CatholicReport.org readers (who have helped me in this effort more than they will ever know)?

Finally and most importantly, I wanted to say that I owe it all to God and His many gifts. Indeed, it is hard to put into words a proper thank you for God the Father, Son, and Holy Spirit. And let's not forget that the article that inspired this book appeared (unwittingly) on the Feast of Our Lady of Guadalupe; she has blessed this project ever since.

May God use this meager work for His greater glory and to bring all of us closer to Him.

Here's what people are saying about *The Tide is Turning Toward Catholicism:*

With the scandals of recent years, all the so-called "Catholic" politicians, and the many threats to Catholic morality from cloning and other such scientific "advances," hopeful predictions for the future of the Catholic faith are often met with skepticism.

But David J. Hartline, editor of Catholic Report, a popular online journal, sees things differently. In his new book, The Tide Is Turning Towards Catholicism, *he makes a compelling case that the Church is gaining in strength and appeal, even in the so-called "post-Christian" West where secular materialism would appear to be the dominant philosophy.*

Hartline argues his case by noting such trends as young people returning to traditional beliefs and pious practices; a new wave of assertively Catholic schools, colleges and universities; impressive growth in books, periodicals, music and other expressions of Catholic popular culture; and even an increased willingness among Catholic public figures (especially athletes) to speak openly about their beliefs.

This highly readable book is an antidote to the doom and gloom that can discourage those of us who love the Church. It is timely and extremely welcome.

> ~ Tom Monaghan, founder, Ave Maria University

The Tide is Turning ... should give families the encouragement, resolve, and hope needed to combat the sinister forces in a society that is increasingly turning its back on God. Hartline's book serves to remind the faithful of Jesus' promise that the "gates of hell" will not prevail against Holy Mother Church.

> ~ Joel Torczon, Catholic writer and father

DAVID J. HARTLINE

This is one of the finest books I have ever read on Catholicism. It is full of facts as well as stories. I found it very thought provoking, and I learned new information not only about my faith but other faiths as well. Catholics need to read this good news book.
  ~ Gerry Faust, former Notre Dame football head coach

Over and over again I meet faithful Catholics who fall into despair thinking that the Catholic Church is "dying." Dave Hartline's book is thus a beaming light in the darkness. It shows the Holy Spirit is alive and active in bringing about a "New Pentecost" in the Holy Roman Catholic Church! This book provides hope, encourages zeal, and displays people's longing for the fullness of truth.
  ~ Dan DeMatte, star of the A&E Television Network's Catholic reality-themed show "God or the Girl."

The Tide is Turning Toward Catholicism *captures the positive efforts of many athletes and coaches as well as their good Christian values and the institutions they represent.*
  ~ Dick Vitale, former NCAA and NBA basketball coach, philanthropist, and ESPN analyst

Dave Hartline has his finger on the pulse of the Catholic Church. In The Tide is Turning ..., *he tells the largely untold story of a vibrant orthodoxy alive in Catholicism and how it is creating a wave that is just now peaking to engulf the universal Church. Hartline's book is an important study examining this rising phenomenon. The "wave" he describes is poised to wash over the Church entire, christening the Church anew with the cleansing, living waters of the Holy Spirit. Catholics had better hold on for the ride!*
  ~ Tim Drake, senior writer, National Catholic Register

THE TIDE IS TURNING TOWARD CATHOLICISM

St. Ignatius of Loyola tells us discouragement is never from God because it clouds faith and hope. Nonetheless, it is true that in today's world we can easily become discouraged by all the negative media reports on the Catholic Church. David Hartline provides us with an encouraging word. By way of inspiring stories and challenging details, he describes all the good things that are happening in the Catholic Church, the good news that normally passes "under the radar" of media reporting. The Tide is Turning ... shows how the Spirit of the Lord is alive in the Church, especially in the inspired initiatives of lay people whose efforts are leading the Church into what Pope John Paul II has called a "Springtime of New Evangelization." David Hartline's work has the power to move some of the clouds away from our faith and our hope as it challenges us to further reflection and discussion.

- His Excellency Robert Kurtz, CR, bishop of Bermuda

Since first visiting Dave Hartline's blog, Catholic Report, (and becoming hooked!), I have eagerly anticipated his book, The Tide is Turning Towards Catholicism.

In it, he examines why a spate of recent conversions, articulate Catholics, faith-seeking youngsters, vocations and many other signs signal hope to the once bare ruined choirs' of the American Catholic Church. The Catholic Church is the only Christian church today that traces directly back to Christ, yet we as Catholics are very frequently offered falsehoods and ridicule regarding our faith. The book addresses the familiar "Are you saved" question, the megachurch fad, and why the largest denomination on Earth keeps springing back from marginalization and persecution.

- Julie Nickell, rural Iowa homemaker and former journalist

INTRODUCTION

The idea for this book came to me during adoration of the Blessed Sacrament and is an extension of an article I wrote for my CatholicReport.org website. The night before I wrote this article, I thought, "Catholics need to hear all the 'under the radar' good news happening in the Catholic Church."

The following day, again during adoration, the words "the tide is turning towards ... Catholicism" came to me. I went home and wrote the article in about an hour. The next day, December 12, 2005, the Feast of Our Lady of Guadalupe, the article debuted on my CatholicReport.org website. It struck a chord with my wife. I e-mailed it to leading Catholic blogger, Amy Welborn.

Amy posted it on her "Open Book" site two days later, as did Catholic author and commentator Mark Shea on his "Catholic and Enjoying It!" blog. That same day, blogs with no discernible connection to Catholicism picked it up (e.g., the sports-oriented "Notre Dame Nation", presumably because the first paragraph mentioned the surging fortunes of Charlie Weis and Notre Dame).

The article took on a life of its own from there. On Fr. Richard John Neuhaus' blog at www.firstthings.com, Joseph Bottum commented on it. It even made the rounds of Catholic blogs in Britain and Australia. A sympathetic Anglican blog picked it up, and the blogger wrote they wished they could say the same thing about their communion.

Of course, not all comments were positive. A couple of atheist blogs mocked it, as did a few pundits on the blog of a liberal retired Episcopal Bishop.

It took a few weeks to decide that I should turn the article into a book. On January 31, 2006, I appeared with authors Michael Dubruiel and Amy Welborn at a talk at my parish. After a conversation with Michael, I decided that the book had to be written and fast. I started on it the next day, February 1, and completed the majority of it before Easter.

Great events are happening in the Catholic Church and many of them are going unnoticed or at least few are speaking of them. I hope this book will help those who read it to see to what extent this is true.

I have attempted to cover many topics in order to demonstrate how the tide is turning towards Catholicism, both generally and specifically. Furthermore, Catholics and people of other faith traditions want and need to hear good news about the Catholic Church, and knowing this good news will help them understand the Church's history, teachings, successes, and its future.

I promise you this: The developments we see today in the Church will encourage you. So will the stories of some amazing people who are faithfully working to spread the good news.

My hope and prayer is that this book will not only inform, but will help usher in the springtime of evangelization John Paul II predicted and thus will bolster faith and love for the Church in those who read it.

May God abundantly bless you and His beloved 'Bride of Christ,'* the Catholic Church.

---

*For those unfamiliar with it, the phrase "Bride of Christ" comes from St. Paul's second letter to the Corinthians, chapter 11. This is what he calls the Church. See also Ephesians 5 and the *Catechism of the Catholic Church*, nos. 796 and 808.

- CHAPTER 1 -

THE EVENTS OF APRIL 2005

During the last few years of Pope John Paul II's papacy, the whispers grew louder until they were practically shouts. Some suggested he should step down, claiming the Church needed a stronger leader. After all, the abuse scandal in America seemed to be sapping the Church's strength, and the scandal threatened to spread further. These were dark days for the Church, and many Catholics – even prominent ones such as Godfried Cardinal Danneels of Belgium and Karl Cardinal Lehman of Germany – thought Pope John Paul II should retire like any other elderly public servant might.

The Polish pontiff would hear none of it. He wasn't a simple public servant. He was the successor to St. Peter, and he would not retire with a farewell dinner or gold watch and gently disappear into the sunset. He would soldier on until his last breath. As he lay dying, his convictions inspired the Church and the world. Never before had millions seen a leader so physically weak yet so strong in spirit.

As April 2005 dawned, the Holy Father lay dying, and the whole world knew it. Unprecedented crowds flocked to Rome. St. Peter's Square in Vatican City was packed with peoples of all nations and of all ages. No one who saw it – either live or on television – could forget the crowds of so many young people flocking to be near such an elderly and infirm man. The assembled journalists were at a loss to explain the phenomena, and it is easy to understand why. One might reasonably ask why the young would love a man who seemed so utterly different than the heroes they were supposed to adore. But such a facile thought ignored a simple fact: Young people are no different than anyone else. They want truth. They may not have agreed with Pope John Paul II on every issue, but they respected him because he was authentic, and he gave them the truth, whole, unflinching, and unfiltered.

From the time the Pope lay dying until his burial in the crypt of St. Peter's, an estimated five to seven million people came to Rome to pay their respects.^a It was the largest throng ever to attend a funeral. This spontaneous outpouring of respect and affection is all the more incredible when one realizes that some 70 percent of those mourners were younger than 25. This and events such as the historic 1993 World Youth Day represent some of the seminal moments in the life of the Church since the Second Vatican Council.

Authenticity is so rare that, years ago, young people started saying, "get real." Young people are accustomed to seeing reality television, which is in actuality quite often phony. Well, no one ever accused Pope John Paul II of being phony. What caused this octogenarian to seem so real to these young people, and what did his life and death mean for the Church?

Pope John Paul II's life was made for the silver screen. He witnessed the horrors of World War II and the Soviet takeover of his native Poland. He saw evil in its most naked form, and his reaction was to turn to the greatest hope he knew, Jesus Christ and His Catholic Church.

This pontiff also knew suffering on a personal scale, as he experienced his mother's death as a boy and the death of his entire family by the time he was in his twenties. While many saw him living out his final days as a "Suffering Servant," he had in fact been doing this nearly his whole life.

This didn't mean he didn't have fun or take an active part in the world in which he lived. An avid outdoorsman, young Karol Wojtyła played a variety of sports. He loved hiking, soccer, and skiing. It was in the outdoors where he most frequently communicated with the young people in the early days of his priesthood. This was best shown in a scene from the CBS movie *John Paul II*, starring Jon Voight.[1]

---

^aThe city's usual population is roughly four million.

The future pope used these excursions to explain life and love to the assembled young people. Every topic – from the mundane, to dating and sex – came up in the conversations. The future pope answered their questions using Church teaching without sounding like a prudish theologian.

This same approach with young people was seen while the world's eyes were on him during his papacy. It was John Paul II who developed the whole concept of World Youth Day, beginning in the 1980s. The most optimistic of Vatican officials could not have predicted the success of these semi-annual events. Indeed, many doubted the Pope. Almost two million came to World Youth Day in Częstochowa, Poland in 1991. An astounding five million came to the 1995 World Youth Day in Manila, Philippines.

Perhaps the most surprising number was the 500,000 who came in 1993 to Denver, Colorado, which, relative to other WYD cities, is remote (although very accessible). Many in the American Church advised the pontiff not to hold the event since they believed few would come.

The young people proved them wrong. Pope John Paul's unique ability to connect with youth made the Denver World Youth Day a huge success. However, after his passing, when many wondered (as they did in Denver) whether the young and faithful would attend the 2005 WYD in Cologne, Germany, over one million attended. This provided another sign that youth's embrace of the Church did not end with His Holiness' death.[2]

The skeptics could never understand (and still cannot fathom) why the young admired Pope John Paul II so intensely. Catholic youth were aware that some doubted both them and their beloved Pope. Their response was to cheer him louder in his last public appearances. The culmination of this saga played out in St. Peter's Square. As Pope John Paul II lay dying, his bedside attendants told him of the huge crowds outside, many of them young. "For years I came to you," he said. "Now you come to me."[3]

DAVID J. HARTLINE

In other words, those who felt indebted to John Paul for his unflinching witness to the truth gratefully and lovingly came in droves as he lay on his deathbed. Few if any had met the man, but he had touched them all in some way.

One of the largest groups to come was the Poles. So many came by train, they created a logjam that overwhelmed the Italian railroads. Frustrated Roman officials would not let any more trains into the already overcrowded city. Observers estimated that between one to two million people were stuck outside of Rome in trains or cars waiting in vain to enter the Eternal City. While many trains were filled with older Poles who remembered Karol Wojtyła from his days as a priest or archbishop, many were middle-aged travelers who wanted to thank him for his support of the Solidarity movement. There were still younger Poles who had been born after that movement's heyday and the fall of the Soviet Empire. They were there to thank His Holiness for the many blessings he had brought their country and the world.

This tsunami of humanity that flooded Rome and Vatican City bewildered those who didn't admire Pope John Paul II. Many of these critics felt that once the pontiff was dying, the only outpouring of sadness would be from older orthodox Catholics.[b] They totally underestimated the love many Catholics and even those of other faiths had for the man. In some cases these critics' exasperation turned to anger, and certain commentaries on the dying man's legacy turned hostile.

---

[b]Orthodox is a term that will frequently appear throughout the book. For those readers not familiar with it, the 1910 New Catholic Dictionary defines being orthodox (or orthodoxy) as something that signifies "correct belief or true faith. Since Christ founded only one true Church, faith is really orthodox only when in conformity with the doctrines of that Church." In other words, if someone believes that the Pope is the vicar of Christ on earth, that Jesus was born of the Virgin Mary, suffered, died on the cross, and rose again on the third day, that birth control and abortion are wrong, and has beliefs that are otherwise in conformity with the Magisterium, that person is orthodox.

4

THE TIDE IS TURNING TOWARD CATHOLICISM

Among the many who could not understand the significance of his papacy were such disparate groups as agnostics, militant secularists, and even some Catholics on the far left. *The National Catholic Reporter*, a liberal Catholic weekly devoted to dissent, ran a series of stories about the Pope. Some columnists such as Sr. Joan Chittister, OSB, felt bewildered by the large percentage of youth in the crowd. She seemed to attribute this to the fact that many children don't have living grandparents or that they don't see them as frequently as they would like. John Paul II was a reminder of that love and leadership they missed, she wrote. While part of her thesis may be true, it seemed Sr. Chittister and other Church liberals could not accept the possibility that the youth actually liked the message of His Holiness.[4]

Andrew Sullivan, the openly homosexual former editor of the *New Republic* magazine, went on a literary rampage against the Pope. Against all evidence to the contrary, Sullivan said the late pontiff's papacy was a failure and blamed him for the world's increasing secularization. Sullivan argued that if the Church had embraced more liberal ideas such as those espoused by some in the gay community, the Church would have grown instead of shrunk.[5]

Sullivan's assertions were fundamentally wrong. While the Church has stagnated in parts of the West (especially Western Europe), the Church has grown by leaps and bounds in much of the rest of the world. We will look at that later, but for now let us examine how Pope John Paul II helped the Church grow.

When his pontificate began in 1978, it is true the other major Christian denominations were experiencing difficulties with growth. However, no one could have predicted the statistical free fall most would go into shortly thereafter. In Western Europe, Lutheranism, Anglicism[c], and Methodism simply lost members to the secular world. In the United States, those denominations lost members to either the Baptist Church or to large non-denominational churches. Dave Shiflett, author of *Exodus: Why Americans Are Fleeing Liberal*

---

[c]Anglicans are generally called Episcopalians in the United States.

DAVID J. HARTLINE

Churches for Conservative Christianity, notes that in the United States during the 1990s, the Presbyterian Church (PCUSA) lost 12 percent of its members, while over the past 30 years, the Methodist Church has lost 1,000 members a week.

In that same period, the United States' Catholic population increased by 15 million. During John Paul II's pontificate, worldwide vocations to the Catholic priesthood increased by an astonishing 76 percent, from 63,882 diocesan priests in 1978 to 112,373 in 2005. Outside of pockets in the western world, talk of a priest shortage is absurd.[6]

Did the Pope have anything to do with these phenomena? He had everything to do with them. The denominations that lost members all bought into a mindset born of the tyranny of relativism that said they needed to change with the times and become a part of the secular society that their forefathers warned them against.

Pope John Paul II didn't buy into this "go-along-to-get-along" mentality. Perhaps this came from his experience in communist Poland where he came to realize people want more than conformity out of a church. The difficult part of that equation is that most people who eventually leave Christianity, end up trying different denominations before they quit it entirely. John Paul tried to prevent that from happening.

Experience also taught him that most people need their religious experiences to be more than academic exercises. The reason so many in the United States left mainline Protestant churches was because these churches deemphasized (and sometimes openly disavowed) some of what their flock thought was holy, principally belief in ancient Christian teachings (e.g., the resurrection and virgin birth). Some churches failed because their leadership failed to understand their flocks and became detached from them.

Pope John Paul II was anything but detached from the people. They saw him as genuine. And while he could entertain, entertainment

6

was not his goal; preaching the Gospel was. The ideas of the man from Kraków were not born out of abstract theological theory or wishful thinking but out of a life lived in personal and observed pain. The Pole who became pope had lived through the horrors of World War II, the Holocaust, the Soviet takeover. He witnessed the growing nihilistic attitude that made so many in the West selfish and self-centered, which in turn left them confused or angry (since self-love is not the thing for which God created us). He saw with an uncanny acuity how false and destructive these things were, and how they offered humanity no hope for anything but the material here-and-now. Thus, when he discussed the gospel, he was able to speak to people with a resonance few could match. He told them things they knew in their heart but which went against what passes for conventional wisdom in our times.

At the Pope's death, the tributes poured in from world leaders and average folk. MSNBC, for instance, posted heartfelt letters about him on its website. These came from Catholics and Protestants, Jews and Muslims, Hindus and atheists. It was a sight to watch across the blogosphere as tributes flooded a multitude of websites.

Syndicated columnist Kathleen Parker had this to say about the Pope in a special column in *USA Today*: "As a non-Catholic, I don't have a dog in this hunt, but I kind of like the idea that somewhere, someone is holding the line taut, setting human ideals above our easy reach. Asking the church to 'get with it' to be more hip to our postmodern whims, puts me in mind of Grandma sporting a navel ring, or Pops with a tattoo – and not the kind that men get while sowing oats in the Merchant Marines. Forty percent of children today live without a father. If you're the child of a broken family, perhaps one without a father – or an adult awed by rare moral courage – a doctrinaire, orthodox pope might seem just the ticket. Perhaps even a godsend."[7]

New York City writer and poet J.J. Haynes-Rivas wrote of the Pope's death in the *National Catholic Reporter's* May 5 online edition. At first he had barely paid any attention to someone he hardly idolized. The deaths of Beatle John Lennon and a host of other rock stars had a far greater impact on him. So Haynes-Rivas wondered why, after several days, he felt conflicted, torn, and depressed. "It was, I think more akin to the loss of a parent with whom you'd barely been on speaking terms for years; the loss of a father whose approval you longed for, but whose hard standards you could never quite live up to. Most of all, I think this was grief of having been on the cusp of finally admitting the old man was right, that you finally understood, and then having him taken away before you could tell him."[8]

The Catholic view of the Suffering Servant (a person who with courage and fortitude offers his suffering for those he serves)[d] has never been popular in or understood by the modern world. Many misunderstand it as an antiquated, outdated panacea to help the poor of the world accept their woeful fate. Others, especially secularists, are outright hostile to the idea since, to their way of thinking, suffering produces nothing of value.

Nonetheless, Pope John Paul II lived the role of the Suffering Servant for all to see during the last 10 years of his life. In a world obsessed with feeling young and comfortable, seeing a leader in pain made many decidedly uncomfortable. By practically dying in front of the TV cameras, Pope John Paul II gave the world a lesson in courage. Every day, until the end, he used what was left of the talents and abilities God had given him for the sake of those he served.

---

[d] See Isaiah 52-53 for a better understanding of this (although Isaiah's Suffering Servant is typically seen as a prefiguring of Jesus the Christ).

THE TIDE IS TURNING TOWARD CATHOLICISM

The Election of Pope Benedict XVI

The election of Pope Benedict XVI was the most closely watched and studied papal conclave in history. Contributing to this was the fact that Vatican Television's cameras caught glimpses of an event never before seen by most in the world: Cameras were allowed into the Sistine Chapel until the assembled cardinals swore the oath of secrecy. Also, the United States Conference of Catholic Bishops' Catholic Communications Campaign used its resources wisely, and the coverage given to the worldwide media was excellent.

Speculation concerning the identity of who the new pontiff would be was intense. Various European betting parlors set up shop right outside the limits of Vatican City. The Irish owner of one such establishment was interviewed against the backdrop of St. Peter's about the latest odds and the scuttlebutt heard in the coffee shops and avenues around Rome and Vatican City.[9]

After more than a quarter century of having a non-Italian in the Chair of Peter, people wondered whether the new pontiff would be an Italian. What about a Third World candidate? If so, who were the top contenders? Francis Cardinal Arinze of Nigeria was a favorite, and the bookmakers gave him good odds.

Although *Time* magazine surprised many by saying he was among the top contenders to become the next pope, a number of Vatican watchers said Joseph Cardinal Ratzinger's chances were scuttled when at the final Mass before the Conclave he gave his famous "dictatorship of relativism" homily.

In that sermon, Cardinal Ratzinger said, "How many winds of doctrine we have known in recent decades, how many ideological currents, how many ways of thinking... The small boat of thought of many Christians has often been tossed about by these from one extreme to another from Marxism to liberalism, even to libertinism... We are moving toward a dictatorship of relativism which does not recognize anything for certain and which has its highest goal one's own ego and one's own desires."[10]

Hearing this, Fr. Richard McBrien, the controversial liberal Notre Dame professor and author of the book *Catholicism* seemed relieved as he told the press, "I think the homily of Cardinal Ratzinger shows he's not going to get elected Pope. He's too much of a polarizing figure. If he were to get elected, then thousands upon thousands of Catholics in Europe and the United States would roll their eyes and retreat to the margins of the Church."[11]

As the television cameras pulled away from the Sistine Chapel and the cardinals went to work, the talking head pundits on the various cable news channels and network outlets took over. According to the media, the longer the balloting took, the better the chances that Cardinals Ratzinger and Arinze would be pushed back. Perhaps a dark horse compromise candidate would be elected at that point, someone such as Milan's Diogini Cardinal Tettamanzi or Jorge Mario Cardinal Bergoglio of Buenos Aires. Pundits debated the appropriate age of the next pontiff. Many Vatican watchers felt another long papacy would be counterproductive, but many commentators saw Cardinal Ratzinger at age 78 as too old.

In many ways, Cardinal Ratzinger had lived as interesting a life as that of Pope John Paul II. Both men were shaped by war and totalitarianism. Cardinal Ratzinger had even been unwillingly drafted into the Nazi Army. The *Sunday Times of London* ran articles about Cardinal Ratzinger's involvement in the Hitler Youth. This was no secret. German teenagers at the time were obliged to be in the Hitler Youth. Now, in addition to being derided as the "Grand Inquisitor," the implication was that Cardinal Ratzinger was a Nazi.

While such analysis may have been raw meat to those who despised orthodoxy and the prospect of his sitting on the papal throne, the cardinals in attendance (especially those from the Third World) knew a different man. During his time as prefect for the

Congregation for the Doctrine of the Faith, Ratzinger had welcomed them, listened to them, and respected their ideas. He even greeted tourists as he roamed St. Peter's Square, often pointing the lost toward their destination in their native tongue. Everyone knew of his towering intellect, but few outside of the Vatican knew of his simple charm and grace, characteristics some say would be rewarded more so than his towering intellect.

As the first day of the Conclave drew to an end, the first ballot had been taken, and Cardinal Ratzinger was already emerging as a strong candidate, garnering a high percentage of votes. Once his strength was evident, opposition to him quickly faded, and he easily won on the second ballot.

It was overwhelming for the man from Germany. This was not what he wanted. Instead, all he longed to do was to retire, go home to Bavaria, and write books. He had told John Paul II this many times. John Paul always replied, "I need you here."

His countryman Joachim Cardinal Meisner said the new Pope looked somewhat forlorn and overcome with emotion once the votes were tallied. However true this was, the new pontiff showed none of it as he appeared for the first time as pontiff on the loggia of blessings, the central balcony of the Basilica of St. Peter. Instead, he wore an ebullient, infectious smile that stretched ear to ear. He had the countenance of a happy child, full of innocence and humble delight. Perhaps it was the joyous crowds demonstrating its full-throated approval and joy, or maybe it was the Holy Spirit strengthening and encouraging him (something he would greatly need now that he had been elected to lead the world's largest religious body).

Crowds in St. Peter's Square are expected to cheer a new pope. But what would be the world's reaction? What name would the new pontiff take and would there be any significance to the name? Cardinal Ratzinger announced he had taken the name Benedict XVI.

What did this name symbolize? Primarily, the Pope chose

the name in honor of St. Benedict, who was born in the late fifth century and died in the early sixth century. Known as the founder of Western monasticism (the Benedictine Order is named after him), he established not only monastic rules but also rules for the everyday Christian layperson. He was a beacon of truth and sincerity who lived during one of Christianity's darkest periods, and many credit him with the salvation of Western civilization. The reason is that while barbarian hordes dismantled the Roman Empire, St. Benedict's monks kept western civilization alive through scholarship, work, and strong adherence to the Faith. His Holiness wanted to have a similar impact on this age of relativism.

The world media had mixed reactions to the news of Cardinal Ratzinger's election. Some passed it off to the frontrunner status he earned through years of working at the thankless job of defending the teachings of the Church amidst a swirl of negative publicity. Other asked if his election was indeed a symptom of a Church leadership that was totally unaware of the feelings of its flock.

Perhaps the best example of this skeptical commentary came from "Scarborough Country" with Joe Scarborough on MSNBC the night of Benedict's election. A conservative former congressman from Florida, Scarborough voiced the concern expressed to him by Catholics at the station that this choice would prove disastrous for the Church.

Although he was a former Republican congressman and an Evangelical, Scarborough has always had a flair for pop culture and even alternative culture. He moves between the liberal and conservative worlds with ease. Sometime later Scarborough had to do a *mea culpa* for listening to progressive Catholics in the studio. Once he talked to rank and file Catholics, he got a positive reaction. So it was with almost all of the media.[12]

Many American Catholics watched coverage of the Conclave on the Eternal Word Television Network (EWTN). There was quite a different reaction and all together different coverage seen on the faithful Catholic network. Indeed, EWTN garnered the highest audience of its nearly 25-year run. Its coverage paired newsman Raymond Arroyo with Fr. Richard John Neuhaus, writer, intellectual and elegant defender of Catholicism. A convert from Lutheranism, Fr. Neuhaus made no bones about his belief that Cardinal Ratzinger would make an excellent pope. He went so far as to promise to sing a *Te Deum* if his hopes came true. So it wasn't surprising that Arroyo and Fr. Neuhaus burst out with unconcealed joy when Jorge Arturo Augustin Cardinal Medina Estévez announced the name of Cardinal Ratzinger as the two hundred and sixty-fifth pontiff.

The day after the election, a full-page headline in a left-wing German tabloid proclaimed, "O My God." The pundits and talking heads failed to realize that the cardinals were not looking at the papal selection as one would a presidential election. The old belief says once the cardinals are locked in the Sistine Chapel, they become so awed by the presence of God and the Holy Spirit (not to mention the profundity of the decision they have to make) that they throw aside political considerations. For many faithful Catholics, the election of Cardinal Ratzinger demonstrates that the Holy Spirit really does move the papal electors.

The first chance for the world to see the popularity of the new Pope occurred the Sunday following his election. St. Peter's Square was once again overflowing with eager onlookers, many from the Pope's native Bavaria. They were visible by the distinctive blue and white-checkered flag of that state that many held. The following Monday, a special welcoming ceremony was held for visiting Bavarians. They serenaded the new pope with a rhyming chant, "Papst Benedikt Gott Geschiskt" (Pope Benedict God Sent.).

As 2005 marched on into 2006, record crowds greeted Pope Benedict whenever he appeared. More people came to see the new pontiff at the beginning of his reign than had seen his predecessor during the Jubilee Year of 2000, another key sign the tide is turning towards Catholicism. The critics scoffed at the huge crowds generated by Pope John Paul II. They labeled these gatherings as merely being an example of the cult of personality. But the huge crowds coming to see Pope Benedict disproved this false notion. Faith had brought them to see Papa Benedetto.

My contention that the tide is turning towards Catholicism, however, is based on more than the record crowds that came to St. Peter's Square for John Paul's funeral and Benedict's election. It is turning because of the impression these pilgrims made in Rome, and the subsequent impact they had on their neighbors once they returned home. The events of April 2005 inspired awe in all those who witnessed it, Catholic and non-Catholic, believer and non-believer. It may prove the beginning of a Catholic Great Awakening.[c]

---

[c]Most scholars agree that there have been three such Great Awakenings in American history, but these have strictly been a Protestant phenomenon. The term refers to a period of a pronounced religious revival.

- CHAPTER 2 -

DEFENDERS OF THE FAITH - LAITY

In the 1950s, Americans recognized Bishop Fulton Sheen as the Church's preeminent advocate for the faith. It seemed as if every American Catholic tuned in to his television show. Today one might ask if any similar defenders of the faith exist, and if so, who are they?

The good news is there are numerous defenders of the faith, many of whom have joined forces in recent years. They spread the gospel using a wide array of media such as the radio, television, books, and the Internet. Those doing this work include Jimmy Akin, the Anchoress, Gerald Augustinus, David and Jonathan Bennett, Joseph Bottum, Tom Craughwell, William Donohue, Tim Drake, Michael Dubruiel, Dawn Eden, Michael Galloway, the Curt Jester, Matthew Kelly, Al Kresta, Rich Leonardi, Patrick Madrid, Matthew Pinto, Mark Shea, Joshua Synder, Eve Tushnet, George Weigel, Scott Carson, and Amy Welborn, to name just a few. They are the new "defenders of the faith."

These people serve the need for good Catholic apologetics by helping Catholics better understand their faith. They come from all walks of life and parts of the country. Some were cradle Catholics, others were not. They may have been teachers, writers or bank employees. They were in rock bands and community theater. Yet faith is now center stage in their life, and they aim to help people understand their faith. What do their efforts mean for the Church?

We can see the impact these defenders have in the newfound respect and reverence many have towards the Church (especially the young). They help laity know their faith, thus making up for the poor formation most received in CCD and confirmation classes. This makes for one of the most important developments in the post-Vatican II Church.

Interestingly, this new defender phenomenon is largely a conservative one. The reason is that most liberal Catholics object to many of the Church's teachings. Who spends time defending something about which they are not passionate? And if one's view of religion is by and large relativistic (e.g., "All religions are the same; you don't have to be Christian to attain salvation"), there is even less reason to spend time defending one's own faith.

Furthermore, even when dissident Catholics endeavor to defend the faith, they find their efforts often fall flat. Since these people typically don't have a total commitment to the Faith as *objective* truth, many will find their arguments unpersuasive. Not only that, but their arguments are often confusing, a trait that frequently characterizes the thoughts of those who refuse to believe in absolutes.

This apocryphal quote of GK Chesterton probably says it best: "It's not that those who don't believe in God believe in nothing. They end up in believing in everything." While some so-called progressive Catholics obviously believe in God, their views on Him are so amorphous that they have a functional atheism. This results in their believing all manner of things that Christians at any other time in history would have found bizarre in the extreme (if not outright heretical). One only need look at the variety of causes and beliefs that those who refuse central authority endorse to see this point.

The Church's orthodox defenders, however, are the antithesis of those who have challenged the Church since the 1960s.

They seek to explain the rich fabric of the Church's teachings, beliefs, history and cultural diversity through the lens of their experience. They seek to provide answers to those who want to better understand their faith. And when the Church is attacked, the new defenders help Catholics to understand the reasons behind this and what they can do about it.

This is crucial because many Catholics in their 30s and 40s received their catechesis in what some call the "warm fuzzy era," when substance wasn't as important as feelings. As a result, the knowledge of Church teachings that many of these people have is rudimentary at best. This generation longs to connect with a faith they have never really known. The good news is that, with the help of the new defenders, those in their 30s and 40s are acquiring that connection. The new defenders explain the faith in ways younger Catholics connect with and understand. They use creative ways to get the Church's message out to an eager audience. The harvest has yet to be seen, but the number of field hands is growing, and the hopes of a promising yield are increasing.

Many in this potential crop are those who left the Church for one reason or another. Many left precisely because of the lack of depth that characterized the warm fuzzy era. While they may have had a warm feeling about their faith, they didn't know that faith, and thus became convinced that Catholicism didn't have much substance behind it. It seems every family knows of a family member or close friend who left the Church precisely for this reason. People such as former Protestant pastors Marcus Grodi and Scott Hahn have enjoyed amazing success in helping these prodigal sons and daughters see just what substance there is in the beliefs they left behind.

A different type of defender is William Donohue, president of the Catholic League for Religious and Civil Rights, whose mission it is to defend the civil rights of Catholics. He saw that Catholic beliefs were being attacked ever more frequently (even as Americans were supposedly becoming more tolerant). Donohue was not worried about attacks perpetrated by rank and file Americans. Instead, he targeted assaults on and denigrations of Catholicism in Congress, courtrooms, and America's living rooms via the media. Donohue is frequently seen on American television news programs defending the

Church or engaging in debate with those who have a problem with her for one reason or another.

Donohue has also defended Catholics who are viewed as less than orthodox. When a radio spoof used the word "molester" and the name of Roger Cardinal Mahony of Los Angeles interchangeably, Donohue rushed to His Eminence's defense, even though Mahony is hardly a friend of orthodox Catholics.

He has also stood up for Mel Gibson and his movie *The Passion of the Christ*, and lashed out at Hollywood for making *The Da Vinci Code* into a movie. In some instances Donohue's efforts have brought immediate results, such as when he encouraged Comedy Central to not show a repeat of the "South Park" *Bloody Mary* episode. This mocked the Virgin Mary, and Comedy Central agreed not to show it again.

But there is not a Catholic League that can come to the faith's defense in other parts of the world. In New Zealand, for instance, uproar ensued when a priest tried to bring up a long forgotten statute of blasphemy against "South Park." In 2006, a Vatican official proposed the creation of an Anti-Defamation League for Catholics to help defend the Church against a rising secular culture that often conspires against the Church. In Great Britain, Catholic schools are under attack for teaching the Catholic faith. Prime Minister Tony Blair was mocked in Parliament for mentioning that he prayed to God over the war in Iraq. These events would seem to suggest that the world's Christians in general might need an Anti-Defamation League.

The Knights of Columbus, while not *new* defenders of the faith, certainly deserve mention. As many service organizations begin to decline because of Americans' busy lives and because many Catholics who once worked near their homes now commute long hours, a new mission was brought upon the Knights of Columbus. After all, it is not a mere service organization it is an organization of faith.

THE TIDE IS TURNING TOWARD CATHOLICISM

In many small towns and city ethnic enclaves, some consider the Knights of Columbus to only be a social organization where men can talk and watch various sporting events over a beer or two. While the Knights do have a social dimension, defense of the faith has increasingly taken center stage. The Knights of Columbus have always taken a strong stand for the defense of life, but they have increasingly been front and center in the struggle. They help Catholic schools and parish schools of religion purchase educational materials. They can also be counted on to help their particular parish with any other needs.

In the realm of the Catholic Internet, Michael Galloway deserves special mention. In 1994, he launched the Catholic Online bulletin board, making it the first Catholic website. Similarly, Kathy Shaidle was one of the first Catholic Internet bloggers. She has now been joined by thousands of others across the world who post news and views about all things Catholic on the Internet. Their pioneer spirit has enabled the Catholic Internet presence to enjoy the success that it has.

Patrick Madrid is also someone worth mentioning. He was one of the first in the post-Vatican II era to be gainfully employed by writing books and speaking to audiences about Catholicism. Like many Catholics, Madrid grew up in a faithful home but not an overly religious one. He considered the priesthood, but ultimately opted for the secular world. Growing up in southern California, Madrid enjoyed all that the Golden State had to offer. However, the Church was never far from his mind. He married while still in his early twenties and joined the workforce.

Life was comfortable for Patrick and his wife, and their family of 11 children kept them busy. However, as the years passed, he felt something missing from his life. He felt he should do something more faith-oriented, but what? While Evangelical groups had many individuals working in full-time ministry, it was almost unheard of for a Catholic to do so. Patrick continued his work in the financial sector until he could no longer resist the call to do apologetics work. It was a moment to which other Catholics who got "the call" could relate. He must have felt he was taking the risk of a lifetime. What would happen if he failed? Would he be able to transition back into the workforce? What about the questions from family and friends? How would he answer those? While the decision had the potential of becoming the proverbial long walk off a short pier, he nonetheless put one foot in front of the other.[2]

And God rewarded that faith. The "godfather of Catholic Apologetics" Karl Keating (also from southern California) came to a similar decision the weekend before Madrid came to his. He would leave his comfortable job as an attorney to start Catholic Answers, the first and still preeminent Catholic apologetics organization. Eventually, God brought the two of them together so others could grow in their faith.[3]

And let us not forget Dr. Scott Hahn. A former Presbyterian minister and seminary professor, Hahn teaches Scripture and theology at Franciscan University of Steubenville. He is extremely popular on the Catholic speaking circuit. His clear insightful teachings on the scriptural roots of our faith have inspired possibly thousands of conversions. To further this work, he founded the St. Paul Center for Biblical Theology.

Modern day defenders are not above relaying personal experiences or sharing aspects of their family life in their writings that they feel might benefit their readers. This is particularly helpful for religious readers because it helps the reader relate to the writer. It helps them to see that those whose job involves religion have the same problems as the rest of us.

One place where this phenomenon is evident is on the Internet, especially on web logs (known as "blogs" for short).

The Catholic blog world greatly expanded as a result of the Terri

Schiavo case. Many of the new blogs were Catholic-oriented and became part of "Blogs for Life," a large site which caters to pro-life views. Terri-centered blogs came to the attention of the news media just as Pope John Paul II's condition worsened in March 2005.

Then, when His Holiness died, Catholic Internet traffic skyrocketed. The unusually high traffic continued throughout April 2005 with the subsequent conclave and election of Pope Benedict XVI.

Unfortunately, the dawning of the blogosphere came with the usual Catholic belatedness. Once again it looked as if Catholics would get beaten to the punch by their Evangelical brothers and sisters. A funny thing happened, however. Catholic bloggers started to show other Catholics how to be Catholic again. One by one their numbers increased. While each of these had their own particular strengths, they were all advancing the cause of explaining Church teaching.

As alluded to above, while the Catholic blogosphere grew, there was a striking lack of liberal Catholic sites. Although the rest of the blogosphere achieved an even balance of liberal, moderate, and conservative political thought, the Catholic realm remained staunchly orthodox. Again, the reason for this lies in the fact that those who have a passion for the Church and her teachings will strive to defend her while those who don't won't.

Catholics are also voting with their keyboards.

What does the Internet tell us about the state of Catholicism? It tells us that many who hunger for the faith are finding those who can explain it to them on the Internet. The Internet's largest audience is those under age 50, precisely the age of those who feel they might have missed out on learning their faith and some of the traditions of the Church. Those traditions – adoration, Corpus Christi processions, Gregorian chant, etc. – began to come back with a vengeance in the 1990s, and this trend has continued during this first decade of the new millennium, often at the behest of those who grew up in the

1970s and 1980s who had no memory of them.

In any event, the ability for likeminded Catholics to be able to contact, converse and find information just a fingertip away on the Internet is a literal godsend. On any number of given Catholic blogs, whether it be Amy Welborn's "Open Book," Mark Shea's "Catholic & Enjoying It," Gerald Augustinus' "Closed Cafeteria," readers have the opportunity to discuss ideas, learn news, and better know the Church's teachings.

The queen of the Catholic blogosphere is Amy Welborn, who used to teach in Catholic schools and worked in a parish as a director of Religious Education. She eventually took her love of writing to the printed page, and she wrote many books, including the early *Prove It* series, which is still in print.

For every new defender, there comes a defining moment not of their making. Amy's defining moment would be *The Da Vinci Code*.

The Da Vinci Code thundered out of the relatively unknown Dan Brown's fingers and onto the world stage. It became the darling of those who seem to rebel against all things that characterize orthodox Christianity. Like so many others, Welborn was flabbergasted by the lack of scholarship underlying the serious charges made by *The Da Vinci Code*, namely that Christianity was a fraud. According to Brown (who used bogus facts and otherwise apocryphal information, all the while claiming that his book was historically accurate),[f] Jesus didn't die and rise again, and at some point He married Mary Magdalene. The apostles were relegated to the role of fools, which meant Jesus was the biggest fraud of all.

Brown claimed the Church had kept this secret for 2,000 years. While his book was published under the guise of fiction, Brown is convinced that much of the tale is true, and wrote the novel in a

---

[f] One of his countless whoppers was that Opus Dei was founded in the Middle Ages and had monks. Neither is true. In addition to Welborn's tome, two great books on the other falsehoods in this book are *The Da Vinci Deception* by Mark Shea and Ted Sri, and the soon to be mentioned work by Carl Olson and Sandra Meisel.

concurrent fashion. This from a man who says his main moments of inspiration come from hanging upside down in his gravity boots. This from a man who says he *knows* the person reputed to be St. John the Evangelist in da Vinci's *The Last Supper* is *really* St. Mary Magdalene because, hold on to your hats, to him it looks like a girl (damn what even non-Christian art scholars say is actually the case or that no one agrees with him).

It was one thing to make such controversial statements; it was another for church-going folks to also believe it, and yet many did. Welborn's answer to *The Da Vinci Code* was *Decoding Da Vinci*, and it served as the first counterattack by Christians. Her book exposed all of the factual errors contained not only in *The Da Vinci Code*, but also in other popular mythological works such as *Holy Blood, Holy Grail*. Her expose would help make her the number one Catholic blogger.[4]

Author and convert Mark Shea has one of the more popular Catholic blogs called "Catholic and Enjoying It!" a unique mixture of apologetics and pop culture tied together with Mark's fun sense of humor. Tom Craughwell, a prolific writer who Michael Dubruiel has dubbed "the walking encyclopedia," has appeared on several networks, including CNN and EWTN, and on a host of radio programs. His 14 books cover a wide variety of topics of faith with both humor and depth. Pick any obscure saint and Tom can more than likely tell you about them. His books are wonderfully informative as well as entertaining.

While on the topic of books, Catholic book publishing is starting to catch up to the world of Evangelical book publishers. Since Protestants outnumber Catholics, and because they see the Bible as the sole rule of faith (which in some way necessitates and encourages owning lots of books explaining Scripture), it is understandable that they sell more books and have more bookstores.

Against this, you have Catholic book publishers, most of whom are small operations. Their hearts are in the right place but they have difficulty playing on the same field as the prominent Protestant and secular companies. However, when Pope Benedict was elected, Ignatius Press – already the largest Catholic publishing house – experienced a boom in sales. The erstwhile Cardinal Ratzinger had published some 20 books with them. Ignatius Press had to make special contracts with timber companies to acquire all of the paper needed to print the books.

And add Ascension Press to the ranks of cutting edge Catholic publishers. Matthew Pinto founded the company after a successful advertising career, first publishing the number one teen book, *Did Adam & Eve Have Belly Buttons?* and now offering the cutting edge *Great Adventure Bible Timeline* Scripture study, amongst many other titles that are helping Catholics to know their faith better. *The Great Adventure* is having two effects that also show the turning tide. One is that parishes that had never had a prior adult faith study are using this program and are seeing attendees come in droves. The other is that many parishes that had held Bible studies for years, attracting at most a dozen people, are now welcoming large numbers of parishioners, all eager to study God's Word. Ascension also offers the popular Theology of the Body resources by John Paul II and explained by Christopher West.[5] These are helping teens and adult Catholics learn this revolutionary way of looking at sexuality and God's plan for marital love. In turn, this is helping single people stay chaste and married people to throw away their birth control.

Matt Pinto had worked with Karl Keating and Patrick Madrid, and, like Keating and Madrid before him, eventually started his own publishing house. In addition, Pinto also formed Maximus Media Group, a public relations firm whose niche is to assist Catholic causes, organizations, and writers to get their word out in the complex world of the mass media.

One up-and-coming Catholic author is Michael Dubruiel.

While his wife Amy Welborn reigned as the queen of the Catholic Internet blog world, Michael was quietly moving up the book charts with *The How to Book of the Mass* (it should be noted that Michael is also an excellent blogger in his own right). To understand the book's success is to understand the secret of the new defenders: The need for knowledge about the rudimentary elements of the Faith from someone the average Catholic can relate to is extremely important. Two generations of Catholics know they don't understand the Church's teachings as well as they should.

Through all of the above mentioned means, the new defenders have become a serious force in the Church, and when they make public speaking appearances, these are often well-attended. Compare this to many mainline Protestant churches, which have great difficulty getting anyone to come to see a speaker.

Furthermore, in part because of the proliferation of these people's efforts, faithful Catholic clergy are now less hesitant to take on controversial topics. As such, though the liberal crowd *claims* to be on the people's side, that claim is belied by how so many Catholics are voting with their feet. Influenced by what they have learned from the new defenders and others, they are attending more orthodox Catholic churches. Many have even begun attending parishes served by traditionalist orders in union with the Pope (e.g., the Priestly Fraternity of St. Peter, the Institute of Christ the King Sovereign Priest, and the Society of St. John Cantius, to name just three).

The Print Media

In the traditional media, several excellent Catholic writers opine about various topics in the Church as well as the religious and political world in general for various publications. Members of this club include Michael Novak, George Weigel, and Joseph Bottum, while John Allen and the Italian Sandro Magister often report breaking news from the Vatican. *The National Catholic Register* is a favorite weekly read for orthodox Catholics, while *National Catholic Reporter* is a favorite among liberals and church dissidents.

Although John Allen, of the *National Catholic Reporter* is respected by many orthodox Catholics, the paper he works for is not. In Fall 2005, the publication's retiring editor Arthur Jones launched a scathing diatribe against Pope John Paul II and Pope Benedict XVI that only added to the low regard in which the *Reporter* is held by many faithful Catholics.

The September 9, 2005, edition of the paper featured the third of three columns written by Jones, and it was met with outrage by many orthodox Catholics. Perhaps the article's title, "The Roman Imposition," should have tipped readers off to its contents.[6] If it didn't, then the unaware were surely in for a rough ride if they were orthodox Catholics.

Jones continually and snidely referred to the papacy of Pope John Paul II and Pope Benedict as the "Wojtyła-Ratzinger continuum." He never mentioned their titles in a respectful manner, something even the most leftist and secularists of columnists typically do.

He talked about a "reclericalized church" and the imposition of child-like attention to "rituals." He went on to say that the "Wojtyła-Ratzinger continuum" made the educated feel unwelcome. He further

---

[6] A point of clarification is needed when speaking of orthodox versus Traditional Catholics.

An orthodox Catholic is someone who holds to and obeys the authentic teachings of the Church (as opposed to the dissenting/liberal/cafeteria Catholic, who either agitates for change or picks and chooses which teachings he will follow). As just one example, an orthodox Catholic would obey the Church's teaching on contraception and abortion, and joyfully follow Pope Benedict XVI's leadership.

However, these people are not to be confused with "Traditionalist" Catholics (who are also generally orthodox). Traditionalists (aka, traditional Catholics) are characterized by their profound attachment to the pre-Vatican II Mass.

I say "generally" orthodox because there are many, many who believe the Second Vatican Council – or at least its Decree on Ecumenism and its Declaration on Religious Freedom – was not valid. Others are attached to various, arguably

lamented the declining activist nature of the Church. He expressed concerns about the declining prospect of women's ordination and the fact that the young are becoming more traditional.

Thus in the space of one article, Jones managed to spell out many of the differences between orthodox and heterodox or liberal Catholics.[g] If Jones' article sounded like the ramblings of a thwarted and frustrated radical who could only watch as his dreams of glorious revolution evaporated into the mists of history, that is because it was. EWTN's Raymond Arroyo has said that attending a Call to Action conference is like going to an American Association of Retired People (AARP) confab after the delegates have just learned their Social Security was being cut.[h] Jones' rant was this phenomenon exhibited on the pages of a publication rather than in the hallways of a hotel.

Perhaps most revealing (and galling), Jones' piece smacked of the elitism that characterizes so much of so-called progressive Catholicism through and through. In it, he implied that if only the Church would listen to the great liberal minds (such as his), the Church would be better. One can only imagine his disdain for the newfound interest in Eucharistic adoration, especially among the young.

Of course, if one wants to see Jones' ideal church, look no further than the many empty Anglican/Episcopal churches. Ask the orthodox members of this ecclesial community if his vision of what a

---

schismatic movements that have routinely rejected both the authority of their local bishops and the Pope. A smaller subset is made up of "sedevacantists." Sedevacantists (adapted from the Latin for "the seat is vacant") are those who believe there has not been a valid pontiff since Ven. Pius XII.

Of course, there are the Orthodox. The capital "O" Orthodox are those Christians from the East who split with the western Church in 1054. So to speak of orthodox Catholics is different than when we speak of the Orthodox.

All of this underscores the need to join our Lord in praying for the unity of all Christians (cf., Jn. 17:21).

[h] Call to Action is an umbrella group for a number of dissident groups agitating to change the nature and character of the Catholic Church, including some of her most timeless teachings.

27

church should be has proved fruitful. Many of these people have left their geographical parishes to attend more traditional ones. In many cases, they have left their communion entirely to become Catholic or Evangelical.

One is tempted to ask, "Where is the clamor for this vision? Where are the new defenders for this vision? Where are the young supporters, and where are their websites and blogs?" We can count their blogosphere allies on two hands (maybe even one), yet there are thousands of orthodox websites. Perhaps Jones didn't see the 2005 Cologne World Youth Day and the love and affection the young expressed for John Paul II and Benedict XVI. Thankfully, Jones' vision has not come to fruition, and the old liberal order is fading into the sunset.

Whereas Jones and his ilk attack and tear down the Church, the new defenders are coming to build and help defend it. Jesus told us, "By their fruits you shall know them." The sheer spontaneity and whimsy of these defenders' work (especially the bloggers) shows the joy they have for what they are doing. Their efforts are bringing many into the Faith.

Sometimes defenders of the faith are those who also defend our country from aggressors. Anyone attending my alma mater Marion Catholic High School will notice the Green Beret and retired high school football jersey of Captain Stephen Chaney who was killed in action in Vietnam. The life and faith lived out by this former Notre Dame football player had a profound impact on those who knew him and many who only knew him by his legend.

West Point graduate Ramon Tancinco was a former captain in the US Army Armor Branch who was fascinated by the knighthood ever since he was a boy. Tancinco who comments frequently on my CatholicReport.org website said, "I voraciously consumed literature about King Arthur, St. Louis the IX, and the flamboyantly dressed Swiss Guards who defend the Pope. And of course, there were the rituals and ideals that surrounded knighthood. A prospective knight had to spend the entire evening before his knighthood awake in fasting and prayer in the local church. Upon his knighthood, he was told that one of his primary duties was to protect women, children and orphans, a direct parallel to what Jesus has told us...fighting for those who cannot defend themselves. Somewhere deep within this concept of knighthood was the seed of 'selfless service' to the point of being willing to lay down one's life for your neighbor."

Tancinco was amazed that during his occasional visits to New York City from West Point, people sometimes asked him how someone of faith could believe in military service.

"No one questions the need for a policeman, so why do they question my call to service?" he asked. "Jesus did not chastise the Roman centurion, He healed his servant. We are reminded of the moving centurion's prayer at Mass, 'Lord, I am not worthy that You should enter under my roof, but only say the word and my soul shall be healed.'"

Tancinco went on to remark, "Today people need clarity and they need leadership through the vacuum of relativism, especially within the Catholic Church. I was witness to these values both in Pope John Paul II and Pope Benedict XVI, and as an officer, the military inculcated these values in me. Part of my challenge today is to translate the 'strategic' leadership from Rome into the 'tactical' action on the ground. Through the influence of the Holy Spirit, I am confident that I will find that path."[7]

One compelling example of why we need modern defenders of the faith occurred in the Ohio State House of Representatives in December 2005. The Ohio State House Judiciary Committee was hearing testimony on a bill for victims of abuse.[i]

It was a contentious issue for the Ohio lawmakers. Some of the

---

[i] While Catholic clergy gets the headlines, most sexual abuse victims do not suffer at the hands of Catholic clergy, but rather at the hands of family members or in the work place.

Ohio House members were asking questions of various people who were called to testify. After Columbus Bishop Frederick Campbell testified, the Democrat ranking member of the House Judiciary Committee, a Catholic, asked him about the secret ceremony she heard of that allegedly took place after a priest's ordination. She was told that in this secret ceremony a priest swears not to protect Christ but the Pope in Rome and the Church from any attack against it. She said she was asking Bishop Campbell this because she was a little rusty on her *Catechism*. This was something right out of Catholic hater Jack Chick's vicious comic books. Bishop Campbell politely said there was no secret ceremony.

Then the committee's chairman, a Catholic Republican and Notre Dame graduate, asked Bishop Campbell about the "hell files," which he heard were kept in the chancery's basement.[j] Again, the chairman repeated an age-old anti-Catholic stereotype, a version of which was perpetuated by the Know Nothing Party in the latter 1800s. This once powerful political party spread fear among Protestant Americans that Catholics were secretly arming themselves by keeping guns in their church basements. The guns were allegedly at the ready for a signal from the Pope in Rome to take over the government.

While I am sure these two Catholic legislators meant no harm towards the Church, their ignorance of their faith was damaging to the Bride of Christ. Furthermore, it was hard to believe that in our time a Catholic elected official from a major state was even remotely credulous about something so ridiculous. They not only failed to defend the Church, they helped perpetuate age-old stereotypes. We need defenders to protect the Church from such lies and falsehoods.

---

[j] Hell files are supposedly documents detailing what priests have told their bishops. The Chairman was referring to files he had been told all dioceses have containing information about predators and other Church secrets.

It got worse. One lawmaker stated that Canon Law of the Catholic Church permitted one lie and that was to protect the Church. Another prominent politician said he was never so ashamed of his Church and claimed that the only time that anyone from it contacted him for legislation was when they wanted to avoid the publicity of the abuse scandal.[8]

Perhaps, he forgot how Church officials had regularly visited him over the years in their fight for legislation for Ohio's poor and marginalized. One can only imagine the kind of political firestorm that would have erupted had such remarks been said about other religious or minority groups.[k] Who knows why some say these things, but the faithful can be comforted by the fact that, in addition to those employed by the Church, there are many times more that number who are lay defenders of the faith. Their ranks are growing in many ways, and they will meet the challenges brought to the Church head on. The tide is turning because faithful men and women have decided to defend the faith they love.

Perhaps the most underrated defenders of the faith are parents who strive to teach their children the Catholic faith. With the hectic nature of the modern world, many Catholic parents still find time to instill in their children the dictum St. Francis taught: "Preach the Gospel always; use words when necessary." The rewards for parents may initially be small: A young child admonishing a sibling for not saying prayers over his or her bowl of Froot Loops or a toddler pointing to a crucifix and saying, "Jesus." However, there is nothing quite like the feeling of accomplishment at seeing one's son or daughter living a wholesome life and helping others along the way.

Before closing this chapter, some small mention should be made of two seemingly unknown (or is it ignored?) developments in the

---

[k] While I'm sure it won't surprise many, none of these outrageous comments were reported by any mainstream journalist. Again, think if these politicians had made similar remarks about other minorities. It would have started a firestorm that would have caused every one of them to resign.

Church, the increasing adherence to the Church's teaching on birth control and the growth in attendance at pre-Vatican II Masses by young Catholics.

Regarding artificial contraception, more and more couples are throwing out their Pills, diaphragms, IUDs, and other contraceptives in favor of letting the unitive and the procreative work together just as God planned it. Through organizations such as Human Life International, the Couple to Couple League, and other groups – not to mention the incredible work done by Dr. Janet Smith and Christopher West (through his *Theology of the Body* series) – a growing number of young people are recognizing the beauty of the Church's teaching on this subject. Through use of the Creighton Method FertilityCare, many are using Natural Family Planning to conceive children that otherwise would never exist.

People are also seeing what a prophet Paul VI was in his encyclical on contraception, *Humanae Vitae*, when he predicted what would happen if birth control became widely available (as it did). As such, they are recognizing birth control for the evil lie it is and are changing their lives. Because of this, society will eventually change. As more people realize this truth, more are defending the Church's teaching on this matter, winning converts to her perspective on this issue, and presenting the world with a badly needed witness to the beauty of God's design.[1]

As for young Catholics and the old Mass, when Pope John Paul II called for a wider application of the pre-Vatican II rite, first in 1984 and more forcefully in 1988, neither he nor anyone else probably imagined that those attracted to the so-called Tridentine liturgy would be mostly young people.

---

[1] It goes without saying that couples have more children when they stop contracepting. Those children, let's say 80 percent of them, will grow up to be like their parents in beliefs and practices. People who do not contracept tend to be religiously orthodox and politically conservative. At the same time, liberals and secularists are not having children or are having them below replacement levels. Therefore, within 100 years, one can expect that a growing number of conservatives and a dwindling number of liberals will have an effect on society.

32

Yet walk into most traditional Masses that are in union with the Church, and while you will see many elderly people there, the shocking thing is how many young Catholics attend, especially those with growing families. These families typically have many children and sometimes take up an entire pew.

Those who attend such parishes say it is a joy to be a Catholic there. These places celebrate saints' feast days, have Rosary and Eucharistic processions, do exposition, benediction, and adoration on a regular (even weekly) basis, have Reconciliation before each Mass, offer young priests who are excellent confessors and give valuable spiritual direction, and provide an unfailingly family-friendly atmosphere. As a result, vocations are being fostered, and children are growing up in a solidly orthodox environment, which will benefit the Church when they grow older by giving her many well-formed Catholics who know how to defend their faith as per 1 Peter 3:15.

Many of these people consider themselves "*novus ordo*[m] refugees." While these people are fully in union with the Pope and wholly orthodox, they decided they had to leave their geographical parish. They had had enough of heresy and uncertain doctrine preached from the pulpit, bad music, and liturgical abuses. Some have said being in a traditional parish is like breathing fresh air again.

While the numbers of such people is growing, it is too soon to tell whether they represent a full-fledged movement. But as more people become exposed to the beauty of the old Mass, the more this trend will develop. And the more it develops, the more the Church will have people who are passionate about defending and leading others into her.

---

[m] "Novus ordo" is Latin for "new order," as in new order of the Mass. Although the Church has never used the term "novus ordo" for the new Mass (i.e., the one instituted by Paul VI after the Second Vatican Council), that is what many now call it.

DAVID J. HARTLINE

- CHAPTER 3 -

YOUTH EMBRACE CATHOLIC TRADITION

Mrs. Josephine Daniels, my high school English teacher at Marion Catholic High School in Marion, Ohio, frequently told us, "Your generation or the one behind you is going to change the Church and society. With all the growing disbelief and vulgarity, society can't go on like this too much longer. You will finally say 'Enough, something has got to give.'"

As much as everyone loved and respected Mrs. Daniels, most of us would probably have said that you couldn't really change the world; you could only hope to contain the bad influences. Little did we know that, as in most matters, she would end up being right.

Many of the teenagers and college students of this first decade of the third millennium are the children of adults who were teenagers and college students in the 1970s. From the end of the Watergate crisis until the end of the disco era, people became more self absorbed in the "me, malaise, and apathy" decade. While one group of these parents may have been listening to the Bee Gees, KC & the Sunshine Band, or ABBA while dancing in a disco, another set of parents was listening to Ted Nugent, Alice Cooper and Foreigner while driving around town looking tough and cool. It would appear that these two groups of parents didn't have much in common.

However, they did. While they may not have been apathetic or lazy, certainly the times gave them the impression that this approach was the way to go. The 1993 movie *Dazed and Confused*, which is about the last day of school in 1976 for the junior class of a Texas high school, is an apt illustration of this.

The malaise theme even turned into a famous speech given by

President Jimmy Carter in 1978. He, too, noticed the trend but wasn't able to do much about it, at least according to the electorate who replaced him with a tough but optimistic Ronald Reagan in 1980. In 1978 a pope emerged who would be the antithesis of malaise. Against all odds, the cardinal from Kraków, Karol Wojtyła, would become the pontiff and ultimately the father and grandfather many Catholic youth never had.

The youth will be (and are) a great catalyst in turning the tide towards Catholicism. However, not everyone had grasped this fact in 1978, even those in the highest echelons of the Vatican. Thankfully, Pope John Paul II and his successor Benedict XVI listened to their own voice and that of the Holy Spirit instead of the prophets of doom and gloom. While the tide has been turning for some time, its genesis in the United States can perhaps be traced back to the summer of 1993 when World Youth Day was held in Denver, Colorado.

As noted in a previous chapter, World Youth Day was another of Pope John Paul II's momentous ideas. Many of these came out of his personal experiences. WYD stemmed from his interaction with young people while he served as a parish priest in the Archdiocese of Kraków, Poland. The CBS movie "Pope John Paul II" did an excellent job portraying the late pontiff's rapport with youth.[1] It showed the then-parish priest Fr. Wojtyła talking with the young people about a variety of topics including life, love, sex, and the outdoors. This was all done within the context of God's gifts to each of us. As pope, John Paul II longed for an opportunity to relive that role. He cherished his position as a "spiritual father" of youth. While he may have been their pontiff, he was still a priest, and he missed the small group learning experiences that so impressed the young people he shepherded during his priestly service in Poland.

World Youth Day started as a yearly event in Rome in 1984. The event took place on Palm Sundays at first, with a large international event held every two or three years. The first international World

Youth Day held outside Rome took place in April 1987. It was followed by events in Spain in August 1989 and in Częstochowa, Poland, in August 1991. Historic crowds have convened outside of each event, and while they were breathtakingly large, they could be explained by the context: They were all big, historic, once in a lifetime events. Pope John Paul II's papal travels to Poland, Mexico, and the Philippines could easily fall into this category.

It is truly awe-inspiring when an immense crowd gathers that is much larger than people anticipated. The World Youth Day held in Denver, Colorado, in 1993 was such an event. Some even called it the "Catholic Woodstock," for it gathered a disparate group of youth who all wanted more from their faith, a faith that many of their peers and even some of their parents were rejecting.

If Pope John Paul II had listened to many "in the know" from the United States, he would never have ventured to Denver. As George Weigel describes in his book *God's Choice: Pope Benedict XVI and the Future of the Catholic Church,* many Church officials warned Pope John Paul II against holding WYD in Denver. They feared no one would show up, and the Pope would be embarrassed.

How could they have so grossly misread the situation? This was a great teachable moment, for it offered one of the earliest signs that many Church officials were out of touch with rank and file Catholic adults and the youth. Certainly, these leaders had the best intentions. Many of the non-clergy church staffers who warned the pontiff not to go were only relaying the lack of dedication to the Church they were seeing among their own children. If an informal survey were done amongst United States parish and diocesan staffs asking if their teenage or college age children wanted to see the pontiff, the answer probably would have been no.[2]

Perhaps another reason why some US Catholics tried to persuade the Pope not go to Denver was the location. While past World Youth Days drew crowds of approximately one million, these events were in or close to major cities. Denver, while well-served by a variety of transportation options, was a city of just a half-million souls, a relatively small city. Furthermore, it is one to two days driving distance from the West Coast and two to three days driving distance from the East Coast. During other World Youth Days, the crowd count exceeded one million because of the many adults who would travel to be part of the final Mass. What was remarkable about the 500,000 who attended the event in Denver is that the majority of the crowd was made up of youth and not adults. The cognoscenti said Denver would be a failure, but Jesus warned us about listening to those who think themselves wise.

The Denver World Youth Day was not only a success, it was a turning point of the Church in the United States. More than 200,000 young people attended the August 1993 event, and a total of 500,000 attended the closing Mass. The American media, including MTV, was there, and they all seemed shocked by the large crowds of young, enthusiastic, joyful young people. It wasn't just the festive atmosphere that impressed observers; the appeal of the sacraments surprised even the biggest optimist. Priests heard confessions for hours on end as thousands of young people received the Sacrament of Reconciliation. Hundreds of young people adored our Lord in the Blessed Sacrament in a perpetual adoration chapel.[n]

The effect Denver had on not only building a positive feeling of

---

[n] Contrast this youthful vibrancy, fidelity, and joy in the Church's orthodox faithful with their counterparts on the other side of the ecclesial spectrum. One night at a Catholic convention, a few attendees and I tried to count all the sons and daughters of liberal Catholic parents who still practice their faith. We couldn't think of any. By and large, they either belong to a very liberal communion such as the Unitarian Church or they belong to no church at all. Some even end up becoming agnostics. We thought of several who have become quite conservative in contrast to their liberal parents and still attend Mass. We also thought of some who attend Evangelical churches. The fact is liberal parenting isn't very conducive to keeping a child's faith intact.

A good case in point is the family of Daniel Maguire, an archliberal and longtime professor of Moral Theology at Milwaukee's Marquette University.

possibilities for the US Catholic Church but also on vocations cannot be underestimated. Tim Drake's book *Young and Catholic* outlines many other wonderful stories from Denver. This book would make very worthwhile reading for those trying to understand the Catholic youth of today.

Pope John Paul II, when seeing then-Denver Archbishop James Francis Stafford at a Rome gathering, said "Ah, Denver. Una rivoluzione! Una rivoluzione!" So many had believed the Church would see its future come from the Asian East, but it was now coming from the West, the American West. Denver itself would remain energized for years to come by World Youth Day. Roxanne King, editor of the *Denver Catholic Register* told Tim Drake, "There has been tremendous growth in youth ministry, to the point where in Denver, it's really cool to be a young adult or youthful Catholic."[3]

While the youth have always been deemed important in many Evangelical circles, the same could not always be said for the Catholic Church, at least not in recent years. Some shuddered to think what the Church would be like without Pope John Paul II's focus on youth ministry. The youth became a source of befuddlement for many who were activists in the 1960s and 1970s. Young people's embracing of the teachings and ancient signs, symbols, and rituals of the Church must leave many who rejected these during 1960s scratching their heads.

Maguire is famous for bashing then-Cardinal Ratzinger. He became infuriated with Ratzinger's assertion that Christianity and Catholicism specifically are the truth. To Maguire every thought is good except for one that talks about specific truth or the concept of suffering. Maguire has rejected the belief that Christ died for our sins. He said God what would have to be a sadistic monster to allow such a thing.

In 1986 Maguire was visiting the Vatican with his teenage son Tom. Although Maguire had attacked Cardinal Ratzinger, the Bavarian prelate was good enough to take a picture with Tom. Tom, like many children of liberal parents, rebelled against his father's rejection of structure. If his dad's form of Catholicism was milquetoast, he would find a religion that was firm in its beliefs, a religion that said what it meant and meant what it said. Tom converted to Islam and now lives in Cairo, Egypt.[4]

When I worked at the Diocese of Columbus, I had a colleague who was a child of the 60s. One day he quizzed me and another colleague Mark Butler, director of Youth and Young Adult Ministry, about why so many young people were embracing these old traditions, including Latin. I can still hear the voice of that fellow staffer saying, "You can have all that hocus pocus and devotions. I will choose my own conscience."

When we asked how well trained his conscience was, he replied, "I trained it well enough. I have read more books than most people will ever read." He tried to lessen the edge of the conversation by saying, "Sorry you missed the '60s, guys, it was a great party. You know the best parties are the ones you can't remember. The '60s were one of those parties." With a smile, Mark and I replied, "Our generation is still paying for your party."

If some of the naysayers were baffled by the youth's response to Pope John Paul II in Denver, they were astonished when World Youth Day came back to North America for the 2002 Toronto WYD. After successes in the Philippines and Europe, Pope John Paul II went back to the continent where the "revolution" began. Many speculated the youth might be seeing Pope John Paul II for the last time as his health was steadily declining. Much like a heavyweight champion whose career seems to be coming to an end, Pope John Paul II gave one last memorable performance in front of the youth assembled in Toronto. Who knows how many lives were changed and vocations developed during those days in July 2002? The Holy Father's message continued to spread despite his failing health, and it made believers out of some who were still doubting Thomases.

In July 2002, Fr. Bill Hahn attended WYD Toronto while still a seminarian. Later, as associate pastor at St. Joan of Arc parish, in Powell, OH, he spoke of the awe, majesty, and wonder that greeted him at the event during a homily:[5]

THE TIDE IS TURNING TOWARD CATHOLICISM

"The Book of Revelation speaks of a 'great multitude from every nation, from all tribes and peoples and tongues, standing before the throne and before the Lamb.'" This is a description of the universal Church. This is something I witnessed for myself in 2002. No, this isn't one of those I almost died and saw bright light stories. I'm talking about a trip to Toronto, Canada, in 2002 for World Youth Day."

There I saw giant fairgrounds with people of every race, color, nationality and language, with flags from all the continents including Russia, Nigeria, Japan and Argentina. They were all united in the essentials, a unity in what matters most – the worship of the one, true God, united under Peter, in the person of Pope John Paul II. Because these were all Catholic Christians, we were united. I knew it mattered most our understanding of who God has revealed Himself as; our Faith, and how we are to respond to that revelation with love; our morals. Maybe we couldn't speak to each other but that didn't keep us from communicating that universal language, the language our Lord has taught us of love and service to our brothers and sisters. It was a city of peace and joy like nothing I've experienced in this world since.

At the center of it all, in a converted greenhouse upon a large stand stood a monstrance, that sunburst shaped vessel that the Eucharist goes in for Exposition, so they can pray before the Eucharist.

Day and night, I would stop by, and there praying were hundreds of young people from every nation, from all tribes and peoples and tongues...before the throne and before the Lamb. Every once in a while you would hear an African song of praise, or worship in German or French or the whole group would sing in Latin, worshipping the Lord. It was the fulfillment of this passage to me. All prostrate, like the Magi, in adoration of the King of Kings, offering Him their gifts of love. This was the meaning of Epiphany - God's revelation to the world.

Another regular event that is having an impact on the Church is the National Catholic Youth Conference. Each year in various cities, it brings together thousands of young people for fun and faith. I attended the 2005 conference in Atlanta and plan to attend the next one when it comes to Columbus in 2007. One couldn't help but feel encouraged at the sight of thousands of energetic young people packed into the Georgia Dome.

The embrace of the sacraments is a sight to behold at these youth events. The participation in the Sacrament of Penance (i.e., Confession) is perhaps the most inspiring. There are no stern lectures about why the youth need to receive the sacrament that compels them toward it. They just seem to gravitate towards the confessional. It is something of a marvel. We hear about the same phenomenon occurring amongst our troops in Iraq and Afghanistan. It is as if they all realize the power the Sacrament of Penance has and cannot wait to receive it. If the old adage is true that there are no atheists in foxholes, then perhaps a similar statement could be made that there are no cynical youth who choose to go to church. If they are cynical, they simply leave. There is no pretense among the young because, unlike adults, their peers wouldn't tolerate it.

My years as a Catholic schoolteacher, coach, principal, and diocesan employee have given me the opportunity to notice trends among the young. Perhaps the biggest trend I noticed from my first years of teaching in the late 1980s until I became a Catholic school principal and diocesan administrator in the late 1990s was the pull towards the traditional. I wasn't alone in this observation. Sr. Melinda Burkhart, OP, and Sr. Josetta Mayer, OP, who were teachers while I was the principal at Holy Trinity School in Somerset, OH, voiced the same opinion. They had seen many trends come and go since they began teaching in the 1950s. They were quite excited that the tide was turning.

The generation that listened to grunge rockers Nirvana, punk rockers Green Day, rappers such as Eminem, Snoop Dogg and Kid Rock, not to mention the boy bands Backstreet Boys, N Sync and 98 Degrees or naughty girls Britney Spears and Christina Aguilera wanted something more. They wanted an anchor to steady their ship in the stormy passage of a world where almost anything goes.

Faith became their anchor and the Church became the ship for these young people.

That is not to say that today's young Catholics aren't part of the mainstream pop culture. Many young Catholics embrace the culture to a point. One example is the "Theology On Tap" program that was started in the early 1980s and spread to many American cities. Young drinking age adults gather at their favorite watering hole to discuss issues of faith or hear a speaker. Many young people would prefer to enjoy a beer and conversation with fellow Catholics than to spend time in the club scene so many of their friends enjoy.

These young people and millions like them are looking for answers, but they often cannot find them in the very place where they should be able to first look for them: their parents. It cannot be overstated how much the youth have been affected by the 1970s malaise of their parents' generation. Having graduated from high school in the early 1980s, I can remember when it was only the oddball family in the neighborhood that didn't go to church. The same definition could be given to the adult parent who in that era acted and dressed like their teenage or college age children. The same cannot be said today. Often these parents who act and dress like Britney Spears or her husband Kevin Federline are part of the mainstream. This behavior makes it difficult for teenagers to admire and respect their parents. Believe me, it did not take too many years of being a teacher and principal to figure this out.

Is it any wonder then that so many Catholic and Evangelical young people have embraced their faith traditions, if for no other reason than as a reaction against the empty and venal (not to mention lewd) things they see in the media or hear from their friends or even parents? These young Catholics desperately want something better. They have witnessed the results from those who have given into the age, the heartbreak, the despair, the loneliness, and the anger, and they don't want to go down that path. They may have seen the shallow lives of the characters in "Sex in the City" and "Desperate Housewives" along with real life characters like Britney Spears, Paris Hilton, or skier Bode Miller, people who are held up as their generation's icons, and they want something different, something better.

This is why meaningful youth ministry and catechetical programs are so necessary in every parish. Many young Catholics want to believe and understand their faith. However, all too often, Catholic parishes and dioceses don't provide the necessary programs for their youth, unlike our separated brethren in many Evangelical churches. I can happily report that is changing but not fast enough.

I am not being Pollyannaish. No one can deny that many young people have left the faith and continue to do so. However, many of these young people grew up in a household where there was no captain to guide the ship of faith.° Thus these young people found their own captain. Sometimes this captain told them they could do almost anything they saw fit (in the Unitarian Communion, for example). Sometimes this captain came in the guise of an overly strict form of radical Traditionalism, Protestantism, radical Islam, or even some form of a cult.

Of course, there can be no denying that young people sometimes leave the faith for no apparent reason. However, when they do, there is a good chance they will eventually return to the faith. I have seen this in my own life as some of my childhood friends who went to the same Catholic school I did who ended up leaving the church for various reasons.

"The Church was too strict," said some who left the world of faith entirely. "The Church was too corrupt and full of too many rituals," was another complaint I heard from some of my childhood friends who left for Evangelical churches. But these people, having undergone the largely vapid catechesis they did, didn't really know

---

°According to US Senator Evan Bayh of Indiana (D), 34 percent of all children are living in a home without their biological father.

their faith enough to know whether these claims were true. After all, if you don't know (much less understand) Catholicism's teaching on marital love, you will think the proscription against premarital sex is "too strict." If you don't know or understand why the Church has the rituals it does, you might find it too ritualistic.

However, with today's emphasis on "being real," the youth have a desire to learn about what they claim to belong to or believe. I believe we will not see these people leaving the church, or at least not to the same degree.

Still, even for the most intellectually curious and pious young people, it will be very difficult to be a good Catholic Christian. Let's not forget that this is a different world than the one in which most adults – even relatively young ones – grew up.

Take schoolwork, for instance. Many parents can probably attest to my belief that homework and school in general are a lot tougher than before. So many parents have told me they often cannot help their high school children with homework. The pace and depth of the subject matter is often overwhelming for them. Kids are learning geometry today at an age when people my age were learning pre-algebra.

But the difference between the world I grew up in and today is especially pronounced in the culture at large. If you are above the age of 35 as I am, you and I did not deal with what is known today as "hooking up" or having "friends with benefits." This refers to the phenomenon that young people will get together with someone of the opposite sex for anything from old-fashioned backseat make-out sessions to intercourse with no romantic attachment (or even attraction) whatsoever. It has become like having a Diet Coke together or playing a match of tennis.

This is fueled by the saturation of sex that bombards our airwaves and other media. It used to be that watching weekend football on television was a family-friendly activity. Today adults have to screen the commercials because of their salacious content. Girls' dolls are given outfits that look like something a prostitute would wear. Immodesty is not only tolerated but encouraged and celebrated.

Standing strong and being virtuous in such an environment of unrelenting temptation is hard for anyone, much less an adolescent or young adult trying to find their way in life. To survive in such a world, today's kids must quickly learn what it is they do or don't believe. This is especially true for their religious beliefs. In response to the emptiness of the world of consumerism and cheap sex, many find themselves longing for symbolism, color, and traditions in a world that denigrates and derides such considerations. It is in part for this reason that so many music videos of the day, especially rap videos, are all about colors, rituals, symbolism, and identity, and sadly they are often the only place the youth can get these things.

Fortunately for those who want something substantive, the Church fits nicely into the equation. Because there is so little tradition in their world, the Church is providing a healthy alternative for many American teens who want to find this while attempting to understand the deeper meaning of life and the world in which they live.

Bishop Robert Carlson of Saginaw, Michigan, believes the best way to help kids in this regard is get them "to know the truth." "We live in a society that is focused on rugged individualism and relativism," he says. "As an immigrant Church, we learned to become like everyone else. Well, now it is time to become counter-cultural.

"I started an apologetics class for our seniors at all of our Catholic high schools this year. Young people are going to have to know the truth when they get to college. They are going to have to answer questions posed to them from the Campus Crusade for Christ. Also, they are going to have to be able to defend their faith from pop culture junk like *The Da Vinci Code* and the Gospel of Judas. We are helping the adults to understand this, as well. We can't evangelize until we know our own faith."[6]

It was estimated that of the five million or so people in Rome for Pope John Paul II's funeral and the countless others who were stuck on the outside of town, 70 percent were under the age of 30. In a special report on the one-year anniversary of his death Francis Cardinal George of Chicago told CNN he was stunned to see so many young people. He asked as many as he could in the streets of Rome and in St. Peter's Square, "Why are you here?" The youth, from many nationalities and races, told him basically the same thing: World Youth Day.[7] CNN interviewed Secretary General of the Vatican Archbishop Renato Baccardo, who was close to the Pope, for a report that referred to the youth as Generation John Paul. When asked why these young people loved the Holy Father so much, he said, "These young people were generous, idealistic, and faithful."[8] They had answered the call that many in their parent's generation had not.

As the Holy Father lay dying, he probably knew that all the youth who had come for his final moments not only were there for him but also for the Church he had shepherded for nearly 27 years.

When John the Baptist knew his end was coming, he told his followers, "I must decrease so He (Jesus) can increase" (cf., John 3:30). In so many words, that is what John Paul II said in his dying words. As he was decreasing, the youth were increasing. The aging Polish shepherd had gathered his flock, and now it was time to go to his reward. With the flock intact and gaining in numbers, he could go in peace to the "house of the Father," as Benedict XVI said in his homily at his predecessor's funeral. They had answered his call and now they were taking spiritual ownership of the Church in the orthodox fashion for which this youth minister from Kraków had hoped, prayed, and worked.

DAVID J. HARTLINE

- CHAPTER 4 -

GROWTH OF ORTHODOXY IN THE CLERGY AND RELIGIOUS ORDERS

During Mass one weekend at my home parish in early 2006, Fr. Bill Hahn, our 30-year-old associate pastor, mentioned there were three nuns available at the end of Mass to talk about vocations and to answer any questions about their growing order. I looked around the church and saw three young women dressed in traditional habits.

Many of those who lament the decline of vocations to the historic, long-standing orders of women religious (which, by and large, have become grossly unfaithful) are often surprised to find out that many newer, very orthodox orders are indeed growing. In some cases they are growing so fast that they are running out of room to house new vocations. In that same vein, many Catholics are surprised to find that the response to questions about a priest shortage in some conservative dioceses would probably be, "What priest shortage?" These places have few problems finding priests because their message of faith is unapologetically Catholic.

The nuns who visited my parish are part of the Dominican Sisters of Mary, Mother of the Eucharist, headquartered in Ann Arbor, Michigan.[1] They were formed in 1996 by four sisters. Today, less than a decade later, they have over 60 sisters with the average age being 28! They are growing so fast they are running out of space to house everyone. I spoke with Sr. Ave Maria Hayes, OP, who came to the community nine years ago because she felt called by God to join a religious community. She said she felt very at home after visiting the Sisters of Mary, especially after seeing one of the sisters with a basketball in her hand. Sr. Ave Maria is a *big* basketball fan.[2]

This is not a unique story. Across the country there are a number of growing convents and seminaries that have seen their numbers rise. While the underlying reason for this is faith, it is also a question of practicality. Why would anyone join a community where they will have to sacrifice so much only to be surrounded by an aging population who often are bitter with the Church?

Those working in Catholic circles can testify that for the last 30 years there has been an increasing number of women's religious orders that have tried to challenge the Church on her teachings and mission. For some orders such challenges might take a more social activist nature, while others might challenge the actual hierarchical structure of the Church.

A priest I recently met told me of an incident that made him both sad and angry. He said two sisters had come to him in tears telling him how their order had become full of rituals they didn't recognize or understand. They called it New Age hooey full of prayers about "Mother Earth" and "Sister Moon." There isn't a left-wing cause the order didn't embrace. They said male bashing is a regular ritual and some refuse to attend Mass unless it is said by someone they deem to be progressive. The two nuns went on to say their community wonders why there are no younger women in their order. "Dave," he told me, "I am supposed to have answers. The only thing I could think to say was that they should approach the bishop. The two sisters have all of their financial retirement locked up with the community. They can't leave and join another one at this point. It just makes me ill."[3]

Stories like this are not unique. Perhaps it was a story such as this that caused the late John Cardinal O'Connor of New York to help start an order of nuns based on a column he wrote in 1989 for his archdiocesan newspaper. The column asked for any women interested in starting an order dedicated to life to contact him. In 1991, eight women entered as postulants for the Sisters for Life. This order is unique because it cares for pregnant women who want to have their babies but have nowhere to go. Some keep the children and some give them up for adoption but none are aborted. The order continues to grow, a living legacy to Cardinal O'Connor.

The Franciscan Sisters of the Sorrowful Mother, an order located in Toronto, OH, near the campus of Franciscan University of Steubenville, has also experienced growth. Maybe it is due to their location near one of America's most orthodox campuses or maybe it is just another sign that the tide is turning. Whatever the case, this group has 27 sisters with the average age being 34.[4]

I have talked to some young women who were considering joining a religious order. They told me they were shocked to hear how few women had even investigated some orders because they were deemed too heterodox or liberal. They felt it an unstated fact that both men and women who were considering religious life knew that any order they might join must be faithful. This observation perfectly illustrates the point Archbishop Edwin O'Brien made: "A person may give their life for a mystery but not for a question mark."

Many are wondering why the growth of orthodox orders is happening in this day and age. Aren't many orders becoming full of elderly nuns whose average age is somewhere around 65? How could orthodox communities be growing and full of so many young women? Perhaps the first clue came from my wife after we talked to Sr. Ave Maria. "They all seemed so happy and easy going," she said. "Sr. Ave Maria was so down to earth and seemed so heartfelt in her excitement about what she's doing."

Sr. Ave Maria told me she had explored other orders but felt most comfortable with this one because the joy of the Lord can be seen on the nuns' faces and in their work. It is worth noting that the common ingredient in the growth of these orders is adoration. It seems to be a universal trait in dioceses and orders that are growing in vocations to the religious life.

I have heard it said that only lost, unsuccessful women turn to a religious community because they can't fit into society and have no skills to offer. One only need look at how educated and successful some of these women are before they make that unsubstantiated charge. There are nurses, teachers, and various kinds of other professional women in many of the orthodox orders.

Convents aren't the only sign of younger people looking for something more traditional. Many young men are also looking for a similar fit. While most young men find the seminary for their local diocese welcomes their traditional beliefs, some find that they are more comfortable joining a particular order such as the Dominicans, the Legionaries of Christ or the Franciscan Friars of the Renewal.

The United States certainly has seen a decline in the number of priests in the last 40 years. However, in dioceses where the practice of the faith is very orthodox, most would simply say there is no priest shortage.

For example, the Dioceses of Wichita, Kansas; Lincoln, Nebraska; Arlington, Virginia; Fargo, North Dakota; and Peoria, Illinois, have been ordaining more men than archdioceses that are five to ten times their size.

The following data was taken from the 2005 *Catholic Directory*. The average number of priests per Catholic in the United States is one priest for every 4,723 Catholics. Los Angeles has the fewest number of priests per population with one priest for every 12,217 Catholic, and El Paso is not far behind with one priest for every 11,927 Catholics. However, the Diocese of Lincoln's ratio is one priest for every 737 Catholics, and the Archdiocese of Omaha is second with one priest for every 1,755 Catholics.

The top 13 vocation-rich dioceses all have fewer than 200,000 Catholics. One could argue this is because their populations aren't growing and their small size allows them to concentrate on potential candidates. While this argument may have some merit, most of these smaller dioceses don't have a full-time vocations director. People in the Diocese of Savannah seem to believe that optimism is a key factor. Fr. Stephen Angell, who was ordained in 2004, made the following point: "Whereas some seminarians from the other diocese have never met their bishop, the seminarians of the Diocese of Savannah know their bishop, and Bishop Boland knows them long before he places his hands upon their heads."

To say that surging numbers in priestly vocations are tied to Church orthodoxy would be an understatement. Two examples illustrate this point. The Diocese of Rochester, which is considered to be one of the most liberal dioceses in America, has a Catholic population of 342,000. They have a total of six seminarians studying for the priesthood. The Archdiocese of Omaha has a Catholic population of 230,000 Catholics with 30 seminarians. In Nebraska, the Diocese of Lincoln (run by perhaps the most conservative ordinary in America, Bishop Fabian Bruskewitz) has a population of 89,236 Catholics with 24 in their local seminary and 10 in other seminaries. Put another way, while Lincoln and Omaha do not have as many Catholics as Rochester, these two dioceses have sixty-four men studying for the priesthood while Rochester only has six men.[P]

Let's look at two large archdioceses, Detroit and Denver. Detroit, home of Adam Cardinal Maida and arguably the most liberal bishop in the nation, Auxiliary Bishop Thomas Gumbleton, has a Catholic population of 1,457,780. They have 32 men in their own seminary and 2 men studying in other seminaries. Denver, home to Archbishop Charles Chaput, another very orthodox bishop, has a Catholic population of 344,042 with 76 men in their own seminary and 2 men studying in other seminaries. Although it is four times smaller than Detroit, Denver has one and one half times as many seminarians studying for the priesthood.[5]

"Those discerning a vocation need to see a happy priest," said Bishop Frederick Campbell of the Diocese of Columbus. When I

[P] The Rochester diocese, once the see of Archbishop Fulton J. Sheen, is run by the notoriously liberal Bishop Matthew Clark.

asked if there were any other secrets to vocations success, he said, "You have to ask. If you don't let people know how important the role of a priest is, they won't come. They have to be asked and so much of what they see in the world tells them to shun this life. We have to tell them why it is a good life."[6]

Several years ago, the book *Goodbye, Good Men*, by Michael S. Rose caused quite a stir. It claimed that many American seminaries were "pink palaces." That is, they were places where the homosexual subculture was tolerated. On his book's web site, Rose says that those running the seminaries were intent on overthrowing "traditional beliefs, standards, and disciplines – especially Church teachings on sexuality."

If you had asked my friend Fr. Bill Hahn about this when he entered the seminary in 1998 for the Diocese of Columbus, he would have probably concurred. Fortunately, however, he saw some drastic changes while he was there.

"My first year at the Pontifical College Josephinum in Columbus... [we] had a few guys who weren't that faithful to the Church's teachings," he said. "We even had some guys who were part of a gay subculture. However, there were some changes in leadership during my first year. [The new rector came in and cleaned house.] Following that, some of the guys who weren't loyal to the Church's teachings were dismissed. After that I had an amazing experience. It was like a smorgasbord. You know there's a lot there, but you still can't get enough. You kind of view the guys that were with you in the seminary as a band of brothers, kind of like being in battle. You are going to help them and they are going to help you."[7]

This is just one bit of anecdotal evidence that things in seminaries are turning around, although it must be said that the orthodox seminarians walk a very careful line, and many purposefully hide devotions such as Eucharistic adoration and praying the Rosary. There is still a long way to go, but things are getting better.

Many American Catholics are shocked to learn that the priest and women religious shortage is predominately a western problem. In much of Africa and Asia seminaries and convents are teeming with candidates studying to become priests and nuns. In one Ugandan diocese, there are three seminaries with 120-200 seminarians each. Seminaries in Poland are also doing well. As a result of this vocation rich environment, many areas of the western world are finding priests and nuns from the Third World. In a strange role reversal, these Third World priests and religious are now evangelizing the West as those from the West once evangelized the Third World 50-100 years ago.

In 1978, the year Pope John Paul II became pontiff, there were 63,882 diocesan priests and seminarians around the world. In a mere 25 years that number had risen 76 percent to 112,373. While some in Europe and North America were blaming their decline in the number of men becoming priests on celibacy, Africa and Asia saw an increase in vocations.[8]

In 2005, 2 percent of American Catholics were of Asian descent. However, 12 percent of students in American seminaries were of Asian descent.[9] Recently, I met Fr. Victor Udechukwu, a young Nigerian priest assigned to the Wheeling-Charleston Diocese. Fr. Udechukwu told me the secret to the packed seminaries in Africa and Asia: Family support. He told me that in his parish alter servers weren't assigned, they just showed up to serve.

"Many altar servers show up more than one hour before Mass so that they can serve," he said. "They want to serve the Church, and their families are glad they are doing it. An Asian or African family is liable to not only support their son or daughter should they decide to become a priest or enter religious life, but also to nurture the possibility with the reverence and piety they model at home. This support is all too often lacking in American or European homes."[10]

In 2006, 57 priests were ordained in Hanoi, Vietnam.[11] The communist country that once tried to wipe away all forms of western life is now seeing men receive Holy Orders, some of whom will tend to the needs of westerners. It is true that many of these men had waited for years for government permission to receive ordination, and that this only came after arduous negotiations between Hanoi and the Holy See. Still, there is such an interest in the priestly life in this former French colony that some believe if all the men who wanted to attend seminary could, there would be 57 ordinations every month. That obviously is an exaggeration, but one that serves the point of how great the interest in the priestly life is in Vietnam.

Unfortunately, the same enthusiasm for the faith is not evident in the very nations that once sent out missionaries to evangelize places such as Vietnam. A 2006 *Catholic World News* story reported on a newly ordained Vietnamese priest who visited Europe and was dismayed to find so many empty churches there. He expected to see churches packed and people excited to see a brother in Christ from a country where the true faith is persecuted. Instead, he found complete indifference, which the empty churches only exemplified. Here he was in the "heart of Christianity," and by all appearances that heart was on life support.

However, this isn't the first time this heart has needed help staying alive. St. Benedict, from whom Benedict XVI took his pontifical name, is thought by many to have re-civilized and evangelized Europe through his monastic movement. Also, during the early Middle Ages, Irish priests kept the continental European Church alive while Viking invasions, disease, and former pagan influences that lingered like a bad hangover took their toll. It is not that the priests being ordained today aren't great representatives of the Church in Europe, but rather that there are so few of them. The low numbers are indicative that the faith there has lost its way, become unsure of itself, and forgotten how to speak to the age and its myriad problems.

Saint Louis University Professor and author Mark Ruff has talked of a disconnect between the youth and the clergy in the

German Church that had existed for many years before Pope Benedict came on the scene. When the youth needed bold claims, certitude, and the truth, their clergy gave them pabulum and feel-good slogans. This (coupled with the cynicism toward religion that was born during the Enlightenment and blossomed full force in the decades following World War II) perhaps best explains the low levels of church attendance in Europe[12] and thus that continent's woeful vocations crisis.[q]

While many might agree that perhaps the Third World has never experienced the type of priest shortage the western world has, and perhaps Europe is worse off than America as far as the need for priests, is there any place in the United States where there isn't a priest shortage? The answer is an emphatic, yes. There are places in the United States where there isn't a priest shortage, and it isn't due to the area becoming economically depressed or to the population shrinking. The one common denominator in dioceses where there isn't a priest shortage is the bishop or archbishop's emphasis on orthodoxy.

Can you imagine a diocese or archdiocese where the bishop or archbishop is not fretting over which parish's pastor can take on the most work and which large parish can get along with just one priest? There are such places in the United States, and they all have orthodox leadership. As previously noted, the Diocese of Lincoln, Nebraska, has seemed to be immune to the priest shortage for decades. While many Church liberals and moderates bristle at the name of Bishop Bruskewitz because of his very orthodox style, he doesn't have the worries that some of his brother bishops do with regard to a shortage of priests. While some dioceses have seen an increase in vocations through collaborative efforts in their parishes, the Diocese of Lincoln has never had to go to the depths that others have had to in order to attract young men to the seminary.

---

[q] However, it must be noted that even in Europe, the number of seminarians has risen, albeit slightly. In 1978, there were just 10 seminarians for every 100 priests; as of 2003, the most recent year for which I could find information, there were 12:100. A fourth of all of these are Polish.

Also, consider the Archdiocese of Denver's vocations. Less than a decade after the 1993 World Youth Day, Denver saw a threefold increase in the number of vocations. Archbishop Charles Chaput, another orthodox bishop, replaced Archbishop Stafford, who moved to Rome and was made a prominent cardinal. Some say Denver's turnaround in vocations was something nearly miraculous, much like the days at Mile High Stadium when Denver Broncos quarterback John Elway led that football team to victory with seemingly miraculous comebacks in the fourth quarter.

Many in the archdiocese would say they are just doing what works by giving potential seminarians what they need to make a good decision. Vocations candidates need something to believe in. Denver has given them this in two ways. First, the archdiocese has provided orthodox leadership. Second, it continues to reverberate the impacts of World Youth Day in the same way a pond continues to experience ripples even after the stone that made them has faded from sight.

To the east of Denver lies another vocations success story, the Archdiocese of Kansas City in Kansas. The recently retired Archbishop James P. Keleher saw a dramatic increase in vocations during his tenure there and attributed his archdiocese's success to perpetual adoration.

There is also the Diocese of Arlington in suburban Northern Virginia. With the hectic nature of life in Washington, DC, one wouldn't think it would have many religious vocations. Yet in a seven-year stretch from 1991-98, the diocese ordained 55 men to the priesthood. Not bad for a place that had relatively few Catholics until the recent population boom hit the Washington, DC, metro area.

The underlying theme running through all the vocations successes detailed above seems to be that people want Church leaders to stand for something and believe what they say. A case in point is the Diocese of Saginaw, Michigan. When Sioux Falls Bishop Robert

Carlson was transferred there in early 2005, there were no candidates for the seminary. By the time Fall arrived, he had 16 men and more coming the next year.

When I asked Bishop Carlson what happened, he said, "I appointed myself vocations director. I think letting the young men know the bishop thinks their job is important says something. However, I don't want you to think I took just anyone. I had to say 'no' to some young men who were interested. The key is knowing what God is calling you to do."[13]

Considering all of this, therefore, the sentiment of the orthodox young men and women entering religious life seems to be reflected in the comments of Nikki Shasserre, spokeswoman for the Catholic campus group Fellowship of Catholic University Students (FOCUS): "We don't want to change the Church. We want the Church to change us."[14]

DAVID J. HARTLINE

- CHAPTER 5 -

DEFENDERS OF THE FAITH –
CLERGY & RELIGIOUS

"If anyone truly knew how close the Church came to imploding in the late 1970s [at the hands of] its own clergy, everyone would experience two emotions. The first emotion would be relief that it didn't happen, and the second would be bewilderment that it ever got so bad."[1]

This quote came from a priest who is not very doctrinaire. Although his politics may be viewed as somewhat liberal, he never bought into the "hallmark" spirituality one often associates with the warm-fuzzy period of the 1970s. This man has always struck me as being very pastoral. He told me this me around 1999, and his words often come to me whenever I hear a story about some clergy member who is advocating something that doesn't seem appropriate to Catholicism. How did the change from a warm-fuzzy Catholicism to a more traditional faith take place?

The first and most obvious answer is this: The Holy Spirit is alive and well in the Catholic Church. For the Church to have survived 2,000 years tells us something about the truth of this statement. In the late 1970s, the Church began to see an amazing turn around in the clergy (although the effects may not have been evident until at least the 1980s). We all know the effect Pope John Paul II and Mother Teresa had on vocations. But there is another person who is responsible for the slow turnaround: Mother Angelica, foundress of EWTN. The woman from Canton, Ohio, who set up shop in the Bible Belt has played a key role in changing Catholicism in America.[2]

How could Mother Angelica inspire Catholics to a religious vocation while more liberal or heterodox clergy could not? Look again at the quote of Archbishop Edwin O'Brien, who answered this question by saying, "A person may give their life for a mystery but not for a question mark." The essence of liberal or progressive thinking is to take the mystery out of the equation. They feel that by being more "relevant" (i.e., more relativistic) and not so rigorous, many will come into the Church.

Conservatives argue just the opposite. Once the mystery is taken out of the equation, the faith becomes a mere social service agency, and the trappings of the faith are replaced with that of political activism.

Faithful young men and women often cite Mother Angelica and her EWTN network as being the reason they entered into religious life. She also inspired some relatively well-known non-Catholic clergy to consider entering the Church, Fr. Richard John Neuhaus, for instance. Once one of the Lutheran Communion's towering figures, he converted to Catholicism and then became an ordained priest in 1991.

EWTN is a towering force in the swing towards orthodox Catholicism. If it were not for EWTN, the somewhat small world of Catholic communications would be even smaller. To read Raymond Arroyo's book *Mother Angelica: The Remarkable Story of a Nun, Her Nerve, and a Network of Miracles* is to read the story of a woman's amazing determination to help shore up the Catholic Church in the United States in spite of some of its leaders.[3] Mother Angelica enlisted the support of all who would help her, whether it was friendly clergy, the laity, or Evangelicals like Jim Bakker (the former PTL minister who sent some employees to help the cause when EWTN first went on the air). Mother Angelica hated to plead for money but did just that anytime it seemed as if the network couldn't keep afloat due to financial strains or when she had run-ins with noted clergy.

Those young men and women and those not so young who are entering religious life nearly all say EWTN strongly aided their recognition of their religious vocation. This shows how one person – even you – can make a tremendous difference in the faith.

Furthermore, the influence the new clergy is having on the young is amazing. One could argue that this could spark even more of an interest in vocations. Indeed, that may already be happening. Fr. Hahn, a young priest all of 30 years old, is quite popular with the young for his involvement in parish activities. He related a conversation he overheard between two high school senior girls. In addition to discussing their college choices, they were also discussing what religious orders interested them. Fr. Hahn's anecdote and Mother Angelica's perseverance are both testimony to what one faithful person can do.

Looks can be deceiving, and in the case of Fr. Mitch Pacwa, SJ, that is certainly so. The cowboy-boot wearing priest may look like a west Texas pastor on a rural sick call rather than a priest who has a PhD and speaks 12 languages, including ancient Greek and Aramaic. A very popular priest among young people, he might have been known as strictly an interesting college professor if it weren't for EWTN. However, his down-to-the-earth style mixed with his broad intellect plays well in front of the cameras. Fr. Pacwa seems equally at home debating an Evangelical on apologetics or chatting with teenagers about their faith.

As noted above, Fr. Neuhaus was a well-known and gifted Lutheran scholar. In the 1960s, he was active in the civil rights movement and was friends with Dr. Martin Luther King. He was pastor of a poor, predominately African-American Lutheran congregation in New York City.

Something wasn't quite right with his ecclesiological barometer, however. Like many Lutheran and Catholic clergy, Father felt Christian unity needed to come sooner rather than later. At the same time, he began to feel more and more comfortable with the Catholic Church. Some suggested that he could play some part in making unity a reality, and if his conversion could be the spark then so be it. Thus, he became Fr. Neuhaus in 1991 when he was ordained to the Catholic priesthood in New York City.

If comfort were involved, Fr. Neuhaus would have never left the Lutheran Church. Well-paid and well-honored, he was a rising star in a relatively small pond. The Catholic Church would be the more uncomfortable place to be because of its ocean-like size (not to mention its ocean-like divisions). But he realized Catholicism was true and that he had no choice but to join the Church Christ has founded.

Fr. Neuhaus reached what may turn out to be the height of his prominence during Pope John Paul II's last days, when he was frequently asked to play the role of commentator. He also narrated EWTN's live coverage from Vatican City. His regular job is serving as editor of *First Things*, a prominent journal of religion and politics. He continues to be looked upon with fascination over his decision to convert and for the intellectual muscle he wields.

But most priests won't find a Neuhaus-like life after ordination. Indeed, the demands on clergy can sometimes get the best of any priest or bishop. Endless meetings and depressing Church politics can easily cause burnout. Surely few clergy expected long meetings on the parish budget or the need to cool tempers over the fine points of their religious education programs when they received Holy Orders. However, such conflicts come with the territory. Priests and especially bishops must quickly learn how to react to the administrative as well as the spiritual needs of a parish or diocese.

Bishop Frederick Campbell of the Diocese of Columbus said, "It is all part of being a bishop, the spiritual, the financial, the paperwork, etc. I found I was surrounded by good and talented people when I came to Columbus [he was installed in January 2005]. You pray that God will provide if a need comes up. A bishop has many things to do, including praying that God will provide. I found He has."[4]

Sometimes affluence means less work for the needy of a bishop's diocese but more spiritual work. Bermuda's Bishop Robert Kurtz, CR, found that his flock has little poverty, but the wealth that some possess can create tremendous resentment.

"Many who have done well here are grateful to God for what they have," he said, "and they see to it that they help the less fortunate. Unfortunately, a good number also believe they alone are responsible for all they have, so they give no thanks to God and assume they are solely responsible for their good fortune. In addition, the wealth creates unrealistic expectations among some who are not well off."[5]

Through an odd series of circumstances too detailed to go into here, my wife and I once found ourselves in Bermuda. I made contact with an old teaching colleague Jim Silcott, who serves as principal of Mount Saint Agnes Catholic Academy there. He and two Sisters of Charity - Halifax – Sister Judith Rollo, SC, and Sister Dolores Sullivan, SC – suggested I meet Bishop Kurtz.

As I walked toward his office for the scheduled meeting, I ask a passerby if this was the right street for the Catholic diocesan office. I was promptly told to go another direction. When I arrived at the location my "helper" told me was my desired destination, I found I was at Bermuda's "dialysis" office, not the diocesan office. I immediately telephoned the bishop's office. Bishop Kurtz answered the phone and told me which direction to take. He told me that in about five minutes I would get to the bottom of the appropriate street. I was told to then look to the top of the hill, and I would see a man flailing his arms. That man turned out to be Bishop Kurtz. The courtesy he showed was unforgettable. He even drove me back to my hotel. He was a true shepherd.

And though the demands of a parish priest can be overwhelming (especially for those in large parishes), a dedicated and inspired laity can provide greatly needed assistance.

"We have so many people who want to help and/or start something new that I never feel overwhelmed here," said Fr. Jeff Rimmelspach pastor of St. Joan of Ark in fast growing Powell, Ohio. "We had 750 families less than 20 years ago when the parish was started. Now we have 3,000, and I find there are many who are willing to help. Sometimes I have to say no. We had a group here that wanted to start a parish yoga club. I have nothing against yoga, but I didn't feel it would have been right for the parish. Sometimes people come up with ideas that I would have never thought of such as a sewing club. I was approached by someone about that idea, and I thought 'This is a young parish! No young person is going to come here and sew.' Yet it has been a tremendous success. They sew blankets for the needy, and they have sewn many of them."

Fr. Rimmelspach came from St. Mary Catholic Church in Bremen, OH, a rural parish that had a history of Catholicism and was steeped in Catholic culture. "The Church there is part of the social fabric of that area," said Father. "People know the faith because not only was it taught in church but also at home. At St. Joan's we are lucky if we have 25 percent of the Catholic youth who go to a Catholic high school or attend high school parish education classes. Sometimes here at St. Joan's we have some very eager Catholics who want to learn what they never did when they were young. Now they have kids on the way or maybe already here, and they want to learn in a hurry. That's why Bible study is so popular here. Also, we are one of the few churches I know, maybe the only church I know, to have Eucharistic adoration and small church communities."[6]

Again, the sign of a successful pastor is that he knows the needs of his flock and tries to accommodate them. The work doesn't stop there, however. A successful pastor also needs to embrace God's plan when he feels he is being pushed into something but doesn't fully understand. Shortly after Hurricane Katrina, a woman approached Fr. Rimmelspach and sought help for her parish in Bay St. Louis,

Mississippi. He saw her again the next weekend and told her he would see if there was anything he could do besides the diocesan special collection. After prayer and reflection, Fr. Rimmelspach came up with a plan to help the badly destroyed parish, although he never saw the woman who approached him again. He was able to start a very successful parish program that sends volunteers to the nearly destroyed Mississippi town to assist with their needs.

Hopefully, no one enters into the priesthood or religious life in hopes that they will be recognized. Pope Benedict said as much when he ordained several men into the priesthood in May 2006.

However, sometimes the Holy Spirit allows efforts to be known by the highest officials in the Vatican, even the Pope himself. Bishop Carlson of Saginaw had this experience in Spring 2006. He was leading a pilgrimage to Rome, and the last thing he expected to do was meet Pope Benedict, but that's exactly what happened. Vatican officials contacted him, and Bishop Carlson hustled his way over to Vatican City to meet the Holy Father.

In an interview for my CatholicReport.org website, Carlson told me the "Holy Father had some questions about our vocations. We have had some successes and he was interested in them. I found Pope Benedict extremely knowledgeable about what was going on in the realm of vocations and in the seminaries. I felt truly blessed to have had the meeting."[7]

Unlike many priests in the past whose autocratic leadership style led to charges of "clericalism," today's clergy are not distant. They don't just unilaterally make decisions, damn what the "benighted" parishioners think. When appropriate, they seek counsel from their flock (most even have a parish council). Nonetheless, they are not afraid to show leadership and to steer their flocks when they feel this is necessary. Thus the new clergy is presenting the faithful with a clear path, somewhat like a successful coach does, even if it isn't always popular on the field. But when all is said and done in the locker room, those who were pushed and encouraged are happy they were. As in the days of Jesus when the apostles and disciples learned His message was not always fun and games, so too the priests who walk in Jesus' footsteps know they must lead, even if it means risking one's popularity. The tide is turning because many clergy realize they must adhere to what Jesus taught. That may not always be popular, but in the end a good coach always gets the respect he earned. So it is with the clergy.

- CHAPTER 6 -

THERE'S SOMETHING ABOUT MARY

Another way the tide is turning toward Catholicism is through Marian apparitions and increased devotion to Mary through means of the Rosary and such. By these means, many are being pulled into a deeper relationship with our Lord Jesus Christ and thus coming into the Church He founded upon the rock of Peter. The visions of Our Lady may also be preparing the way for the conversion of those of other faiths, including Islam.

For years many Protestants and secular thinkers accused Catholics of seeing the Virgin Mary everywhere. She was reported to be appearing to the young and old the world over. Bumper stickers popped up saying, "See Mary here, see Mary there, Catholics see Mary everywhere." However, by the first decade of the first millennium the whole world, Catholic and non-Catholic, actually were seeing Mary everywhere.

She was in the movies and on television shows and it seems leading many to the Catholic Church. For numerous converts to Catholicism, Mary was one of the leading reasons that they came to the Catholic Church. Even Muslims revere her as evidenced by her prominence in the Koran. How could such an exalted woman, the world's only virgin woman to give birth, not be more highly revered by other Christian denominations? How can they so deeply misunderstand the devotion the Catholic Church shows to her?

Catholics do not worship Mary. Church teaching, since the time of Christ, points to Mary as interceding to God for Christians (cf., John 2:1-5). She intercedes just like any other saint (cf., Rev. 5:8, 8:3-4). Yet, she's not just any other saint. She was deemed worthy by

God to bear His Son, Jesus. For devout Catholics there's something peculiar about a Christian who recognizes the virgin birth yet doesn't think Mary is otherwise any different than any other woman. The earliest Christians had the greatest reverence for her, and early Church holy days revolving around her were held in the highest regard (they still are). Yet, some fundamentalists don't look upon her with the same esteem. Even though they came on the scene 1,700-2,000 years later, they believe they know better than the earliest Christians.

The reverence early Christians had for her is evident in the early Church. Take, for instance, the *Protoevangelium of James*, which was written circa 120 AD. It offers some remarkable, in-depth accounts of Mary's life. Origen talks of "Mary ever-Virgin" in 248 AD. St. Athanasius wrote in 360 AD about the evils of the Arian heresy, saying, "Let those, therefore, who deny that the Son is by nature from the Father and proper to His essence deny also that He took true human flesh from the ever-virgin Mary." Sts. Jerome, Ephraim of Syria, Irenaeus, John Damascene, Ambrose, Augustine, and other early Church Fathers wrote lovingly and convincingly of her special status.

Yet it wasn't just the ancient Christians who admired Mary. The leaders of the Protestant Reformation Martin Luther, John Calvin and Ulrich Zwingli all revered her and believed in her perpetual virginity.[1]

Marian Apparitions have occurred since the early Christian era. However, one of the most famous sightings occurred in Lourdes, France, in 1845. The most famous of the twentieth century apparitions occurred at Fatima, Portugal, in 1917. The messages young children received in both cases warned the world that power of God's love could not be tested forever. Our Lady confirmed that Hell is a real place, and the visions served as a warning of sorts. The Fatima visions were a foreshadowing of world events that would take place in the twentieth century. While the skeptics scoffed, the barely educated children warned of events that later occurred but hardly seemed possible in 1917. They foresaw another global conflict after the devastating World War I, the so-called "war to end all wars." They also predicted the emergence of communism as a world power, its demise, the brutal world atheistic regimes it would spawn, and an attempt on a future pope's life.[2]

These events gripped Catholics, and while few others paid attention to them, many would start to years later after the assassination attempt on Pope John Paul II, the end of communism, and in 2000 when Pope John Paul II revealed the third secret of Fatima.

Before all this, most non-Catholics had no knowledge that Mary sometimes appeared to the faithful. For many, especially the elderly and movie buffs, *Miracle of Our Lady of Fatima*, a 1951 film directed by John Brahm, or the more well-known *Song of Bernadette* were perhaps their only exposure to Marian apparitions. Outside such pop culture offerings, or perhaps a sermon against them by a very conservative fundamentalist pastor, few non-Catholics would have any knowledge of these phenomena.

Then, on May 13, 1981, Mehmet Ali Ağca shot Pope John Paul II. This Turkish hitman seemed to have had a number of high-level contacts in the various radical groups in Europe as well as the Bulgarian Secret Police. His arrest set off alarm bells in many western capitals. He seemed to know too many people to be merely a gunman or a deranged psychopath who wanted to kill the Pope.[3] How did he fail in his mission, and how was he caught? Most importantly, how did Pope John Paul II survive? The answer to this and other questions seemed obvious to many Catholics who were interested in Marianology or prophecy.

May 13 is a historic day in the history of apparitions. On May 13, 1917, the apparitions to the little children in the small village of Fatima began. Pope John Paul II knew the history of Fatima well. Thus he believed his survival was no coincidence. He was always convinced that the Virgin Mary had interceded on his behalf and kept the bullet that hit him from taking his life.

One year to the day after the shooting, the Pope flew to Fatima and placed the bullet into the crown that rested on the head of Mary's statue there. Pope John Paul II also knew he must do one more thing in order to fully repay Mary for interceding with her Son Jesus to spare his life: He had to consecrate Russia to her Immaculate Heart (as per Our Lady's request to the Fatima seers). Why was this necessary? The answers lie in the secrets that were told to the children at Fatima.

Our Lady told the children Russia would fall to communism. Indeed, this is one of the most puzzling aspects for skeptics about Fatima: How could the relatively uneducated children have known that Russia would be swept up in a communist revolution? After all, in the years leading up to the apparitions, most would have predicted that highly industrialized nations such as Germany and the United Kingdom would have fallen to communism before the backwards, barely industrialized agrarian state of Russia. To the believer, however, no explanation was necessary. God had taken an impossibility of history and revealed it to these appointed children. A faithful Catholic would have no problem believing the hand of God was involved in this momentous event. Our Lady indicated that the way to release Russia from communism was to consecrate that nation to her Immaculate Heart.

Thus, it is believed that Pope John Paul II consecrated Russia to Mary's Immaculate Heart sometime in 1984.[5] As if on cue, major changes began to occur in the Soviet Union. Constantin Chernenko was the last of the old guard, hard line communist leaders. The Soviet KGB and the aging Politburo knew they had to do something drastic to stop the downfall of communism. Already alarm bells were sounding in Moscow about the pace of the West's technological advances. While many in the West scoffed at President Reagan's Strategic Defense Initiative (SDI), or Star Wars as it was referred to, the Soviet Union's power structure panicked and decided it needed to have a younger leader who might cajole the West into concessions or at least appear less menacing.

Mikhail Gorbachev became that leader. He proposed a new system of openness towards the West called *glasnost*. At first, he was received cautiously, but when Britain's Iron Lady, Prime Minister Margaret Thatcher said he was someone with whom she could do business, many in the West rejoiced. People of faith began to wonder if something else was afoot. It was learned that Mikhail Gorbachev, although officially atheist, was baptized when he was a child.

During the subsequent years, many chinks in the armor of the old Soviet Bloc countries began to appear as Pope John Paul II's trips to his native Poland early in his pontificate began to bear fruit. Communism's grip on society had never been as strong in Poland as it had been in East Germany or many of the other Eastern European communist states, and it began to weaken even further with the growth of the Solidarity movement and the advent of Gorbachev's *glasnost* policy.

Then in 1989, these and other events led to one of the greatest bursts of freedom in history. The Berlin Wall fell, and with it communist regimes throughout the East Bloc started to crumble. Poland, which had the East Bloc's first free elections, led the way. What political scientists thought would never happen in young people's lifetime had occurred in their own. What could have caused such a miraculous series of events? For many Catholics no explanation is necessary: The Fatima apparitions had been true.

While the Marian apparitions of Fatima may have seemed distant and long ago to most, the events in Medugorje, Yugoslavia, were playing out right in front of many Catholics' eyes. Medugorje would be a rallying cry for many in the Church in the 1980s. Many parishes were gripped by talks about the apparitions. People traveled to Yugoslavia to see for themselves what these visions were all about.

On June 24, 1981, several small children from the village of Medugorje, located in what is now Bosnia-Herzegovina, said the Virgin Mary appeared to them. They contend she continues to appear to some to this very day. The Church has not ruled on the subject, as the investigation continues. The local bishop believes they are not true. Nevertheless, Medugorje has led to many conversions and has encouraged people to explore other apparitions that the Church has approved.

For Catholics, Mary has always intervened in times of trouble. Historically, the trouble came in many forms, whether it was the early days of the Roman Empire when pagan emperors persecuted the Church or modern examples such as communist and Islamic aggression. The events of September 11, 2001, and subsequent attacks left many Catholics wondering if the Virgin Mary had helped them before in other times of Islamic extremism. Many Catholics may not be aware that when they recite "Our Lady of Victory, pray for us," they recall a historical battle that happened in the Mediterranean Sea in the sixteenth century.

The Ottoman Empire was trying to expand eastward, and the Ottomans (present day Turks) had their sights set on the rich Italian trading cities such as Milan and the destruction of the Church of Rome. Christian nations resolved to meet them on the sea at a place then known as Lepanto.

The Christian forces aligned against the Ottomans hardly presented a picture of unity. They were a disparate group of defenders who were thrown together out of fear of the consequences of an Ottoman victory. The cast of characters, included Don Juan of Austria and Cervantes (who went on to write *Don Quixote*).

During the darkest hours of the battle, Pius V, who had ordered all of Rome to pray the Rosary, saw out of his window a vision of the battle, including the galleon on which hung a banner with an image representing the apparition of Our Lady of Guadalupe.

At this precise moment, the Muslims began to lose the advantage that had heretofore been theirs in the battle. Against all odds the Christian forces overpowered the Ottoman fleet, which culminated in the destruction of nearly 75 percent of their navy and the freeing of thousands of Christians galley slaves from the holds of Ottoman ships. The Ottoman Empire and expansive Islam would not threaten the west again for some time.

Unfortunately, the battle became something of a cautionary tale for the victorious Christian forces as pride, greed, and a need for power would prohibit the Christian forces from fully taking advantage of their victory and creating an alliance many had hoped would promote greater unity among the West.[4] Nonetheless, Our Lady had interceded on behalf of her children at Lepanto. This was proof to many that, when needed, she would always be there to rescue the Faith.

The connection between Marian apparitions and Islam began long before the 1500s, however. The first connection happened in the late 9th century when the Moorish commander Mirat surrendered to Charlemagne at Lorus, France. Lorus centuries later became known as Lourdes, the site of the famous apparitions of 1858. Through such occurrences, many Marianologists believe Mary is reaching out to the Muslim people. This is not a sign of conquest, but a plea for unity.[5]

The miracle and apparitions of Fatima also might reveal a significant connection between Islam and Catholicism that few realize. Fatima is the only town in Portugal with an Islamic name. Not only is it the only town with an Islamic name, it is the name of Mohammad's favorite daughter. The Koran calls her the most exalted of all women, surpassed only by the Blessed Virgin. Of all the thousands of towns in Portugal, why did Mary appear in the one town that had an Islamic name? I believe it was to reach out to Muslims to welcome them into the Church to which many of their ancestors in the Middle East and North Africa once belonged. Just like Fatima foretold the end of communism before it began, maybe Fatima is also a sign that Muslims will soon return home to the Church in which their ancestors once worshipped.

The connection to Islam doesn't stop there. The patroness of the Americas is Our Lady of Guadalupe. The word Guadalupe is a Spanish-Arabic word meaning "wolf river." Some may remember that Mary appeared to Juan Diego in 1531 when few in the New World were Catholic. The people of the New World all believed in indigenous, pagan religions. In a few short years after the apparition, however, nine million indigenous Mexicans became Catholic, an astounding development in an era where the only form of communications was word of mouth.

In the image preserved on the tilma (poncho) of St. Juan Diego, still housed in a basilica near Mexico City, Mary is standing over a snake and a crescent moon. Catholic theology believes the snake symbolizes Satan. Muslims use the crescent moon as their symbol. Does this symbol mean that one day Mary will bring Muslims back to the Church of their ancestors?[6]

One of the most interesting Marian apparitions occurred in the predominately Muslim country of Egypt. The pictures of the apparitions were some of the most dramatic ever taken.

In 1968, millions of Egyptians, the majority being Muslim, witnessed the apparitions at Zeitoun. None other than the famed Egyptian nationalist President Gamal Abdul Nasser saw them as well. Islam has always held out a special place for Mary. She is mentioned dozens of times in the Koran, which calls her a virgin. One could argue that Muslims revere Mary more than some Protestants do. They even call her "il-Sittneh" or "Our Lady." It should be noted that many Muslims in Egypt visited Zeitoun, even some who were sick and in need of healing. Again Zeitoun is another example of Mary reaching out to the Islamic world.[7]

But while some Muslims have been receptive to Marian visions (some even make pilgrimages to Fatima), the same cannot be said of most Protestants. The various apparitions have drawn a storm of protest from many Evangelical leaders. Perhaps because of the growing Evangelical-Catholic unity on many political and social issues, many Evangelical leaders have politely chosen not to discuss the issue. However, this accord does not prevent some fundamentalist television personalities – John Ankerberg, for example – from stating that Satan, not God is behind these apparitions. Ankerberg says he is convinced that many sincere Catholics believe what they are hearing and seeing, but Satan is playing a cruel trick on them. Apparitions, says Ankerberg, are not from God, and in fact he claims the New Testament warned about such trickery.[8]

Obviously, the subject of Mary is very touchy for most Protestants. Because the issue of Marian apparitions is not explicitly mentioned in the New Testament, those who have a *sola scriptura* view of the Bible might not see God's hand in these great events. For Catholics, however, God continues to show His love and guidance in many ways, apparitions being one of them. Certainly if God deemed Mary worthy enough to bear His Son, then Mary is worthy enough to continue to spread her Son's mission. While many mainline Protestant leaders may feel the subject of Mary has not been emphasized enough in their communions, few are sufficiently interested to pay her much attention, much less concede the points made by the Catholic Church about her.

The subject is much more difficult for Evangelical leaders. As mentioned above many won't even discuss the matter, but some will and their views often upset Catholics. John Ankerberg is obviously not the only fundamentalist leader who will denounce the Catholic Church's view of Mary.

One of the more dramatic anti-Marian groups is the Street Preachers Fellowship. This national group actually shows up at

Marian events to tell Catholics that they are going to hell for their beliefs. One of the more dramatic events took place in Carey, OH, at the Our Lady of Consolation Shrine, during an Assumption Day in August 2005. What actually took place is dependent upon who you believe. However, no one would disagree that it was a riot.

The Carey Chief of Police Dennis Yingling and Pastor Rod McRae of the Street Preachers Fellowship agreed that it was the Catholic worshippers who started the riot.[9] They put the blame on young Chaldean worshippers from Detroit.[t]

Many Catholics in the procession had an entirely different view of what happened. Fr. John Hadnagy, pastor of Our Lady of Consolation Shrine, says it was the Street Preachers who started the melee by telling Catholics they were going to hell for worshipping Mary. Brother Jeffrey, a Franciscan friar at the Shrine said a member of the Street Preachers yelled at him that he was leading people to hell because of he wouldn't reject the Church's beliefs on Mary.

Radical Protestant rejection of the Blessed Virgin is not just an American problem, either. For some years Northern Ireland Protestants have taunted Catholics by calling Mary unspeakable names. Not surprisingly, therefore, the Reverend Ian Paisley of Belfast, political leader of the radical Democratic Unionist Party, has had political ties with some of the more radical elements of American fundamentalism.[10]

Paisley has justified the burning of Catholic homes, claimed that the IRA was the military wing of the Catholic Church, and even heckled Pope John Paul II when he visited the European Parliament in 1988 by saying, "I denounce you Anti-Christ." Bob Jones University in South Carolina, which is known for its anti-Catholic views, has had ties with the Northern Irish leader for years. According to John Leo of *Jewish World News*, Paisley has visited the school 50 times

---

[t] The Chaldeans are mainly Iraqi-American Christians who came to this country after World War II or fled the regime of Saddam Hussein in the 1980s and 1990s. The Chaldean rite, which traces its lineage to the apostles, is one of the oldest in Christianity.

and even received an honorary doctorate there.[11] It was only in the year 2000, after several presidential candidates were taken to task for visiting the campus, that the school's president announced on CNN's "Larry King Live" that Bob Jones University would allow interracial dating. However, the school's views on Catholicism remain as defiant as they always were. To it, Rome is the harlot of Babylon mentioned in the Book of Revelation.

Furthermore, an odd silent alliance seems to be forming between some fundamentalist figures such as Ankerberg and radical secularists, who claim there is not a God to begin with, let alone apparitions. The Amazing Randi, a former magician who is now a professional skeptic, has taken to the road to denounce all things religious. One has to ask why Christians would forge an alliance with non-believers to denounce fellow believers over their views about Mary and her role in Christianity.

With the steady stream of miracles and healing that has been reported through the years at various apparition sites around the world, one thing is clear: A lot of people must be lying for all of these events to be false. Only one miracle has to be proven true for the skeptics to realize that there may be another dimension that they refuse to acknowledge. The previously referred to miracle of Our Lady of Guadalupe is one such unexplained miracle.

In 1531, the Blessed Virgin appeared to St. Juan Diego Cuauhtlatoatzin and told him to go and see the bishop. Although he didn't know it, Mary's image had become transposed on his cactus cloth tilma, which today hangs in a basilica outside Mexico City.

Normally cactus cloth would have disintegrated centuries ago, but the tilma and the miraculous colors on it remain vibrant to this day. Furthermore, scientists examined the eye of Mary and found an image that appears to be a bishop looking at Juan's tilma. But the miracles don't end there.

Mexico was afflicted with a militant anti-religious government in the 1920s. Some radical partisans of this movement thought if they destroyed the tilma, they could destroy the Faith. They placed a bomb under the altar over which the tilma hung. The explosion was massive. It severely damaged the basilica and blew out windows far from the bomb. However, the tilma remained unscathed, protected by an iron crucifix that sheltered the tilma from the blast. The symbolism of Jesus protecting his mother was undeniable.

Countless apparitions of the Virgin Mary have appeared through the centuries. The Church takes extra time to examine the validity of these claims. For instance, it is still investigating the apparitions of Medugorje. The apparitions in all of the other cases mentioned here – Guadalupe, Lourdes, Fatima, and Zeitoun – have all been deemed "worthy of belief" by the Church. To achieve this distinction, an apparition must endure many years of scrutiny starting at the local diocesan level. Then it must pass the inspection of Vatican investigators. As a result, it can take many years or even decades before an apparition it proved "worthy of belief." Sometimes, the visions are not approved or are even counted as false. Indeed, the overwhelming majority of apparitions reported by individuals or groups are not deemed "worthy of belief."

One has to ask oneself, "At the above places, were all of these people wrong?" According to secularists and many Protestant skeptics, they are either lying, delusional, or being misled by Satan. Could that possibly be the case in every instance? There have been countless religious and even secular news programs that have shown healings that cannot be explained by medical science. How can a rational person weigh the evidence and think that Jesus is not working through Mary's intercession?

As noted above, John Ankerberg has said these apparitions are the work of Satan, and he is not alone in this belief. One can visit a plethora of websites dedicated to denouncing the Catholic view of Mary. One particular site I visited, Rapturewatch.com, had a string of web threads pointing out that Catholics needed to be saved because Satan was appearing as Mary in the apparitions.

However, I would ask the reader to consider the following thought: If our Lord said to judge a tree by its fruits, and if the fruits of the apparitions are a return to righteous living and a respect for God and His laws, then perhaps Mr. Ankerberg and his fellow travelers need to recall the words of Jesus, "How can Satan be against Satan" (cf., Lk. 11:17-18)?

Another point worth considering for our fundamentalist friends: For centuries, especially in the Middle Ages, Christians collected relics of saints. These were obtained through scrupulous and unscrupulous agents. Throughout the world, there exist pieces of bone, clothing, and other fragments related to saints.

Yet there is one important person for whom there are no relics to be found. Catholics and Eastern Orthodox are the only Christians to believe that Mary was bodily assumed into Heaven. Belief in her bodily assumption was solemnly defined as a dogma on All Saint's Day 1950 by Ven. Pius XII, and has been believed since the apostolic age (more on this belief later). If Catholics and Orthodox made up the idea of the Assumption, then where are her relics? One can logically deduce that the ancient Catholic belief that Mary was bodily assumed into Heaven is historically accurate.

Mary hasn't just appeared in apparitions, but in recent years has appeared in the pop culture as well. Not only have many contemporary books been written about her, but Mel Gibson's movie *The Passion of the Christ* featured Our Lady as a central character. Many Evangelicals who flocked to the film saw her in a way they might never have before. Some believe that because of the increasing role of women in Protestant churches, especially Evangelical churches, Mary is finding a home in these places. It is not uncommon to find images of Our Lady in Protestant churches that have a large Hispanic population. Even the somewhat sacrilegious pop star Madonna is fascinated with the Virgin Mary. The author Stephen King (who is not Catholic) is said to wear a medal honoring Mary because he says he has always had a special devotion to the mother of Jesus.

Although some people think women are demeaned in the Catholic Church, the devotion Catholics have towards Mary disproves this ridiculous notion. Catholic culture has elevated women in every culture where Catholicism holds sway. One only need look at Islamic, Hindu, and animist cultures to see the difference between the way women in those faiths are treated compared to those in Catholicism. A look at Catholic Third World countries shows this to be the case, as well. Catholic women in these cultures are not forced into arranged marriages while still children or forced to endure painful female castration. Women in Catholic cultures are not beaten or treated worse than domesticated animals. The same cannot be said of non-Christian societies.

For instance, a friend of mine did military service in Afghanistan. He was told that when coalition soldiers first arrived and were attempting to give rural people inoculations against diseases, they were met with an astonishing request. The village elders asked if the men and boys could be inoculated first, their domesticated animals next, and, if there was still enough left, then the women and girls last. The village elders seemed quite surprised when they were told humans first, animals second. This would never happen in a Catholic country.

The Rosary

At Fatima and in other apparitions, Our Lady has asked the faithful to pray the rosary as the way to bring about world peace and the conversion of souls to a life in her Son Jesus. However, the rosary has been a powerful weapon in the hands of Catholics for centuries before our own age. Through it, countless conversions have occurred, hundreds of millions of people have experienced profound meditations on the life, death, and resurrection of our Lord Jesus Christ, and God has wrought miracles.

Of this great devotion, Archbishop Fulton J. Sheen wrote, "The rosary is the book of the blind, where souls see and there enact the greatest drama of love the world has ever known; it is the book of the simple, which initiates them into mysteries and knowledge more satisfying than the education of other men; it is the book of the aged, whose eyes close upon the shadow of this world, and open on the substance of the next. The power of the rosary is beyond description."

At one point, this sacramental was a staple part of Catholic life. For instance, "Catholicism in the Twentieth Century," a study conducted by the Cushwa Center for the Study of American Catholicism at the University of Notre Dame, noted that "In the early 1950s, Detroit boasted some 3,000 block rosary clubs, while an estimated 200,000 Catholics gathered their families together and prayed along with the Radio Rosary Crusade.

Today, turn on Catholic radio anywhere in the nation, and you can hear the rosary being recited several times a day. Rosary prayer groups meet regularly, and even some Protestants have started to join these. More and more seminarians and university students at both Catholic and secular campuses have incorporated the Joyful, Sorrowful, Luminous, and Glorious Mysteries into their prayer life, and it is becoming more common to see people saying it before Mass. Even more important, an increasing number of families have resuscitated the beautiful habit of a daily family rosary.

As Scott Hahn wrote in his beautiful work *Hail, Holy Queen*, "Pray the rosary! This is what I urge Catholics and all Christians of goodwill. Pray the rosary, and realize that every recitation is plugging you into the permanent things, taking you out of the transitory and ephemeral, the things that matter most to people who really don't know what matters.

"Put time aside to pray the rosary in a concentrated, dedicated way. But pray the rosary again when you find time that would otherwise be badly spent — when you're stuck in a doctor's office waiting room or delayed in rush-hour traffic. The rush hour is unreal in comparison to the reality you're praying, the mysteries of the ultimate reality. Your beads and your prayers are more real than the cars in front of you and the horns that are honking.

"Once [when I was a Protestant] I looked down with disgust upon a string of rosary beads. I saw it as a noose that choked off true devotion in countless Roman Catholics. When I held Grandma Hahn's rosary, I couldn't break that loop quickly or forcefully enough.

"Now, when I look down at my own beads, I see the same circle, but it is different. It suggests a queen's crown, a mother's encircling arms."[12]

Mary, Mary, quite contrary?

Something should be said about various beliefs on Mary that Protestants have trouble with. By learning how to counter our separated brethren's objections to these beliefs, Catholics are providing a crucial and badly needed witness to our age and drawing people into the Church. This is another sign the tide is turning.

For instance, take the dogma of the Immaculate Conception, proclaimed by Bl. Pius IX in 1854. This defined as binding upon all Catholics and Christians of goodwill the certainty that Mary was preserved from original sin from the moment of her conception by a singular grace given her by God. She still had need of a savior, but she was "redeemed 'by the grace of Christ' ... in a more perfect manner than other human beings."[13] Bl. Duns Scotus said (and the Church teaches) she was redeemed in anticipation of Jesus Christ's sacrificial death.

The biblical foundation of this has two fundamental parts. The first is Gen. 3:15, where God tells Satan, "I will put enmity between you and the woman, and between your offspring and her." If Mary had any part of sin, then Satan would have had some part of her. How, then, would she have been a fitting vessel for the One who was to relieve us from the effects of sin?

The second is Lk. 1:28. The original Greek reads, "*Chaire kecharitomene.*" St. Jerome translated St. Gabriel's words into Latin as, "*Hail, full of grace! The Lord is with you.*"

One source says this about the passage, "The latter word, *kecharitomene,* is the Passive voice, Present Perfect participle of the verb "to grace" in the feminine gender, vocative case; therefore the Greek syntax indicates that the action of the verb has been fully completed in the past, with results continuing into the future. Put another way, it means that the subject (Mary) was graced fully and completely at some time in the past, and continued in that fully graced state. The angel's salutation does not refer to the incarnation of Christ in Mary's womb, as he proceeds to say: 'you will conceive in your womb ...'" (Luke 1:31).

Another hotly contested Marian dogma is the Assumption. Catholics and the Orthodox believe that at the end of her earthly life, she was assumed body and soul into heaven. The biblical foundation for this doctrine is found in the fact that Enoch, Elijah, and Moses were all assumed into heaven (for Moses, see Jude 1:9 and the ancient Jewish but apocryphal work, the Assumption of Moses). There is also Rev. 12, which Catholics and Orthodox believe shows Mary as the woman in heaven wearing a crown of 12 stars.

Interestingly, neither of these dogmas was solemnly defined until recent times. Then again, the doctrine of Transubstantiation was not solemnly defined until the Council of Trent in 1551, nor was the word even used until 1079, when it was employed by Archbishop Hildebert de Savardin of Tours. For that matter, there was no defined canon of books in the Bible until the late fourth century. Up until that point, some still considered the First Epistle of Clement to the Corinthians, the Shepherd of Hermas, and other writings as Scripture.

To some Protestants, these late definitions are not only a scandal, they prove their unreliability (aside from the fact that they find them unbiblical, which they are clearly not). But very often, things aren't given precise definitions because people at the time see no reason to do so.

Consider transubstantiation. The Council of Trent had to define this precisely, but only because the so-called Reformers were vociferously and relentlessly attacking this doctrine. Before that point, it was simply accepted as truth. The Assumption of Mary is one of the oldest doctrines in Christianity. However, it was not officially defined as a dogma (i.e., binding upon all Christian faithful) until 1950, when Pope Pius XII infallibly defined it as such. In this case, there was no dispute compelling the definition. The Pope was simply making official what has been believed and practiced since the earliest days of Christianity.

Governments often make decisions based on similar reasoning. My home state of Ohio entered into the Union in 1803. However, in 1953 when the state was preparing to celebrate its one hundred and fiftieth birthday, Ohioans suddenly realized that Congress had never officially ratified their state into the Union. So in 1953, President Dwight D. Eisenhower signed a document that had been delivered to him by horseback from the former Ohio state capitol of Chillicothe. This retroactively made the 1803 date official. All of Washington was full of laughs because of the obvious century-plus oversight. No one doubted Ohio had been a state for 150 years.

Yet when the Catholic Church did the same sort of thing three years before, many acted as if this was the first they heard of a belief that dated back to the first century AD.

Conclusion

Mary has appeared through the centuries to all peoples and to all religions. As previously mentioned, the most recent verified apparition occurred in Zeitoun, Egypt. Egypt is 90 percent Muslim, and millions of Muslim and Christians came to see her. As previously noted, many Muslims embraced these appearances by bringing their sick for a possible cure while the apparitions continued; they did not say this was Satan. Yes, there were reports of healings and cures among Muslims as well as Christians.

Mary is the one who bore the Messiah, the one who said, "Yes," to God. She held a very significant place in the faith for 15 centuries prior to the Protestant Reformation. In light of her recent apparitions as well as her significance in the world of film, music, and literature, one hopes she will soon be given her due by all Christian denominations.

Mary is helping people turn to Catholicism because they see how important she is to their faith, and they realize that Catholicism is the primary faith that has her in her proper place of distinction. It is not hard to see how she is attracting them. She unconditionally accepted God's will for her despite the consequences. Most importantly, she is the *Theotokos*, the "God bearer," the mother of the Son of God. Many people have realized how they revere their own mothers and believe it is only fitting that the mother of our Lord be revered as well, for without her fiat, where would we all be?

I remember talking with former Notre Dame football coach Gerry Faust. He told me an interesting story about giving up on a prized recruit because of the way this recruit treated his mother. "Dave," he said, "you can tell a lot about a person by the way they treat their mother."[13]

May we always try to act like her obedient children who are growing in our faith in Jesus Christ.

DAVID J. HARTLINE

- CHAPTER 7 -

THE EUCHARIST AND THE CATHOLIC EMBRACE OF IT

The Real Presence refers to how Christ is present Body, Blood, Soul, and Divinity in the bread and wine consecrated during Mass, and it has always been source of debate between Catholics and Protestants.

However, a few years ago its importance was even debated among Catholics, as those who are more liberal began criticizing the practice of Eucharistic adoration. They felt it was an exercise steeped in so-called pre-Vatican II theology that didn't need a resurrection. Despite this, Catholics have lately begun to see its importance.

This development also signals that the tide is turning towards Catholicism. More and more Catholics are learning about what the Real Presence of Jesus in the Eucharist really means, and they are embracing the sacrament. Consequently, Eucharistic adoration is becoming more frequent around the world and especially here in the United States, and many new believers are being made as a result.

For purposes of illustration, it might help to explain the difference between the Catholic belief regarding the Eucharist and the various teachings of the Protestant churches. For instance, Martin Luther's beliefs (and that of the Lutheran and Anglican communions) were closer to Catholic theology than the other Protestant founders.

In 1529, shortly into the Protestant Revolt, Martin Luther and other leaders of that movement held a summit known as the Marburg Colloquy, which Bruce Heydt wrote about in an article for *Christianity Today* magazine.[1] Luther was shocked to learn how different their beliefs were regarding the Eucharist. His fellow conferees believed Jesus was only speaking symbolically when He said, "This is My Body".

Luther grabbed a piece of chalk and wrote on a table, "This is my body." Then Luther asked the Swiss Reformation leader Ulrich Zwingli to tell him what he thought of the Eucharist. When Zwingli said it was just a symbol, the already heated debate grew more intense. Luther shot back, "You're trying to dominate things. You are in [the German state of] Hesse now, not Switzerland." Luther left utterly frustrated with Zwingli and the others, but not before making a pointed comment: "I would rather drink blood with the Pope than wine with the Swiss." Unfortunately, more Protestants believe as Zwingli did than Luther.

However, while he believed the Eucharist was the Body and Blood of Christ, Luther's view and the Church's view were still very different. Luther could not wrap his mind around transubstantiation[v] (indeed, the only way to see the truth of this doctrine is through the eyes of faith). Instead, he invented a new doctrine called "consubstantiation."[w]

Many have speculated that as Luther entered the twilight of his life, he began to wonder about what he had started. Perhaps the events of Marburg show a bewildered Luther wondering where the Reformation was headed. He seemed to have embraced some of the beliefs he initially threw out at the beginning of the Reformation. (As noted in the previous chapter, one of those was his devotion to Mary.)

It is also important to note that the Episcopal Communion in the United States (called the Anglican Communion elsewhere in the world) has a very different history than other Protestant denominations. As a matter of fact, some high church Anglicans resent the term "Protestant." They see themselves as part of the one, holy,

---

[v] Transubstantiation is the term the Church uses to define her belief in what happens during the sacrifice of the Mass. Although the elements of bread and wine appear to the senses as bread and wine, they are in fact transformed in their substance by the Holy Spirit into the Body and Blood, Soul and Divinity of our Lord Jesus Christ. Nothing of the bread and wine remains after the priest speaks the words of the consecration (i.e., "This is My Body ..." and "This is My Blood ...").

Catholic, and apostolic Church with the archbishop of Canterbury as their leader. They were not present for the above referenced meeting on the Eucharist. While their views on the Eucharist are different from Catholics, they are much closer than any other denomination.

Many Protestant churches, especially the large non-denominational congregations, do not have Communion as part of their service. For many Catholics, this omission is unthinkable because the Eucharist is the source and summit of our spiritual life. But as noted above, most Protestants think of Jesus' words about the Eucharist as pure symbolism. However, Jesus faced similar disbelief among the Jews who said, "How can this man give us (His) flesh to eat" (John 6:52)? To which Jesus replied, "Amen, amen I say to you, unless you eat the flesh of the Son of Man and drink His blood, you do not have life within you. Whoever eats My flesh and drinks My blood has eternal life, and I will raise Him on the last day. For My flesh is true food, and My blood true drink. Whoever eats My flesh and drinks My blood remains in Me and I in him" (John 6:53-56).

The varying beliefs about the Eucharist create a huge obstacle to Christian unity, and some feel overcoming this is an impossible task. However, Catholics believe Christ's Real Presence in the Eucharist can bring about unity.

---

[w] According to the 1913 Catholic Encyclopedia, this is "an attempt to hold the doctrine of the Real Presence in the Holy Eucharist without admitting Transubstantiation. According to it, the substance of Christ's Body exists together with the substance of bread, and in like manner the substance of His Blood together with the substance of wine (hence the word Consubstantiation). How the two substances can coexist is variously explained. The most subtle theory is that, just as God the Son took to Himself a human body without in any way destroying its substance, so does He in the Blessed Sacrament assume the nature of bread." However, once the service is over, the bread and wine revert to their original being. Fr. Richard John Neuhaus explained the difference between the beliefs of Catholics and Lutherans this way: When his father, a Lutheran pastor, finished with his service, he took the remaining altar wafers, put them in a box, and placed them in a sacristy cupboard. When a priest finishes the Mass, he takes any unconsumed hosts and places them with reverence and veneration back in the tabernacle to be worshipped and adored by the faithful.

Pope Benedict XVI, then Joseph Cardinal Ratzinger, wrote about St. Paul's view that ecclesial unity is unthinkable without "remaining in the teaching of the apostles" in his book *Pilgrim Fellowship of Faith: The Church as Communion.*[2] He goes on to say that fellowship in the Body of Christ and in receiving the Body of Christ means fellowship with one another. Catholics see the Mass as a communal celebration and sacrifice where at the end we are called to the "table" to celebrate with Christ, who is present. He told us He would always be there for us in spirit at Mass. He is there in person as well. During his March 29, 2006, general audience address, Pope Benedict called Communion "the fruit of the Holy Spirit nourished by Eucharistic bread and expressed through fraternal relations, a kind of future glory."[3] Though Jesus ascended into Heaven, He remains here with us in the Eucharist. Jesus told us that at the Last Supper, and Paul reminds us of it in 1 Corinthians 11:23-29.

It might be helpful for Protestants (or even disbelieving Catholics) to understand what the enemies of Christ believe about the Eucharist. Perhaps seeing this will help those who are truly Christian but don't understand this most special of sacraments.

Stealing consecrated hosts and desecrating them has always been a standard practice of the myriad groups vowing some sort of adherence to Satan. They never take something that was a mere symbol at a Protestant communion service. Instead, Satanists only use consecrated hosts in the Black Mass, the antithesis of the Catholic Mass. Usually, some defilement takes place alongside it on the satanic altar, usually an animal sacrifice or sexual act, which is meant to mock the sacrifice Christ made. One has to ask: If Satanists realize what the Eucharist truly is and represents (i.e., the source and summit of the Christian life), why can't those who claim Christ see the same thing?

If this isn't enough to convince, then what about the earliest Christians? I sometimes wish I could go back in time to converse with Jesus or at least His apostles to discuss these vexing issues. We can't do that, obviously, but we can do the next best thing, which is see what those who learned the faith from the apostles and those who learned the faith in turn from them had to say.

I'm referring, of course, to the Church Fathers. For instance, St. Ignatius of Antioch, who died in the first decade of the second century, learned the faith from St. John the Evangelist and succeeded St. Peter as bishop of Antioch. This man was no slouch as a believer, and if he learned the faith from two of the principle apostles, you can be sure he was orthodox. Indeed, he was condemned to death rather than renounce his faith in Christ and was sent to Rome for execution. Along the way, he wrote several letters, seven of which still exist, where he discussed various points of Christian belief in a way of bolstering the faith of his correspondents.

In his Letter to the Smyrneans, he wrote this about Christ's Real Presence: "Take note of those who hold heterodox opinions on the grace of Jesus Christ which has come to us, and see how contrary their opinions are to the mind of God. . . . They abstain from the Eucharist and from prayer because they do not confess that the Eucharist is the flesh of our Savior Jesus Christ, flesh which suffered for our sins and which that Father, in His goodness, raised up again. They who deny the gift of God are perishing in their disputes."

Writing in 151 AD, St. Justin Martyr (who, as his name implies, also went to his death rather than renounce his faith in Jesus) observed, "We call this food Eucharist, and no one else is permitted to partake of it, except one who believes our teaching to be true and who has been washed in the washing which is for the remission of sins and for regeneration [i.e., has received baptism] and is thereby living as Christ enjoined. For not as common bread nor common drink do we receive these; but since Jesus Christ our Savior was made incarnate by the word of God and had both flesh and blood for our salvation, so too, as we have been taught, the food which has been made into the Eucharist by the Eucharistic prayer set down by him, and by the change of which our blood and flesh is nurtured, is both the flesh and the blood of that incarnated Jesus."[5]

In his book *The History of Eucharistic Adoration*, Fr. John Hardon, SJ, tells us of many early accounts of the Eucharist. We know that the custom of the *fermentum*, during which a particle of the Eucharistic bread (which sometimes has been dipped in the Precious Blood) is transported from the bishop of one diocese to the bishop of another, took place in the third century AD. By the opening of the Council of Nicaea in 325, the Eucharist was already reserved in church tabernacles much like it is today. We know from a narrative that St. Basil, who died in 379, is said to have divided the Eucharist into three parts, one for him, one for the monks, and a third was placed in a golden tabernacle suspended above the altar.

We know the power the Eucharist held not just for believers but also for non-believers. In 601, pagans attacked St. Comgall, and, seeing a small receptacle used for carrying the Eucharist called the Chrismal around his neck, fled because they surmised he was carrying his God. St. Comgall was so moved that he exclaimed, "Lord you are my strength, my refugee, and my Redeemer."[6]

Through the centuries the Eucharist became a subject of fascination even for the non-believer. Fr. Benedict Groeschel, CFR, relates a story of a young priest who visited Albert Einstein for the sole reason of wanting to talk to the world's smartest man. Little did the young priest know that Einstein would spend a great deal of time during that visit probing him about the Eucharist. It had not been the first time that the great mind of Einstein had contemplated this matter. Einstein had also asked several other priests to recommend the best books on the Eucharist to him so he could further understand the concept of Real Presence. Even though Einstein was a Jew he was still fascinated with the Eucharist.[7]

So when Christians who profess belief in the Bible as the inerrant word of God mock the sacrifice of the Mass (Eucharist), one has to wonder if they have ever read 1 Corinthians 11:23-30. The most telling part reads, "So it is the Lord's death that you are heralding, whenever you eat this bread and drink this cup, until He comes. And therefore, if anyone eats this bread and drinks this cup of the Lord unworthily, he will be held to account for the Lord's body and blood. For anyone who eats and drinks without discerning the body eats and drinks judgment on himself."

It might be hard to believe that Evangelicals, the very ones who demand such strict observance of the words of Christ, would not obey Scripture's very clear words regarding the Eucharist. There are those, however, for whom the scales drop from the eyes and who see what God is trying to tell them. It is therefore small wonder that belief in the Eucharist is not a great stretch for many converts to Catholicism. The words are plain to see in the Gospels and especially in this passage from 1 Corinthians.

To show just how poorly (even blasphemously) some Christians discern the Body, take popular Christian music star Kirk Franklin's February 2002 appearance on "The Bill Maher Show."[4] He told Maher (who himself has said religious people "have a neurological disorder"), "We gotta move people away from religion. I think religion is one of the worst things that has ever happened to America." According to a March 5, 2005, press release from the Catholic League, "Franklin ... then attacked the Eucharist by complaining, 'gotta take the cracker.' To which Maher replied, 'Gotta take the cracker from a cracker.'"

Fr. Groeschel says disbelief in the Real Presence started during the Protestant Reformation when the founders of this movement tried stripping it of its mystery. "Once you depart from the mystery given by Christ and interpreted by the early Fathers," said Fr. Groeschel, "you are out on the sea without a compass or a map."[8]

It does appear that Fr. Groeschel is right in his observation. And if the Reformation's intent was to demystify religion, the movement succeeded. Some years ago there was a general outcry against a proposed effort to find out once and for all if there was a Loch Ness monster. Scientists thought the true story of the monster could be discovered with their advanced tracking devices. Newspaper editorials spelled out their reasons against the expedition, stating that many felt it would demystify something special and relegate it to the mundane.

In a sense that is what happened because of the Protestant Reformation. While those leading the Reformation perhaps thought they were doing the people a favor by demystifying Jesus in downplaying the importance of the Eucharist, they did a great disservice to them. While Evangelicals rightly voice their displeasure when they encounter liberals who feel they know what God and Jesus meant in the New Testament better than the experts, those who deny the Eucharist could be accused of doing the same in light of all the biblical evidence. They have demystified what worship is supposed to be, which was celebrating the Real Presence of Jesus. One often hears an Evangelical calling such worship idolatry, but it is not; it reflects the words of Jesus.

Could Jesus have been any clearer during the Bread of Life discourse in the Gospel of John 6? In Jn. 6:32-35, we read, "'What sign can You do that we may see and believe in You? What can You do? Our ancestors ate manna in the desert it is written.' So Jesus said to them, 'Amen, amen I say to you, it was not Moses who gave the bread from Heaven; My Father gives you the true bread from Heaven. For the bread of God is that which comes down from Heaven and gives life to the world.' So they said, 'Sir, give us this bread always.' Jesus said to them, 'I am the bread of life; whoever believes in Me will not thirst.'"

Later on in verse 41, the Jews murmured about the meaning of the bread of life. The same thing happened in verse 52. The Jews murmured again, and Jesus answered even more forcibly in verses

53-58: "Amen, Amen, I say to you, unless you eat the flesh of the Son of Man and drink His blood, you do not have life within you. Whoever eats My flesh and drinks My blood has eternal life, and I will raise him on the last day. For My flesh is true food, and My blood is true drink. Whoever eats My flesh and drinks My blood remains in Me and I in him. Just as the living Father sent Me and I have life because of the Father, so also the one who feeds on Me will have life because of Me. This is the bread that came down from Heaven. Unlike your ancestors who ate and still died, whoever eats this bread will live forever."

Are not those who deny the Presence of Jesus in the Eucharist like those Jews who murmured?

About the decline of belief in the Real Presence, author Tom Craughwell said, "All Protestant leaders going back at least to Wycliffe rejected the Real Presence because they said it was idolatry. They were reacting to something you and I are always delighted to see – profound reverence and devotion among the faithful for the Blessed Sacrament. The intensity of devotion for the Host at Mass, exposed for veneration, or reserved in the tabernacle was very strong in the 16th century. And so Luther, Calvin, Zwingli, Knox, Cramner, et al. launched major attacks against the Mass and the Real Presence, and they did so not just verbally and in print, but in the way they reorganized the churches and created new Sunday services. Strip the churches bare. Get rid of the tabernacle. Rip out the altar and put in a table. Face the people. Tell the congregation they are at a communal meal. Ban Benediction. Lock the churches up except on Sundays. Put the bread in the hands of the communicants. Downplay the sacred character and exclusive role of the priest.

"And it worked. Once all sense of the solemn and the sacred was gone, faith in the Real Presence among one-time Catholics vanished too."[9]

Because so many so-called Reformers thought of the Eucharist as idolatry, many priests were killed in the early days of the Reformation. The impending fear caused by this onslaught led to what Fr. Groeschel and Tom Craughwell talk about, a decline in mystery and reverence, not just among Protestants but among Catholics too.

This doesn't mean there weren't great defenders of the faith in the centuries that followed the Reformation. St. Alphonsus Liguori and St. Teresa of Avila were two such champions of the faith. Others were St. Robert Bellarmine (whose intellect the Protestants were said to fear), St. Francis de Sales (who converted whole sections of Switzerland back to the true faith), and Servant of God Stanisław Hozjusz (who converted Holy Roman Emperor Maximilian II and kept Poland from becoming Lutheran).[x] Of course, St. Therese of Lisieux or the "Little Flower" wrote extensively about the Eucharist and implored all those who would listen to receive the sacrament often.

Eucharistic Adoration

The practice of Eucharistic adoration declined during the 1960s and 1970s. It simply belonged to a bygone era in the minds of some ultra modernists. Little would these people realize that in a few short years, not only would the aged continue to participate in Eucharistic adoration, but the young would embrace the practice as well, especially at faithful Catholic colleges such as Franciscan University.

Eucharistic adoration and perpetual adoration have been an integral part of Catholicism for centuries. Each is the practice of praying before the Real Presence of Christ. Catholicism teaches that in front of the Real Presence, we can more easily pour out our prayers of joy and sorrow. Even in the first few centuries of the Church, adoration was beginning to manifest itself as a holy ritual.

We see this ritual beginning to take place when St. Augustine

---

[x] Consider the ramifications of Hozjusz's actions: If Poland had gone over to the Lutherans, no Pope John Paul II (and possibly no St. Stanisław Kostka or St. Andrew Bobola, for that matter).

said these famous words about the Eucharist in 414, "Not only do we not sin by adoring it, we sin by not adoring it." St. Katherine Drexel inherited a fortune in the late 1800s and gave it away to Native Americans and African-Americans. She founded Xavier University in New Orleans, which became a premier university for blacks in the South. After many years of diligent work for the Church, her dreams came true as she ended her years taking part in daily Eucharistic adoration. She died in 1955 at the age of 96.[10]

During the 1980s and 1990s, as many Catholics became increasingly alarmed at the dwindling number of religious vocations, adoration in all forms began to experience a renaissance. Archbishop John Donoghue of Atlanta started emphasizing adoration after he became the ordinary of that city in 1993. In the next 11 years, he ordained 98 men to the priesthood, an impressive number for that decade. Perhaps it was the 10 parishes participating in perpetual adoration and the 46 parishes participating in regular Benediction and adoration that made the difference. Whatever the case, by the time Archbishop Wilton Gregory took over from Donoghue, Atlanta had a higher number of priests per capita than many other dioceses in the United States.[11]

At his diocese's 2003 Chrism Mass, Brooklyn's Bishop Thomas V. Daily said, "I challenge you to adore Jesus Christ perpetually in the Eucharist." Bishop Daily went on to say, "The Eucharist contains all the mysteries of the Church because it contains the complete Jesus Christ. It is the source and summit of the whole Christian life." Brooklyn's diocesan newspaper *The Tablet* reported that Bishop Daily stood out in the blustery chill to greet each and every clergy and lay person who left the Chrism Mass in order to demonstrate the seriousness of his message.[12]

Saginaw's Bishop Carlson said Eucharistic adoration is "what it's all about it, isn't it, the Real Presence of Jesus? How anyone cannot embrace this, I do not know. This is not some abstract theory. We are talking about the Real Presence of Jesus. Wherever you see this happening, you see great things taking place in the Church. You see vocations, parish involvement, and greater respect for one another. I could go on and on."[13]

In 2005, WCCO television in Minneapolis-St. Paul ran a story about St. Timothy Catholic Church in Maple Lakes, Minnesota, which was participating in perpetual adoration along with 40 other Minnesota parishes. "It's a bottom-up phenomenon," said John Boyle, a professor of Theology and Catholic Studies at the University of Saint Thomas in St. Paul. "It's been remarkable to watch it grow over the past 20 years, especially the last 10 years." WCCO went on to mention that people from all over the world have been contacting another nearby parish, Epiphany Parish in Coon Rapids, inquiring about the specifics of organizing adoration in their parish.[14]

Msgr. Joseph Schaedel, vicar general for the Archdiocese of Indianapolis was quoted by his archdiocesan newspaper *The Criterion* as saying, "In every parish that I'm aware of that established Eucharistic adoration, people will tell you that great blessings have come in terms of spiritual awakening and interest in vocations to religious life and the priesthood." Cathy Andrews of St. Vincent DePaul Parish in the Indianapolis Archdiocese said that Eucharistic adoration has caused a change in her parish. "We've just come together and just gelled so wonderfully," she said.

At Holy Family Catholic Church in Oldenburg, Indiana, Dennis and Pat Schrank stored part of their church's altar in their barn after it was removed in 1987, the era when the feeling of trying to demystify the church was well underway. The altar was put back in the church in 2005. This was another strong symbol that tradition was being taken out of the mothballs and being put back into practice.[15]

Chris Kelly, parishioner at St. Joan of Arc Catholic Church in Powell, Ohio, was stunned when a fellow parishioner told him that because of the abuse scandal, he was leaving the Catholic Church for

THE TIDE IS TURNING TOWARD CATHOLICISM

a popular local non-denominational megachurch. "I was stunned," he said. "'But you are walking away from the Eucharist.'" He could tell the man didn't know what he was talking about.

"I have attended adoration ever since 1999. I cannot imagine my life without it. I responded to a call for those interested in adoration and I choose the 1 a.m. hour. I wanted an hour that could not be taken away from my family, and I wanted a time that would cause a sacrifice to remind me of Christ's sacrifice. Even in exhaustion, I feel His love while I sit in His presence."[16]

Many attribute the rise in adoration to Pope John Paul II. In 1991, the pontiff urged people to start perpetual adoration in their home parishes. Speaking to a group at Christendom College in 2001, Fr. Groeschel said he was glad to see adoration coming back: "How can anyone be opposed to praying and kneeling before the presence of the Son of God?"[17]

Yet there has been some debate in Catholic circles about the presence of Christ in the Eucharist. Nothing will get an orthodox Catholic more fired up than if a fellow Catholic seems to challenge the idea of the Real Presence in the Eucharist. A verbal battle ensued between two Catholic powerhouses, Roger Cardinal Mahony of Los Angeles and Mother Angelica of EWTN for this very reason. The spiritual war of words went on for years, and it essentially divided Catholics into two camps, faithful and so-called progressive.

Mother Angelica never said Cardinal Mahony didn't believe in the Real Presence of the Eucharist, but when she suggested he was promoting the ideas of people who thought as much, the battle was on. She noted that his pastoral letter "Gather Faithfully Together" contained several objectionable statements. His implication that the Eucharist was merely a representation of the Last Supper really angered Mother Angelica. Cardinal Mahony was furious that Mother Angelica had questioned him on international television, and demanded that she apologize. Mother Angelica did apologize, saying perhaps his words weren't fully understood.[18]

Eventually, Cardinal Mahony dropped the matter but not before many in the Catholic world rallied around Mother Angelica. This episode gave heart to many rank and file Catholics because it was another sign that tide was turning. The Eucharist was being embraced and defended in the most passionate of ways.

Also, it might be worth noting the lengths some have gone in past history in order to receive the Eucharist. A few centuries ago, Britain banned the Catholic Mass in its own country and in conquered Ireland as well. Shortly after the Reformation, edicts were issued outlawing the belief in the Real Presence. It would seem an odd thing to do if you didn't believe it was true. This was somewhat akin to atheists banning belief in God. If atheists didn't believe in God, why do they care if others do?

Catholics have believed in Christ's words in John 6:48-56 for 2,000 years: "I am the bread of life. Your ancestors ate manna in the desert, but they died; this is the bread that comes down from Heaven so that one may eat it and not die. I am the living bread that came down from Heaven; whoever eats this bread will live forever; and the bread that I will give is My flesh for the life of the world."

"The Jews quarreled among themselves, saying 'How can this man give us (His) flesh to eat?' Jesus said to them, '"Amen, amen I say to you, unless you eat the flesh of the Son of Man and drink His blood, you do not have life within you. Whoever eats My flesh and drinks My blood has eternal life, and I will raise him on the last day. For My flesh is true food, and My blood is true drink. Whoever eats My flesh and drinks My blood remains in Me and I in him.'" These words are as true now as they were 2,000 years ago when Jesus said them.[19]

Some say the concept of the Eucharist is hard to grasp. Fr. Hahn offered the following advice for those who have a problem with the Eucharist: "We love to devour many things we enjoy to make it a part of us. [Understanding this, why] is the Eucharist such a problem?

Occasionally, one can hear someone of another denomination proclaim, we don't have the Eucharist, we pray to God directly. Yet would this same person not leave their house of worship if their pastor said, 'Look everyone, Jesus is out in our parking lot!' There would be a mad dash of people leaving that sanctuary to go out and see Him."

In the Catholic Church, Jesus is present at every Mass. He asked us to make Him a part of our lives. He did so because He loves us. When asking Fr. Hahn how I could better explain the Real Presence or Transubstantiation to those Catholics and non-Catholics who feel it is too complex for them to understand, he used this example: "Think of how we greet different people. We shake hands with people we don't know that well and gently hug people we know a little better. However, think of a child who sees a grandparent. Look at how the child and the grandparent beam when they see one another. Doesn't that child usually run over to that grandparent and hug him or her with all of their might? That loving embrace is what Jesus wants to do with us. He wants to embrace us with the same love. He does that in the Eucharist. He wants to embrace and love us in the same fashion that a grandchild hugs his or her grandmother or grandfather."[20]

DAVID J. HARTLINE

- CHAPTER 8 -

CATHOLIC SCHOOLS

Catholic schools were in many ways the building blocks of the Catholic Church in America. They arose during the late 1800s at a time when Catholic school children attending public schools were often subject to a Protestant-influenced curriculum that was often anti-Catholic. Some rural schools even brought in the local minister to warn the children about the evils of Catholicism and the Pope in Rome.

When Catholic schools eventually emerged, they became one of the most successful American educational systems in the United States and also helped to lift various ethnic groups out of the ghetto and into the American mainstream. The same continues today in the inner city. Thousands of African-American students graduate from America's inner city Catholic schools. They go on to lead successful lives and join the middle and upper-middle class. It is arguable that without Catholic schools, Catholicism would not be the force it is today.

The American Catholic school reached its zenith in the baby boom years of the mid-1960s. In 1965, there were 5.7 million children enrolled in Catholic schools in America or about 47 percent of the total Catholic school age population.[1] Today, 40 years later, there are roughly half as many students in Catholics schools, although there are also less children today than there were back then. Partly because of this reason, Catholic schools currently face a crisis of both costs and leadership. The rising costs of salaries combined with skyrocketing health care costs have made it very difficult for poor and rural parishes to compete with public schools. Most Catholic schools hire almost all lay teachers (who need relatively competitive salaries and benefits), as compared to 40 years ago when the students were primarily taught by nuns whose salaries were a fraction of what secular teachers earned. As a result of this development, pastors and even some bishops have occasionally viewed Catholic schools as a financial burden rather than a spiritual grace to their parish or diocese.

Many Catholic parents haven't been too happy, either. There are often complaints about the cost of a parochial education. For a wealthy family, several thousand dollars a year per student may not be a stretch. But consider that represents a cost of several hundred dollars a month per student. Such a considerable expense often means that parents of lesser economic means must work two or more jobs to pay the tuition.

However, as noted above, the high tuition imposed by a parish or diocese is because of a new situation. It is not as though these schools are turning a profit or that its teachers and administrators are earning excellent incomes. Indeed, many of these people work for salaries that are 60-80 percent of those of their public school counterparts. When you had a cheap labor pool made up of men and women religious and priests, it was easy to offer a parochial education for nothing or next to nothing (and compared to other private schools, a Catholic education is still a bargain). Sadly, times have changed.

Given these difficulties one might ask how Catholic schools can survive. Since religious orders that used to serve as teachers in the Catholic schools have all but disappeared, how are parochial schools maintaining and expressing their Catholic identity? The encouraging news is that during the 1990s, as religiously trained teachers continued to disappear from the schools, many Catholic schools began making a concerted effort to bolster their Catholicity through not only visible means, such as signs and symbols but also through their curriculum.

While many people may be aware of how successful parochial schools in the inner city have been, few it seems are aware of rural

America's success stories. Holy Trinity School in Somerset, OH, is one such example. Nestled in southeast Ohio, this Appalachian school (along with the two parishes that assist it) has a long history of support. Somerset has less than 2,000 residents. Yet these venerable Dominican parishes (St. Joseph Catholic Church there is the oldest Catholic parish in the state) find a way to make sure their faith and history continue.

St. Mary Grade School and Marion Catholic High School in Marion, Ohio are two more examples. Marion Catholic High School is one of the smallest high schools in the state to offer many of the academic programs and extracurricular activities that many larger schools do. St. Mary Grade School's building is 100 years old, yet it has not lost any of its functionality. The common bond that unites these examples is faith, a faith that enables graduates to live the Catholic message they were taught. The communities these schools serve will not abandon them even though economically their regions have seen better days.

"Catholic identity" became the chant of many Catholic school administrators during the late 1990s and this first decade of the new century. On a personal note, having been a student, teacher, coach, principal, or diocesan administrator from the early 1970s until recently, I can vouch for the fact that Catholic schools are certainly emphasizing their Catholic identity more in recent times than they have in the not too distant past.

Superintendent of Schools for the Diocese of Columbus Lucia D. McQuaide said, "Having been in the Diocesan Schools Office since 1975, I have seen many changes, especially in the area of Catholic identity and culture. In the late seventies and early eighties, we began to lose sight of the emphasis on being Catholic. When I became superintendent in 1998, I felt the need to switch our primary emphasis back to Catholic identity. We began to concentrate on operational gospel values that permeate all we do. We made the director of Catholic Culture position more visible. We emphasized our Catholic identity through goal setting in our accrediting plans. Catholic schools provide a unique education. They provide the formation of the person towards holiness, which no other system can provide."[2]

I have also heard many orthodox Catholics observe that parochial schools are full of students whose families do not attend Mass and who do not take their faith seriously. There is certainly some truth to this statement. However, one has to ask would you rather these students attend schools where no faith will be discussed or a Catholic school where faith is discussed daily? There's always the hope that some of what the students hear in the Catholic school will make an impression on them. My answer to questions posed to me from parishioners who are skeptical about what help Catholic schools were providing as far as daily spiritual growth was the same. The outside world gets these kids for 138 hours a week out of a possible 168 hours; we get them for 30 hours and we do the best we can with the time allotted.

The ability to talk about faith openly in the classroom is a source of great comfort for many parents. Sandy Lape, a parishioner at St. Mary Magdalene Church in Columbus said, "My children have gone through Catholic schools, and I think that their experiences [there] are invaluable as far as helping them make the right choices as they grow older. It is a little easier when you have Jesus present in your daily life at school and not just at home. It's as if you have a loving parent at school always present trying to smooth some of the bumpy path."[3]

As noted previously, Catholic school salaries are often drastically less than public school salaries. Given the pay disparities, working for Catholic schools can obviously require some sacrifices. The challenge of finding the right people (who are willing to do as much or even more work for less compensation) can be overwhelming. Kitty Quinn, director of Leadership Effectiveness for the Diocese of

Columbus states, "Leaders for today's Catholic schools have to have a vision of the Kingdom of God—right here and right now."[4]

However, God always seems to find a way to deliver people where they are needed. Dianna Dudzinski, who has worked for the Catholic Schools Office in Columbus for nearly 30 years says, "The common bond in God and Church as well as similar stories growing up in Catholic schools makes us want to continue that with our own families."[5] Even those of other faiths such as diocesan office secretary Susan Shaver said the purpose of providing a spiritual basis for a child unites all in their work. "I have always felt very welcomed by my co-workers."[6]

The good works of many hard working Catholic schoolteachers and principals are evidenced in data collected by the National Federation of Catholic Youth Ministry. When asked "is religious faith important in shaping daily life," 55 percent of Catholic school students said "very" or "extremely important" while only 40 percent of Parish School of Religion (e.g., CCD or Sunday School) students felt the same. When asked, "How important is your religious faith in shaping daily life decisions?" 48 percent of Catholic school students said "extremely important" or "very important," while only 40 percent of Parish School of Religion students felt the same.[7]

The most important statistic is not mentioned here. It is believed that between one-third and one-half of Catholic high school age students don't attend either a Catholic high school or a parish school of religion. Of course, there have always been a substantial number of Catholic children who have not received the benefit of a parochial education. The difference, however, is that those kids generally received good catechesis, both from the parish priest and from their parents. This is no longer universally true. Many parents do not ensure that their children receive a religious education. Furthermore, even such tried and true programs such as CCD do not reliably transmit the faith.[y]

Now there are deficiencies in parochial school religious education, to be sure. All of us can probably recount stories of the person who went through 12 years of Catholic education and cannot recite the Ten Commandments or the Hail Mary. Nonetheless, graduates of parochial schools generally have a foundational knowledge of what the Faith teaches, but the same cannot be said anymore of their Catholic public school counterparts. Therefore, when these two universes mix, it is often the case that these latter students negatively impact the two previously mentioned questions, especially if they or their parents feel it is not necessary to learn about their faith past the eighth grade.

Something needs to be done about this, obviously. I cannot speak for parochial catechesis programs, but for parochial schools, I have personally observed that the tide is turning toward having better catechized students, and thus eventually better formed adults who will live their faith in edifying and impressive ways.

And all of us know that this has historically been the case. This explains in part the unparalleled success of Catholic schools in American history. Catholics who were at the bottom of the societal totem pole are now suddenly at the top. With the help of Catholic schools, many minority groups, especially African-Americans, are working and studying their way out of the same inner city areas that Catholics once called home.

As evidence of this, consider the following: Only about 50 percent of African American students graduate from high school as compared to almost 75 percent of Caucasians. However, 95 percent of African American youth enrolled in Catholic schools end up graduating. In a Heritage Foundation study done, 60 percent of African American youth enrolled in New York City's Catholic schools scored above the national SAT average for African American youth. At the same time,

---

y Walter Cardinal Kaspar alluded to this in an October 2006 speech he gave at a small Pennsylvania college about the effectiveness of Pentecostals in leading Catholics out of the Church. Today's Catholics don't know their faith well enough to challenge the accusations made against it by such sects.

70 percent of African American youth in New York City's public schools percent scored below the national SAT average in the same category.[8]

Director of Assessment for the Diocese of Columbus Jeri Rod has to make sure schools are performing well in all areas. "Many notice the academic excellence of Catholic schools," she said. "Some may think it is because the Catholic school teachers are excellent, which is true. Others may think it is because Catholic schools only accept the best students, which is not true. The truth lies in the Catholic culture of the schools. The culture has foundational tenets of respect for oneself and others, and recognition of the uniqueness and importance of each individual. These tenets are based on the 'gospel values'" of Christ, and they set an atmosphere in Catholic schools that is conducive to learning. It is this permeation of Catholic culture that permits students to grow academically and spiritually strong."[9]

Another thing about Catholic schools is that they prove that money is not necessarily the key to giving a child a great education. Often, the per pupil cost to educate a child is half that of a public school, especially those in many large inner city districts, the same districts that often rank at the bottom of academic achievement. Unlike those districts, Catholic schools have less bureaucratic red tape with which they have to deal. As a result, the National Catholic Education Association has found that Catholic schools, by their very existence, save the federal government $19 billion a year.[10]

It is unfortunate that given this institution's track record, there are many bishops and priests who don't seem to value Catholic education more highly (judging by the few new schools that are opening and the many old ones that are closing).

There are some, however, who see the need to build the Kingdom of God through parochial education. One such person is Bishop Robert Carlson. He is leading the charge in his diocese for

Catholic education. "We need strong Catholic schools to teach the faith and to evangelize," he said. "We need to keep the schools going, all the while paying a just wage." As mentioned previously, he has established an apologetics course for Catholic high school seniors.

He has also directed that all parochial grade school students write diocesan seminarians. "I have them doing this not because the seminarians are lonely," he said, "but to connect [them] to different levels of Catholic education."[11]

Furthermore, there are some pastors who recently have taken bold steps to build new schools, often in areas not normally considered wealthy. Fr. Tim Hayes of Blessed Sacrament Church in Newark, OH, is one such leader. His school is located in Newark's east side, which is working and lower class. In 2004, his parish found itself with a school community that used classroom space that was outdated and nearly 100 years old. As a result, a decision was made to build a new school. Bishop Frederick Campbell dedicated the Blessed Sacrament Centennial Building in August 2005, just in time for the school's one-hundredth anniversary.[12]

That spirit of community evidenced in Newark has always been found in Catholic schools, whether in large cities or small towns. Single mother Joy Patterson found out how strong that community was as family and friends assisted her in sending her children through Catholic schools. "I wanted to give my children the same faith and opportunities that were given to me," she said. Thankfully, with the help of the Catholic community, it was accomplished.[13]

While Catholic schools are located in all areas of America, it may surprise some to learn that some of this country's premier Catholic schools are located in many inner cities. Many families in Washington, DC, and New York don't think twice about sending their children to Catholic schools even when public schools are close by because public schools are often havens for gangs and drugs. In September 2004 the *Washington Times* reported that 33 percent of

New York City's public school teachers sent their children to private schools, many of which are Catholic. In Washington, DC, the figure was at 28 percent, in Baltimore 35 percent, and Philadelphia topped the list with 44 percent.[14]

More importantly than even excellent academics, however, is that even the most excellent public school cannot allow discussion of prayer or of how God fits into life's ups and downs for fear of a lawsuit by a group like the American Civil Liberties Union (aka, ACLU).

Catholic schools, on the other hand, can answer the fundamental and crucially important questions students have when life is turned upside down. Rocco Fumi, principal of St. Mary Magdalene School in Columbus, explained, "When devastating events happen in the world, people have a tendency to immediately turn to God for guidance, comfort, and prayer. At St. Mary Magdalene, we teach our students that God is with them in bad and good times. We try to explain what some schools dare not: God is with us always."[15]

Bishop Hartley High School in Columbus serves an area that has pockets of very wealthy as well as very poor persons, though most students come from middle class homes. The school is nationally known for its technology plan implemented by two faculty and alumni Ken Collura and Stephen Trovato. Principal Mike Winters says his school is so successful because, "We might have the most diverse socioeconomic school in the state. The thing that ties all of this together is our Catholic identity. [It is not simply] our excellent academics. From retreats to helping the local community to our Stations of the Cross and Our Holy Family Memorial located in our courtyard, all of this reminds us of who we are and what God calls us to do."[16]

St. Francis DeSales High School located on Columbus' northeast side also relies heavily on faith and tradition (i.e., its Catholic identity) as the foundation for its excellent academics. When alumnus Patrick Rossetti retired as principal in 2004, he had been principal for more than half of the school's existence. Following him as principal was another alumnus Dan Garrick, who said the success of the school "is rooted in three simple yet powerful words: faith, family, and tradition. Simply put, our school community has always embraced the fundamental reason for our existence as being to celebrate our Catholic faith. It is in the context of celebrating that faith as community that we join together as an extended family. And finally the rich traditions of our Church serve as a tremendous guide as we attempt to embrace our God-given gifts through our daily effort in all that we endeavor to do."[17]

The closing paragraph of Fr. Hayes' e-mail about Catholic schools says it better than anything I could write: "We are committed to the future of Catholic education because our faith teaches us its value. Our children, their parents, the extended families, and wider community all benefit from what has been accomplished. It has shown us what God can do when there are hearts open to His grace."[18]

- CHAPTER 9 -

CATHOLIC HIGHER EDUCATION

If one were to judge Catholic higher education in America by the best-known schools, one might tempted to despair. Boston College, Georgetown, and storied Notre Dame among others all seemed to have abandoned part of the Catholicity that helped make them into the powerhouse institutions they are.

At Notre Dame, teachers of questionable orthodoxy such as Theology Professor Fr. Richard McBrien and History Professor R. Scott Appleby have many students and parents wondering why they are paying princely sums each year to have their faith undermined. Even though the school hired the supposedly more orthodox Fr. John I. Jenkins, CSC, at its new president in April 2004, he allowed the putrid play *Vagina Monologues* to be performed on campus.

DePaul University has initiated a Queer Studies program. Boston College's newspaper called on administrators to remember that its identity was more Jesuit than Catholic. Georgetown University had to be shamed into putting crucifixes back on its classroom walls (something even many Muslim students at the school did not find objectionable). And Francis Cardinal Arinze caused a huge uproar among that school's faculty when he detailed the Church's teachings on abortion and homosexuality during a commencement address.[1]

The unifying thread that binds together all these institutions is that each has compromised their Catholic identity and thus missed a unique chance to evangelize and provide a witness our world desperately needs. As a result, many college students are losing or have lost their faith at a time in their lives when they need it the most. A study by University of California Los Angeles' Higher Education

Research Institute of freshmen in 1997 and seniors in 2001 showed that by all measures, students at Catholic colleges were much less likely to believe the tenets of the Church by the time they graduated than their secular school counterparts.

However amidst the despair there is some good news at these well-established colleges and universities. Often it is the students themselves who are taking matters into their own hands by forming prayer groups, attending daily Mass, and helping the less fortunate in the local community.

For instance, Notre Dame has initiated the ACE (Alliance for Catholic Education) program. Under the leadership of Fr. Ron Nuzzi, this endeavor helps students pay off their college debt if they work in impoverished areas. Often, this program sends young teachers to the inner city or Appalachia to assist those students with their faith and skill sets. And even though Notre Dame has people like McBrien and Appleby, it also has great minds such as law professors Charles Rice and Rick Garnett. Both are widely respected by orthodox Catholics for their sharp legal minds. The latter also contributes to the Mirror of Justice website which discusses Catholic legal issues. Rosary and other prayer groups are very prominent at Notre Dame, as well.

And when the crucifix-less walls at Georgetown first came to light, it was because a Catholic students' association began to protest the situation.

The best news in Catholic higher education, however, is not coming from the historical schools. Many may not know of the dramatic rise of the more orthodox colleges and universities that are quickly gaining prominence. For instance, Franciscan University of Steubenville in Ohio has steadily gained a solid reputation since the late 1970s for its faithfulness and concern for the holiness of its students. Franciscan University now houses the largest undergraduate Theology program of any Catholic institution of higher learning. The university is unapologetic about such traditional practices as

Eucharistic adoration. Young, traditionally-minded students are flocking to Steubenville, many drawn because of the youth conferences the school puts on several times each summer at its campus and in places across the United States.[z]

Franciscan is not alone, however. As noted by Michael James, associate executive director of the Association of Catholic Colleges and Universities, the five Catholic universities that have opened in last five years are quite orthodox. "The startup institutions have all aligned themselves (with) what they term fidelity to the Magisterium of the Catholic Church," he said.[2]

Others include Aquinas College in Nashville, Thomas Aquinas College in California, Benedictine College, the University of Dallas, Belmont Abbey College, Wyoming Catholic College, and fresh from its move from Michigan to Naples, Florida, Ave Maria University. Tom Monaghan, the man behind Domino's Pizza, was also the man behind Ave Maria University (as well as its law school, which will remain in Michigan) and their move to Florida.[3]

Catholic students and their parents want truth. They have found it in places such as Thomas Aquinas College, which is about 70 miles northwest of Los Angeles. Students there address each as Miss, Mister, or Misses in the classroom. There are no lectures by a professor or textbooks, but rather discussions on great books that helped form Western civilization by the likes of St. Augustine, CS Lewis, Marx, Locke, Virgil, Chesterton, Tacitus, Shakespeare, Euclid, Sophocles, Newton, and others moderated by a tutor, all with the aim to discover truth. The 35-year-old school continues to grow, and it seems each year's freshman class is its largest.

Catholic life is also very evident on many of these faithful Catholic campuses. At Benedictine College, more than 200 students

---

[z] It used to be that the easiest way to not get a job with a parish ministry or diocesan chancery was to list a degree from FUS. Those who ran such offices falsely accused graduates of being "fundamentalist" and "rigid" when what they really were was faithful and in love with the Church and her teachings. Thanks be to God, the fantastic job done by Franciscan grads is steadily eroding the baseless prejudice they once faced (and sometimes still do).

attend daily Mass out of a total student body of 1,700. At Franciscan University, it is estimated that 75 percent of the student body attends daily Mass.

Many Benedictine students also skip lunch once a week so the proceeds can go to the area's needy. Other orthodox Catholic college students also are engaged in acts of charity and obedience. Whether it be praying in front of abortion clinics or working in soup kitchens, many of these students are showing their good works and assisting others in the process. Some upper-class women at Franciscan University even have a "What Would Mary Wear" presentation for some of the incoming freshman.[3]

Tim Drake's book *Young and Catholic* talks about some of the independent student Catholic newspapers that are published on Catholic campuses such as Georgetown University, Gonzaga University, College of the Holy Cross, and Villanova University, among others. With the help of the Cardinal Newman Society, which promotes Catholic identity at Catholic schools, these periodicals give students an alternative view to what they might read in their campus-run newspaper.[4]

Lest one think that only Catholic colleges are seeing such positive signs, it is important to note some of the uplifting stories coming out of secular campuses through the help of the Greeley, Colorado-based Fellowship of Catholic University Students (FOCUS). At schools such as Texas A&M, and Florida State, 200 or more students attend daily Mass. FOCUS has found that many students want something more than just the party scene. They often were weak in their faith, but because of FOCUS' Bible studies, now spend some of their free time studying Scripture and in Eucharistic adoration. A learning process of a whole different kind is underway with these students. They are putting the knowledge they receive from the Bible studies to daily use. These students and the lives of those with whom they come in contact are better for it.

In just eight years, the group has founded chapters on 27 campuses in 15 states. Phenomenal doesn't begin to describe the growth of vocations due to FOCUS. It took a few years for the group to get a start, but in those few short years the group already has had 80 men who are priests or who have entered the seminary and 25 women who have entered religious life or are studying for it.

The group was started by Curtis Martin, who left the Church while at Louisiana State University and came back five years later. He credits God with placing him in Josh McDowell's Campus Crusade for Christ. He feels he learned much from the group, but after doing much reading about the early Church, he came back to his childhood faith and credits the Eucharist and apostolic succession for this return. Each campus where FOCUS is present has four missionaries, two men and two women. They are entirely responsible for raising their own salaries, and they usually do this through donations and pledges from supportive parishioners near the campus. They see the Bible and Catholic apologetics as the focus of their ministry. Martin was able to meet Pope John Paul II in the early days of the group. The pontiff told him "to be a soldier of Christ" and gave him a rosary. The meeting had a profound impact on Martin and those involved with FOCUS.

Nikki Shasserre, spokeswoman for FOCUS, said college students often get caught up in the college party life and become unmoored as they grow older. She related to me that she felt emptiness in her life while a senior in college. FOCUS was just getting started and her involvement with the group puzzled many of her family and friends. "My family became very supportive after they realized how happy I was becoming, but I did lose friendships," she said. "I wouldn't preach to my friends, but when we would go out to have fun, there were things I wouldn't do anymore and I guess that made them uncomfortable."

When reminded that there are so many who want to change the

Church to be more reflective of the world, she said she had also met them. However, she then said something very profound: "We don't want to change the Church; we want the Church to change us."[5]

Shasserre's words offer a great lesson for all of those who wonder why small, relatively obscure Catholic colleges and universities are growing. Perhaps these smaller schools are starting their own tide, a tide that is beginning to envelope the larger tide by pushing it, albeit sometimes unwillingly, ever closer to the shore for all to see.

- CHAPTER 10 -

CATHOLICISM AND POPULAR CULTURE

In recent years, the world of Catholic communications has been woefully behind that of Protestants, especially the Evangelicals. Evangelical books, websites, and television programs far outnumber Catholic ones. While one can watch a televised Catholic Mass on Sundays, the program is often designed for shut-ins and is likely to be shown before dawn (indeed, it would seem only the most faithful shut-in could get up at such an early hour). With the emergence of EWTN and Catholic radio programs such as "The Al Kresta Show," however, this situation is changing. At long last, Catholics are receiving information and inspiration through the media, and that development is helping the tide turn towards Catholicism.

Perhaps the growth of Catholic radio most acutely shows this trend. When EWTN radio was launched in 1996, there were only 14 Catholic radio stations in the United States, but Catholic radio is now growing. In 2006, the number of Catholic radio stations have topped 120, although this is still modest compared to the roughly 2,000 Evangelical radio stations.[1] Radio networks like Ave Maria Radio and syndicated shows like the Kresta program began to make inroads into the booming talk radio business.

Another way the tide is turning is the way high profile people of faith in athletics and entertainment are causing people to take notice of Christianity's importance.

Catholics are blessed to have many stars of the stage, screen, and athletic field who give of their time for the faith. Some have a very inspiring and charismatic presence. While there are many Catholics whose faith has burst into the limelight recently, none has had a magnifying glass on him the way Mel Gibson has. The American-born and Australian-raised Catholic was a major star in the 1980s and 1990s. He could have easily spent his remaining years in the spotlight, occasionally talking about his faith and playing the good Catholic, all the while not rocking Hollywood's boat. Mel Gibson not only rocked Hollywood's boat but also those on which many people throughout the world were traveling.

A traditional Catholic, Gibson always wanted to make a movie about the final 48 hours in the life of Jesus Christ. He decided to do so and spent a year preparing for and shooting the movie. Rarely has a Hollywood film made news a year before it was released, but almost as soon as Gibson announced his plans in 2004, a barrage of negative stories appeared.

First there was the story of Gibson's film being based on the visions of an eighteenth century nun, Bl. Anne Catherine Emmerich, whom some Jews considered to be anti-Semitic. Then there was the completely gratuitous story on Gibson's traditionalist faith and his father Hutton Gibson's alleged denial of the Holocaust. As Christmas and the release of his movie approached, rumors filled the air that Gibson would be blackballed from Hollywood. There were fears the film would renew long-dismissed notion that the Jews were solely responsible for Christ's death.

As the film approached its Ash Wednesday 2004 debut, Gibson met with a large group of Evangelical pastors. The irony for religion news followers and pundits was plain to see: Gibson was meeting with the very people he vehemently disagreed with on a host of theological issues. The same could be said for the Evangelical leaders as well. However, they met with each because of what united them, a faith in Jesus Christ as their only savior. This unity made them stronger in the face of withering criticism that came from some in the secular world.[2] It was starting to appear to be a showdown of biblical proportions.

Before the film's release, Gibson tried to show his film was not anti-Semitic in meetings with the Jewish leaders. In doing so, he found some support from people such as Rabbi Daniel Lapin, who said he felt the film's Jewish critics were secular Jews who were more upset with a perceived conservative political agenda than with the stated religious differences. In the final cut, Gibson even withheld certain scenes that he thought might be offensive to Jews or that he thought might take away from the overall message of the film.

Regardless, Gibson began gaining a great deal of support from Christians across the board. This support would get even more interesting when those Christians who were not Catholic saw what in the end was a very Catholic film. A great deal of the movie was focused on Jesus' mother, Mary. Mary's role was something that was somewhat unfamiliar to many Protestants, who might have known precious little about Jesus' mom.

As a result, an event unfathomable 20 or 30 years ago occurred. Evangelical Protestants were taking their congregations by the busload to movie theaters to see a Catholic portrayal of the last 48 hours of Jesus Passion, His death on the cross, and His subsequent resurrection. Evangelical leaders defended Gibson's Catholic movie most vociferously to a host of secular critics that the Evangelicals viewed as enemies of Christianity. A strange interdenominational alliance that had been growing in political circles for years was now making its presence felt in the realm of entertainment. Catholics and Evangelicals started working together even more closely, and it took an essentially Catholic film to make that happen.

Jim Caviezel, the Catholic star of the film, was also emerging. He had appeared in several films and had even co-starred with Jennifer Lopez in a quickly forgotten movie *Angel Eyes*. While Caviezel's openness regarding his Catholicism might have worked against him in some circles, it greatly helped his cause when Gibson cast his eyes around for the film's lead.

Furthermore, because Caviezel played basketball in college,

this caused many sports reporters to interview him who might have otherwise not paid much attention to the star of *The Passion of the Christ*. It was a great opportunity for him to subtly talk about his faith in a non-intrusive manner. Many heard a witness to Christ from a faithful young man who many women considered to be heartthrobs.[aa]

In any event, Gibson's film was a tour de force for Catholicism in that it showed the human and divine side of Christ from a Catholic perspective.

If anything could kill the good feelings that resulted from *The Passion of the Christ* for orthodox Christians, it was *The Da Vinci Code*. Ordinarily a book that posits preposterous claims doesn't make it to the silver screen, to say nothing of being met with eager anticipation. *The Da Vinci Code* was the exception.

As noted in a previous chapter, the book and movie basically asserted that Jesus was a fraud, and if that was the case, then so was Christianity.[3] Once again the entertainment industry was taking another Sunday punch at Christianity. This time, though, it was a one-two combination. The combination was meant to question the essence of Christianity while also attacking the Catholic Church, in particular the Opus Dei prelature.[bb]

The popularity of *The Da Vinci Code* was seen not only in its sales but also the magnitude of its message. Many Christians began to seriously consider the previously unthinkable idea that Jesus had married Mary Magdalene. Stories of *The Da Vinci Code* being discussed at parish book clubs surfaced. There were even stories of bewildered priests and parish directors of Religious Education having to field questions as to why no one had ever taught them that Jesus was married.[4]

[aa] Caviezel followed this up by appearing in an ad opposing a 2006 Missouri state ballot initiative that would have allowed embryonic stem cell research in that state. Appearing with him were fellow Catholics Patricia Heaton (former star of "Everybody Loves Raymond"), St. Louis Cardinals' star pitcher Jeff Suppan, and Kansas City Royals' slugger Mike Sweeney.

THE TIDE IS TURNING TOWARD CATHOLICISM

The release of *The Da Vinci Code* was quickly followed by another skeptics' delight, *The Gospel of Judas*. The National Geographic Channel promoted their documentary about this Gnostic book as if it was an unknown and great historic find. Neither was the case. It seemed the Gnostics wrote about and challenged just about anything they could in the early centuries of the Church. Their characterization of "Judas the hero" was in this vein. But to portray Judas as actually being a good guy was ridiculous even to early Christians. That is why no one in the early Church read this Gnostic Gospel of Judas. It seems the early Christians were far more intelligent than the goofy modern theologians who were all aflutter over this Gnostic text. Some of the media could also hardly contain their glee over a possible rift in Christianity.

---

bb According to its web site, Opus Dei is a personal prelature of the Catholic Church that helps people seek holiness in their work and ordinary activities. They strive to help people do ordinary things in extraordinary way out of love for God. If you want to grow in sanctity and faithfulness to the Church, lay movements such as Opus Dei and others are an excellent way to go.

The founder of Opus Dei, St. Josemaria Escriva was born in 1902 and died in 1975. His dedication to the Church and to the salvation of souls should be commended not condemned by our pop culture's glitterati. Yet Brown and so many others have unjustly vilified this group and many have accepted this vilification as gospel truth. Why?

"I think [it's because] we live in a conspiracy driven society," said Terri Carron, the prelature's spokeswoman. "[Brown] went after us because [some] claim we are a secretive group. You know, 200 years ago, it would have been the Jesuits. Now it's our turn. However, we are just like the many other Catholic lay groups who are trying to defend the Church and live out her message."

In case you were wondering, I am not in any way affiliated with Opus Dei. Not only have I never attended one of their evenings of recollection, they don't even have them in my area. I simply admire the work they do, and it makes me angry that such a fantastic organization whose only concern is growing saints has taken such an unfair rap. For a fair treatment of the organization, read John Allen's book, *Opus Dei: An Objective Look Behind the Myths and Reality of the Most Controversial Force in the Catholic Church*. Scott Hahn has also recently released a book on the group.

The good news with all of this, however, was that it forced many Catholics to investigate the claims of both Brown's book and the apocryphal Gospel. To aid them was the aforementioned "Jesus Decoded" website by the United States Conference of Catholic Bishop, along with a book of the same name. While Amy Welborn wrote *Decoding Da Vinci*, Carl Olson and Sandra Meisel penned the popular *The Da Vinci Hoax*. Both books tore apart Brown's claims point-by-point. Additionally, Dr. Edward "Ted" Sri released a popular talk called "The Da Vinci Deception" that did much the same thing, and Jimmy Akin of Catholic Answers issued a little user-friendly booklet called *Cracking the Da Vinci Code* that followed the path blazed by these other titles.

As a result, many Catholics learned things about their faith they had never known before. They learned things about Church history, the teachings of various councils, and how the Bible was codified. They learned how to defend Jesus' divinity. Perhaps most important in an age where Gnosticism is once again rearing its ever-ugly head, they learned what this heresy entails and how to argue against it.

But there have been some orthodox portrayals of Catholicism in the mainstream media, too. In the spring of 2006 the A&E cable network ran a five-part series called "God or the Girl."[5] The show featured four young men discerning a call to the priesthood. At first, some Catholics were turned off by the title, envisioning a reality type TV show that turned vocational discernment process into something tawdry. However, the show quickly won over most skeptics. Indeed, it became quite a hit for A&E and showed these men up close and personal.[cc]

One of the men featured on the show, Dan DeMatte, related to me the following in an interview for my CatholicReport.org website: "I was always interested in my Catholic faith. However, I remember

---

[cc] Ironically, with all the attacks launched against Catholics, ranging from movie producers to book writers (many of whom claim to be Christians), the show was produced and written by Jews and agnostics. Indeed, the Lord does work in mysterious ways.

when I was a senior at St. Charles [High School in Columbus, Ohio], I thought I really don't understand the Eucharist and the Real Presence as much as I should. So I asked for some help and I was directed to some books and articles. I think I had a true religious experience as I began to understand Christ's presence."

Dan agreed to be on the show but he admitted the decision to do so wasn't easy. "It was very difficult. There were days when I could barely find one half hour to pray. I had to watch what I said because in the back of your mind you don't want to say anything that would draw negative light to the Church. However, I knew that God had a hand in all of this so I accepted it as His will."

During the show, a fundamentalist confronted Dan. This man said he couldn't participate in group prayer with Catholics because they were leading people "astray." Dan felt frustrated that he couldn't go toe to toe with the fundamentalist in the Bible quoting department so he started to brush up on his scriptures and attended a local non-denominational Bible study group that he heard had a propensity for being anti-Catholic. Dan witnessed to this group over various Scripture quotes and felt he helped them better understand the Church's teachings. "At first I think they were surprised that a Catholic was there," he said. "I think some of them have never personally interacted with a Catholic before. I think they appreciated my testimony."[6]

Fr. Jeff Coning, with whom I worked at the Diocese of Columbus, talked about Dan's experience with the fundamentalist and the similar situations Catholics go through.

"It's not who memorizes the most scriptures," he observed. "It's who loves God and serves God. That's what our faith tells us."

Father Jeff also told me in an interview for my CatholicReport. org website that discerning a priestly call takes time. One cannot make demands of God. The answer will come in His time, not ours.

I asked Fr. Jeff about one of the most powerful scenes of the entire series. In it, Fr. Jeff asks Dan to carry an 80-pound cross over 20 miles to help with his discernment concerning the priesthood.

"Well, I have gotten beaten up over that," he said. "I am really not an ogre. We tried to work with the producers and Dan's time constraints, and this was the best way we could show what carrying a cross means in light of a priestly vocation. I wouldn't ordinarily recommend something like that, but it worked out best for this situation."

In our interview, Fr. Jeff went on to say that those discerning a vocational call must have a spiritual mentor.

"I have young men who come into my office and are gung ho about the priesthood," he told me. "The next week maybe they are not so gung ho about the priesthood. You can't demand an answer from God on your time. You can't walk into a chapel and say, 'OK, God, by the time I am finished praying, I want an answer.' St. Teresa of Avila said she always spent time reading in the chapel. She would pray and read and pray and read." In other words, discerning an answer take time, reflection, meditation, and prayer.[7]

The benefit provided by the show is that it got many Catholics thinking and praying about their own vocations and life choices. It seems hard to imagine how something so positive and balanced in its portrayal of the Church could not turn hearts and minds and even lead to conversions.

The Catholic writer JRR Tolkien made a splash on the big screen with a trilogy of his three-volume book *The Lord of the Rings*, initially printed in 1954. For years, Tolkien has been a favorite amongst Catholic and other fans of the fantasy genre. However, it wasn't until 30 years after his death that his books were translated into a powerful series of films. Tolkien was now part of a pop culture world that he took great measures not to embrace while he was alive.

As with the books, the movie version had many subtle Catholic references in it. While it was open to debate as to what the author really intended, certain allusions to aspects of redemption and even a rarely used metaphor for Purgatory were believed to have been used in the films. The Church would do well to use that scene to explain the concept of Purgatory to a Protestant world that is often very skeptical about it.

Tolkien's influence spread far and wide. While some who read his books might not catch all of the Catholic symbolism, at least the opportunity is there. The 1970s rock super group Led Zeppelin used many Tolkien inspired images in their songs. Many wondered about the rumors that guitarist Jimmy Page dabbled in the occult.[dd]

However, the group's lead singer Robert Plant was a huge fan of Tolkien. Who would have guessed that classic rock tunes like "Ramble On," "Misty Mountain Hop," and "The Battle of Evermore" had some of Tolkien's influences spread about them. If the rumors of occult beliefs were true about Page, at least some of the group's songs had a counter-balance because of Tolkien's influence. There is even some evidence that perhaps the classic rock song "Stairway to Heaven" might have had some unintended Tolkien (i.e., Catholic) images in it.[8]

Perhaps Tolkien's biggest claim to fame, according to CS Lewis, was that it was Tolkien who was chiefly responsible for Lewis' conversion to Christianity after many years spent as an atheist.

Catholic Musicians

A few years ago, the Catholic contemporary music scene had a lot of catching up to do with its counterpart in the Evangelical world. However, recent developments show that great strides have been made as more and more Catholic musicians such as John Angotti

---

[dd] Indeed, he bought the late and legendary Satanist Aleister Crowley's estate precisely because Crowley had owned this. He has often spoken of how he chan-neled music, although he is always vague about saying from who or what he did the channeling.

and Aaron Thompson emerge as up-and-coming stars.

When one remembers pop music from the 1970s, one doesn't have to try hard to recall anti-religious lyrics in songs performed by big time rock groups (e.g., "Cathedral" by Crosby, Stills, Nash & Young and "Imagine" by John Lennon).

Perhaps it was in part because of these anti-religious songs that the Christian rock era began with groups such as Petra, Larry Norman, Randy Stonehill, and Mason Profit's John Michael Talbot, who eventually became a Catholic.

Catholics took whatever small victories they could get in music in the 1970s and 1980s. When the Beatles released the single "Let It Be" in 1970, everyone knew the group was just about to break up. In the verse, "When I find myself in times of trouble, Mother Mary comes to me, speaking words of wisdom, let it be," many Catholics thought (perhaps hoped) that Paul McCartney was singing about the Blessed Mother since he was raised Catholic.[ee] However, Catholics couldn't be blamed for trying to find some kernel of truth in the world of popular music. "Let It Be" was even played at some churches' guitar Masses.

For those Catholics who were looking for a spiritual bent in contemporary music during the rest of 1970s and 1980s, however, there was little to get excited about. "Jesus is Just Alright," by the Doobie Brothers and "Spirit in the Sky" by Norman Greenbaum, plus "Put Your Hand in the Hand" by both Ocean and Loretta Lynn were nice exceptions but they hardly started a trend. Some Catholics took whatever positive news they could get, like the fact that the rock guitar virtuoso Eddie Van Halen and his actress wife Valerie Bertinelli mentioned that they liked to go to Mass when they were on the road in the 1980s.[ff]

There were some rock groups who had positive messages in their songs like "Roll With the Changes" and "Keep Pushin' On" by Midwest rockers REO Speedwagon, as well as "Fight the Good

---

[ee] It appears not; "mother Mary" refers to his own deceased mother.

Fight" by Canadian rockers Triumph. Also, Irish band U2 had loads of Christian imagery in their songs, and even put Psalm 40 to music. Bruce Springsteen's Catholic upbringing clearly gave some of his songs a feeling of hope. Other than these limited offerings, however, one had to look long and hard to find groups with positive or somewhat faith filled messages.

Fortunately, the Christian music scene began to come on strong in the 1980s with groups such as the metal band Stryper. It really took off in the 1990s, however, with groups such as Jars of Clay, dc Talk, Third Day, Michael W. Smith and Amy Grant. These artists had an appeal that moved them beyond the Christian music audience to the wider pop audience. Catholics were looking for a figure to do the same for them.

The "godfather" of the Catholic music scene may be Tony Melendez, the armless singer-songwriter and guitar player (yes, you read right, an armless guitar player). Tony was a victim of thalidomide and grew up learning to do with his feet, toes, and mouth what most people do with their hands. Many Catholics might recall the inspiring performance he gave before Pope John Paul II in Los Angeles in 1987. After the performance, John Paul made his way over to Tony to personally thank him and tell him how strong his witness to Christ was.

I spoke with Tony in Atlanta at the 2005 National Catholic Youth Convention. His ability to witness was greatly aided by his down-to-earth nature and easy-going way of explaining the hardships he had conquered. As we walked toward a table where I could do the interview, he bought a bottle of water, opened it with his teeth, and drank it by grabbing the bottle with his mouth and drinking it like he was doing the most mundane of routines. He noticed my amazed expression, laughed, and said, "I bet you never saw anyone open and drink a bottle of water like that before." I replied, "No. I guess you learn something new everyday."

---

ff Sadly, the couple has since divorced. Let us keep them, their son, and all such families in our prayers.

Shortly after I interviewed him, he made an appearance near my home in Columbus at Bishop Watterson High School. When I arrived at the school there he was, standing near the large electrical cords needed for his performance and harmlessly directing the students away from them. To put the students at ease, Tony tried to put a humorous spin on his disability by telling the students various scenarios as to why he didn't have any arms. This technique gave him the perfect set up to talk seriously to the students about their faith and purpose in life. Melendez talked about overcoming obstacles and concluded his remarks with a demonstration. He took a Frisbee, and, with his toes, flung it across the large high school gym, hitting the basketball scoreboard on the far end. It was truly a remarkable feat and put some action into his words.

Melendez's sincere nature could be seen in his desire to be taken seriously as a musician. He did not simply want to be seen as some sort of sideshow personality that could play the guitar with his toes. Indeed his version of the Lord's Prayer, along with original songs including "Ways of the Wise," "You Are His Miracle," and "Never Be the Same," are considered Catholic classics. Melendez also had some interesting insights on some other topics. He spoke emotionally about how Pope John Paul II changed his life after the performance at which the pontiff embraced him and told him how inspirational he was.

When asked why Christians fall in their faith journey and what causes evil, he responded, "Sin is [attractive] and causes us to do stupid things. The first time you drink a beer you might cringe, and then in college you're drinking it like there's no tomorrow."[9] Melendez continues to tour across the United States and Latin America telling crowds his story and hopefully encouraging them in their faith journey.

"Many new Catholic musicians are hitting the music scene," said Larry Nolte, host of a Catholic radio program and organizer of the CrossRoads Catholic Music Festival. "Whatever musical genre you're into, it's being done by Catholic-based musicians. I am 51-years-old so my musical tastes steer to rock and folk. I am not really into rap. However, six or seven years ago there was one Catholic rapper; now there're about 12 established acts. Whatever type of genre you like, rock, folk, jazz or hard rock, there's a Catholic band for your taste. Sometimes Catholic bookstores and radio stations won't carry or play Catholic artists that perform something besides liturgical music. There are still so many barriers to overcome but Catholics have made tremendous progress."[10]

Fr. Stan Fortuna, CFR, has been a staple of the Catholic music scene for some time, while Cheer Up Charlie is a remnant of the Catholic group Scarecrow & Tinmen. Cheer Up Charlie are rising stars in the Catholic music world, and their music is cutting edge. Nothing about it is simplistic, and they sing about faith from a different angle. The Canadian Catholic rockers Critical Mass have gone through some different incarnations. They are fronted by David Wang, who makes his living as a science professor at the University of Waterloo in Canada. If it weren't for that and music, this husband and father of eight could probably be a theologian.

During an exchange of e-mails Wang said, "I really stumbled into the music ministry. It just started from listening to Christian music in my own faith life. In 1997, with a group of friends, we decided to introduce a more contemporary sound to youth groups. We released a demo recording called *Faith Looks Up*, and it took off. We followed up with two albums, *Completely* and *Grasping for Hope in the Darkness*, which both garnered Best Rock Album honors from the Gospel Music Association Canada. We also performed for the Pope in 2002 in Toronto for a cumulative audience of over one million youth! Despite this, the Catholic music ministry for an audience is a very difficult path. Unlike Evangelical Christians who nurture their industry into one that challenges the secular music scene, Catholic laity and clergy are difficult markets to figure out.

We tend not to support our own for some strange reason."

Although frustration can sink in for still emerging Catholic musicians, Wang wrote that "What keeps me going is the knowledge that, from our e-mails and correspondence, our songs seem to be making a difference in our listeners' lives. In 2006, when we are inundated with the 'culture of death,' I feel that the Church needs Catholic artists to continue to shine with a different message. Hopefully, some time in the future, the flame will catch fire and help the Church into another revival, where more than a small percentage of Catholics understand their faith, particularly about the Magisterium, Confession, and the Real Presence of Jesus in the Eucharist."[11]

John Angotti, a former West Virginian and current Memphis parish music director has a voice that sounds like a cross between Billy Joel and Marc Cohn. He travels the country and the world sharing his music, and in his parish stops, Angotti often has his family accompany him. He shares personal heartfelt stories of family life along with its joys and struggles. It certainly is a genuine witness to which many families can relate and appreciate.

Young, Catholic, and on fire for the faith is Janelle Reinhart (known simply as Janelle), who sang for John Paul II at World Youth Day 2002 and won the Best Pop/Contemporary Album of the Year in 2003 for her debut effort *New Day* from the Canadian Gospel Music Covenant Awards and three different best new artist awards that same year. In 2005, Janelle released the single "Be Not Afraid - Open Wide Your Heart," an inspiring song that honored Pope John Paul II. Its release resulted in over 25 radio and television interviews following the passing of His Holiness John Paul II, including "Dateline NBC."

Aaron Thompson is another parish musician who takes his faith on the road. He resides in Arizona but travels the country spreading his witness. He has traveled to Poland, where he appeared before

20,000 of the country's faithful at Częstochowa.

While many of the previously mentioned artists cater to a relatively young demographic, Kassel & Company is quite unique. Their feel-good music, a cross between John Michael Talbot, Peter Paul & Mary, and the Oak Ridge Boys, might skew to a little older demographic than the average Cheer Up Charlie fan. Whoever listens to it, however, can't help but feel better about life.

Because of these people and their music, interest in the Catholic music world has increased by leaps and bounds from what it once was. Catholics would not only be helping these dedicated musicians but also their own spiritual growth by purchasing some of this inspiring music.

Faith isn't limited to Catholic music artists, obviously. Jerry Elliott, co-host of Columbus' leading morning radio show "Wags & Elliott" on QFM 96, states that amidst all the zaniness of a rock-n-roll morning show, his Catholic faith is very important to him.

"When I was a young man traveling across the country with other comedians [e.g., Tim Allen and Sinbad]," he told me, "I wasn't as faithful as I should have been. My mother died when I was 20 years old, and it took me a while to sort through that. When my children arrived, I realized that I needed to get back to where I should have been for those missing years. I wanted to give my children the same faithful Catholic upbringing that my parents gave to me. I started to understand Pope John Paul II's words about being a cafeteria Catholic.

"I was certainly one of them. I would take a little here and take a little helping there. I am not that way now. I still have a long way to go but I am getting there. All of my family is involved with the Church. One of my brothers is a dentist, and he and his wife have traveled to India with a Catholic group to help children who need dental work. His living example of faith has really helped me."[12]

Slowly, the world of Catholic entertainment is catching up

not only to its Evangelical counterpart but to where it used to be. Archbishop Sheen's radio and television shows, publications like *Our Sunday Visitor*, and publishing houses like Image books were part of a "Catholic Golden Era," an era that featured memorable Catholic-themed movies like *Going My Way* and *The Bells of St. Mary's*. Fr. Patrick Peyton, CSC's "Family Theater" ran for 10 years on the Mutual Broadcasting System, had a huge following, and attracted huge stars such as Bob Hope, Lucille Ball, and Jimmy Stewart to appear on its popular programs.

Things have obviously changed over the last few decades. However, today Catholic radio, television and books are once again showing signs of growth as many Catholics feel the call to minister to the Church using the gifts God has given them.

Some mention must be made about the infinitesimally small but growing "garage schola" movement, which is promoting traditional music (e.g., Gregorian chant and polyphony).

Although it is not well known, the Second Vatican Council asked in its first document that chant be given "pride of place" in terms of Catholic liturgical music. It also lauded polyphony.[gg] That was all largely ignored in favor of the "Kumbaya" style '70s folk music that continues to predominate today. Granted, beautiful music was not unknown in the '70s, and some songs from this era are quite lovely. However, while many parishioners don't mind one or two of these tunes during Mass (it's hard to call them "hymns"), and while most would agree they are nice for listening to in the car, some argue such a style of music is generally inappropriate for the most sacred, holy event on earth, especially when it is at the exclusion of timeless "standards," if you will, that once helped create saints but which are now largely forgotten.

Today, because of the work of people such as Ave Maria University Professor Susan Treacy, Fr. Joseph Fessio, SJ, and his Adoremus Society, *Crisis* magazine, Jeffrey Morse, Arlene Oost-

---

[gg] *Sacrosanctum Concilium*, promulgated by His Holiness Pope Paul VI on December 4, 1963. See Article 116.

Zinner, Jeffrey Tucker, and many others, sacred music is making a slow, slow comeback. You can hear it in a growing number of parishes across the country (of course, when you start from zero, any increase can be defined as "growing"). For the past several years, there has even been a sacred music conference at Franciscan University, and the *Adoremus Hymnal*, with its mixture of chant and timeless hymns, is increasingly found in Catholic churches.

It is too early to tell whether the tide is turning in this fashion. However, because of chant and polyphony's unique capacity to lift and dispose the soul to God, this budding resurgence is something for which we should all pray and work. It is also something we should celebrate at every turn. And if what is happening now does lead to a full-blown resurgence, it will mean many more souls undergoing conversion and receiving the great gift of salvation because this music has the power to lift and order the soul (and thus dispose it to God's grace) like no other.

Finally, a growing number of Catholic artists, art groups, and architects are seeking to reclaim the mantle of excellence practiced by such forbearers as Bouguereau, Michelangelo, Caravaggio, Guido Reni, El Greco, Lanfranco, and so many more. Catholicism has such a rich patrimony of great sacred art and architecture, a patrimony that has been largely ignored over the last 60 or so years in favor of the stark aesthetics of the modernist movement.

Those helping turn the tide include artists Natalia Tsarkova, James Langley, Jed Gibbons, Michael O'Brien, Daniel Mitsui, institutions such as the Foundation for Sacred Art, Talleres de Arte Granda Liturgical Arts, the Chicago-based Society of St. Barbara web log, and architects such as Franck Lohsen McCrery, Quinlan and Francis Terry, Thomas Gordon Smith, Duncan G. Stroik, Nancy Keane, and James O'Brien. Let us pray that the efforts of these individuals and entities (and those like them) continue to grow and flourish for the good of souls.

DAVID J. HARTLINE

- CHAPTER 11 -

CATHOLIC ATHLETES AND COACHES

The sports world is filled with heroes who are Catholic and not afraid to talk about their faith or share their beliefs with those who want to hear about them. True, some Catholic athletes don't act very faithful, but that shouldn't detract from the many who are role models of the faith. Many Catholics would be surprised to hear about the athletes and former coaches who try to give something back by speaking and making appearances across the country. Stories about their experiences reveal their faith and inspire listeners.

In the 1920s, many Catholics longed to be a part of the middle class. Up to this point, Catholics had long been relegated to the bottom of the economic totem pole. During that decade, however, the University of Notre Dame (especially its football team) gave them hope that status would soon change for the better.

Thanks to Knute Rockne, the Norwegian immigrant who coached the Fighting Irish, Catholics from diverse ethnic backgrounds began cheering for Notre Dame. During the succeeding decades, men such as Rockne, George Gipp, the fabled Four Horsemen (Harry Stuhldreher, "Sleepy Jim" Crowley, Don Miller, and Elmer Layden), Paul Hornung, Johnny Lujak, Leon Hart, and Angelo Bertelli, Notre Dame was a force in college football. It didn't hurt that many Americans identified with the various ethnicities of those names.

Notre Dame athletics continues to captivate today's Catholics. Although there have been some slumps in their record, that hasn't stops a national fan base of all faiths and ethnicities from cheering on the Fighting Irish. This largely universal appeal has enabled two of Notre Dame's former coaches to spend a good deal of their time doing public speaking.

One is Coach Lou Holtz, who led the Irish to a national championship during the 1988 football season. He told me about the various Catholic people who influenced him while he was growing up in East Liverpool, OH (just north of Steubenville). He rattled off the names of several nuns who taught him in grade school as if no time had passed between his elementary school years and his career as a college football coach.

Coach Holtz stated there is not a doubt in his mind that if it were not for the Sisters of Notre Dame pushing and prodding him, he would have never gone to college, let alone become a national coaching legend. He related that sometimes living the Catholic way and doing things right can be challenging, but it ultimately is rewarding.

He spoke of the different rules at a Catholic school like Notre Dame. "Winning a national championship was just a cherished experience," he said. "However, I was brought back down to earth at the start of the next season. University officials told me that three players, including [All-America linebacker] Michael Stonebreaker, were ineligible to play in the season's first game. I think Michael Stonebreaker's case had something to do with a violation of bringing a car on campus when he shouldn't have. However, those were the rules, and rules at Notre Dame mean something. Those are things that set Notre Dame apart from some places."

Holtz speaks at men's conferences and is gracious enough to be interviewed by people like me. To this day, the Coach Holtz interview is one of the most read articles from the archives of my CatholicReport.org website. Holtz gave me some pertinent advice that he said he found out the hard way living in this fast paced world. "It has taken me a long time to figure this out," he said, "but I now live by the belief that if something isn't going to bother you on your death bed, then it shouldn't bother you now." Coach Holtz is a great storyteller and ended the interview by reminding the CatholicReport.

org readers to remember the words of St. Francis: "Preach the Gospel always; use words when necessary."[1]

Coach Gerry Faust was a high school coaching legend at Archbishop Moeller High School in Cincinnati, before he made the leap from the high school to the college ranks at Notre Dame. In the modern era no coach had ever made the leap from a successful high school program to a major college program. Faust had not only achieved great success on the high school level, but he was the model of a saintly coach. He was full of energy and enthusiasm, one minute yelling out encouragement and the next saying an appropriate prayer for the situation. It wasn't uncommon for him to say an "Our Father" and a "Hail Mary" in the locker room or on the sidelines. Sometimes he would throw in a "Glory Be" for good measure.

Unfortunately for Faust, the storybook ending never happened. He never achieved the success in the college ranks that he had enjoyed at Moeller.[hh] After five seasons at Notre Dame, he resigned as head coach prior to his inevitable firing. He loved the University so much that he didn't want to put it through any more turmoil. In addition to his love for Notre Dame, his love for his faith would never be extinguished. The fire of the trial would only sharpen his love of the Church.

Coach Faust's honesty would be refreshing enough for most Catholics, but his public support of the faith is even more so. I also interviewed him for my CatholicReport.org website. When I asked him about any mistakes he had made at Notre Dame, he replied, "I should have been a little tougher with the kids. I thought, well, they're in college. They will be more disciplined than in high school, and I wasn't concentrating on discipline as much as I should have.

[hh] As noted by Wikipedia, his "remarkable 174-17-2 record [at Moeller] was highlighted by seven unbeaten seasons, four national prep titles, and five Ohio state titles in his last six seasons." At Notre Dame, his record was 30-26-1, and his teams went to two bowl games and had a win at the 1983 Liberty Bowl against Boston College. From Notre Dame, he went on to coach at the University of Akron, where his record was 43-53-3.

I had a great coaching staff, but the chemistry in coaching is very important. I keep in touch with the former players and coaches. They are all good people, and many have done great things."

Coach Faust's daily spiritual life was evident for all to see at Notre Dame. Often he would walk to the famed grotto and pray. One time he noticed a tearful young woman who told him she was having some difficulty adjusting to her new surroundings and the Indiana chill. He found out she was from southern California and told one of his players who was also from that area to visit her. Some 25 years later, the two are happily married with children. This level of concern was typical of Coach Faust.

In Coach Faust's last game, his team was getting pounded by the Miami Hurricanes coached by the famed Jimmy Johnson. When Johnson ran up the score 58-7, some on the sidelines told Coach Faust not to shake Johnson's hand. "I never judge people, the Lord does that," Faust said. "I shook Jimmy Johnson's hand and left it at that."

Today Coach Faust gives selflessly of his time, so much so that his friends often pleaded with him to say no. I saw an example of this generosity myself. Coach Faust was gracious enough to give me a telephone interview for my CatholicReport.org website. Lo and behold, I spotted Coach Faust a few weeks later at a high school football game between his former team Archbishop Moeller and Columbus' St. Francis DeSales High School. I introduced myself to him, and once again he recited the names of the people he knew from my hometown of Marion, OH. "How's my old classmate Fr. Tobin doing?" he asked.

After we exchanged pleasantries, I went back to my standing perch alongside my wife. As the game concluded, Coach Faust caught a glimpse of me and came over to say goodbye and said hello to my wife Theresa. He told her I was a great guy for doing what I was doing with my Catholic website. I don't remember ever being treated so graciously and sincerely by such a well-known person. I don't know who was more impressed, my wife or me.

At his various talks Coach Faust outlines his life and his faith, as well as his coaching mistakes. Never was there a major college football coach with a record as wanting as Coach Faust's who was nonetheless more beloved. If it was said once, it was said a thousand times by various football fans, many of whom might have normally hated Notre Dame: "Why did God let this man lose? He was such a great spokesman and role model for the Catholic faith." Coach Faust would go on to explain his mistakes and admit that he was at a loss himself to understand the defeats. He would often say, "I wanted more than anything to win and be successful, but it didn't happen. I am sure God had a reason for it. Now I must continue to pay Him back for all the blessings He gave me."

Coach Faust may have found answers to the purpose of his losses. In a day of spoiled athletes and coaches, many of whom seldom have time for God, Coach Faust never wavered in his faith. He admitted his mistakes and proclaimed them for all to hear. Whether they were athletes or not, he gave all people a roadmap for handling adversity and for dealing with losing their dreams just when they seem within reach. Coach Faust wished he hadn't traveled this road. If Satan's desire were to break this man of his faith in front of the entire world, Coach Faust would have none of it. He would live his life as faithfully as if he would have won a national championship.

Coach Faust is a popular speaker at Catholic men's conferences. I understand his talks about faith are very inspiring. While many a coach who didn't have a successful career at Notre Dame would have ordinarily been less than well received, Coach Faust is still warmly embraced, especially when he returns to his beloved Notre Dame. "I speak about 150 times a year. I get more out of the conferences than those who attend," Faust told me.

Faust went on to sum up his feelings by saying, "You know, as Catholics we have so many special gifts. Unfortunately, not everyone takes advantage of all the blessings, like the presence of Our Lord in the daily Mass, the renewal that comes with Confession, the intercession of the Blessed Mother, and prayers like the rosary. I just want to pay God back by telling others about all of these great gifts of our faith."[2]

The Fighting Irish of Notre Dame had fallen on controversial times during the late 1990s and the first decade of this new century. The Irish did not play poorly compared to most football teams, but Notre Dame isn't most football teams. People have a higher standard for the Fighting Irish, and the late '90s teams played far below expectations. After the Lou Holtz era ended in 1995, Bob Davie and Tyrone Willingham coached the Irish. They were both honorable men, but their records did not suffice for Notre Dame. After Notre Dame fired Willingham in late 2004, it hired alumnus Charlie Weis to succeed him. Weis seemed to exemplify the spirit that had been missing at Notre Dame.

Weis has a very interesting story. A Notre Dame graduate who didn't play football for the Irish, he nonetheless went on to achieve great success at coaching football. Indeed, his story seems like something right out of one of Knute Rockne's inspirational talks. Some people even dubbed him the coaching version of Rudy Ruettiger (more on him later.).

A former high school English teacher, Weis' lucky break came when his New Jersey high school team's offensive prowess came to the attention of New York Giants head coach Bill Parcells. After a few years with that team, he moved up the eastern seaboard to become the offensive coordinator for the New England Patriots under head coach Bill Belichick. Charlie Weis was the offensive mastermind for the New England Patriots and has two Super Bowl rings to show for it.

Tragedy struck in 2002 when his gastric bypass surgery went awry and almost cost him his life. He even received the sacrament of Extreme Unction. Weis was deeply affected by this experience, and many feel it led him to pursue the Notre Dame job when it became available. Weis made it clear he had no desire to coach anywhere else. He wants to coach at Notre Dame at least until his son finishes college, which will be in eight years. After that his plans are to retire.

Weis has seen other hardships that life can dish out. His daughter Hannah was diagnosed with a rare form of autism that required intensive tutoring. As a result, Weis and his wife set up a foundation to aid children afflicted with this condition. He has stated he has no desire to go anywhere else but home when his long workday is done. While others duck out to play golf or visit friends, Weis is eager to head home to his family.[3]

While Weis' first season was an immense success, it was a story of death and hope that left many in and outside of the sports world talking.

Weis learned of a dying 10-year-old boy named Montana Mazurkiewicz who had an inoperable brain tumor and only a short time to live. The boy had simply asked if a Notre Dame player could drive by the house and give him a signed football. Weis decided to drive over himself and see the boy.

After a brief unpublicized visit, Weis saw firsthand that the boy would soon die. Before Weis left, he promised the boy he could call the first play of the game that Saturday, something that seemed rather innocuous at the time. Montana requested a pass to the right. However, Notre Dame started the game at its own one-yard line. What had been innocuous before now seemed almost impossible. When quarterback Brady Quinn asked what he was to do, Coach Weis told him to pass right. Quinn did just that and the rest will be written in Notre Dame lore. Tight end Pete Fasano caught the ball and somehow leaped over smaller more agile defenders to make a first down.[2]

Montana died shortly before the game, and Weis wanted no publicity for the visit. However, when word got out the following week, the University received numerous positive media reports. Weis and the boy's mother were interviewed about the visit and Montana's dying request. She couldn't have spoken more highly of Weis, and the whole event added to the Notre Dame football mystique.

Weis just seemed like another burly looking football coach who had a somewhat crusty demeanor to some. A number of football fans couldn't understand the fascination with this man besides his winning ways. Why were Notre Dame fans and the Catholic faithful so entranced by him?

One reason is that for many, Weis' blunt leadership and no-nonsense ways made people long for the day when the Church said what she meant and meant what she said. Some felt the Church had become too touchy-feely by the 1970s. By trying to please everyone, the Church lost its edge. However, Weis could never be confused with being too touchy-feely and trying to be all things to all people. There are many similarities between those who want to win football games and those who feel their faith should be guided by something more than just warm feelings. Each desires some discipline, demands certainty, and seeks a purpose. Many feel the Catholic Church in America can learn a thing or two from Charlie Weis about leadership.

Another amazing story of faith and perseverance on the football field is that of Rudy Ruettiger. The 1993 feel-good movie *Rudy* tells the story of his dream to go to college at Notre Dame and play football there, though he had limited athletic skills and was not a good student. The film seems to be on some cable channel once a week, especially during football season. While everyone might remember his quest to make the Notre Dame football team and his two minutes of fame that came from playing in a game after all those years of struggle, few realize what it took to get there. In an interview for my CatholicReport.org website, Ruettiger let me in on his behind-the-scenes religious life.

"Dave, you have to understand that I came from a big Catholic family," he told me. "Faith was and still is very important to us. You can never be the person God intended you to be if you are not right spiritually. I mean, you can never use all of your God-given talent and achieve your goals if you are not right spiritually. I see angry and bitter people, and I think, 'Well, there's another person that could be doing so much more in life.'"

Rudy went on to talk about his childhood mentors, including his friend Pete who was killed in a steel plant accident, and Coach Gordon Gillespie, his legendary high school football coach at Joliet Catholic High School in Joliet, Illinois. Rudy was also eternally grateful for both head coaches he played under at Notre Dame, Ara Parseghian and Dan Devine. Rudy also talked about the two players – Pat Sarb and Ivan Brown – who personally met with Coach Devine to convince him to let Rudy play in one game.

Rudy believes God sends these types of people into our lives to assist us. Unfortunately, we don't always see these gifts from God because we are caught up in negative thinking. "I loved the spirituality of the campus and the many people who were being positive and thinking about what they do to make their lives and the lives of others better, but there were some negative things," said Ruettiger. "There were some guys on the team that had tremendous talent and never used all of it. You have to understand with my size I was doing about all I could, so I could never understand those who weren't. I also think about some of the students that I got to know who were negative and disrespectful. I have no appetite for negativity and people being disrespectful."[4]

Danny Abramowicz is another man who felt the call to take to the road to tell others about his Catholic faith and the importance of it. The former New Orleans Saints professional football player retired from the game in 1974. He spent the 1980s battling alcoholism, a battle he eventually won. Since then, Abramowicz has spent much of his time speaking about his religion. He often speaks of the importance of his faith through his "spiritual workout plan," a concept he turned into the book, *Spiritual Workout of a Former Saint.*

Abramowicz uses sports analogies to talk about Catholic Christianity. He talks about Head Coach Jesus Christ and His coaching staff, the Apostles, and the "Personal Trainer," the Holy Spirit. Analogies like these help him connect with sports-minded Catholics. In his book and his talks to audiences, Abramowicz often tells people that those of faith need to take a time out and question how often they pray. He also likes to quote from the *Catechism of the Catholic Church* and remind people they must intimately know the teachings of the Church. Otherwise, like an athlete or coach who doesn't know the rules, we can never fully be successful.[5]

Another Catholic who has made a name for himself in the world of sports is college basketball guru Dick Vitale, who many know for his enthusiastic commentary on ESPN. However, there is another side to Vitale that many do not know. He is a devout Catholic who can't remember the last time he missed Mass, even though his travels during basketball season would have given some plenty of reason to.

Vitale told me, "I have had great role models of faith ever since I was young. My parents were not educated as we think of today, but they had a PhD in love. My mother went to daily Mass at St. Leo's in Elmwood Park, NJ. Because she had a stroke, she would have to literally drag one of her legs the two or three miles it took to walk to get to Mass.

"I try to set aside prayer time for the Lord daily," Vitale continued. "In my bedroom, I have four prayer cards I recite daily: St. Anthony, St. Francis, St. Jude, and the Virgin Mary. In addition, whenever I travel I have St. Jude tucked in my left pants pocket at all times. Faith is more than just doing something on a personal level; I believe you have to care for people as well. That's why I like to help charitable groups."

In saying that he likes "to help charitable groups," Vitale is being quite modest since he has played a key role in raising $51 million for cancer research through the Jimmy V. Foundation (named after the late North Carolina State basketball coach Jimmy Valvano, who died of cancer in 1993). When reminded of this fact, Vitale answered he was only playing a small part.

When I asked Vitale if he had noticed as I had that many athletes and coaches were actually quite faithful people who cared about others, unlike the prima donnas featured on the news, he said yes he had.

"You know just last week we had 300 people here at the house for a fundraiser for the Jimmy V. Foundation," he said. "There were basketball coaches like national champion Billy Donovan of Florida, Mike Brey of Notre Dame, and Tommy Amaker of Michigan, and football coaches such as Urban Meyer of Florida, hockey's Scotty Bowman, baseball's Fred McGriff, and tennis guru Nick Bollettieri. They paid their own way here and also made a donation, as well. This event won't make the papers, but it's indicative of the good people you find in the sports world."

When asked about the tough luck fortunes seen in the 2005-06 Notre Dame basketball season and Coach Mike Brey, Vitale responded by weaving in his own faith-based interpretation of Brey's season.

"You know, Coach Brey lost so many games because of a bad bounce here and a missed shot there," said Vitale. "If the bounce had been right and just one of those shots per game would have gone through the hoop, he would be a genius. Yet we have some people grumbling about his season. When you are a faithful person, you don't have to worry about bad bounces and missed shots. You see life for what it is. I know many good people of other faiths, but I am very happy and content in my Catholic faith. It is very special to me, and I try to give back because God has given me so much."[6]

The 2006 Winter Olympics in Torino, Italy, showed the great difference between those athletes who turned to faith and those who lived like they were ancient Greek epicureans. While the incredibly talented skiing sensation Bode Miller was unfortunately making more news for what he did in the bars than what he did on the slopes, athletes of faith were showing a great example of sportsmanship and faith.

United States biathlete Carolyn Treacy, for instance, prayed a novena to the Infant of Prague before competing as a result of her special devotion. Her sport combines cross-country skiing with target rifle shooting and is one of the most grueling endeavors in the Winter Olympics. Yet she trains with the joy of someone truly living out her faith. She proudly told the Catholic News Service she was born on the Feast of St. Joseph and loved attending Mass at the Games even if she didn't understand the language.[7]

Sometimes, faith and athletics work in a way to feed off each other inspiring individuals and teams to do great things. While principal at Marion Catholic High School, I was privileged to know Nate Smith. He was a student of great courage and faith as he battled a recurring brain tumor. He came to my office one day and asked if we could talk. He told me the tumor had come back, and he wanted me to keep an eye on his mother and brother. While he felt strong and full of faith, he worried it would be difficult for his mother and brother to once again see him go through the long drawn-out treatment fighting his disease would require.

Sadly, Nate passed away a couple of years later. I wasn't principal when he died, but Principal Fran Voll, Religion teacher Bill Thomas and many others told me of the courageous struggle Nate waged on a daily basis. In doing so, he taught many about faith and perseverance. After a moving funeral homily by Fr. Rod Damico, the football team vowed to do what was seemingly impossible for the smallest high school in Ohio that had a football team. They vowed to make the state playoffs, which they eventually did by bringing the courage, faith, and perseverance of Nate Smith with them.

All of these Catholic athletes and coaches are proud of their faith as evidenced by the time and travel they give to the Church. This pride is also demonstrated by some of them who were more than willing to grant me an interview for my CatholicReport.org website even though they had no idea who I was. In some ways most of these star athletes and coaches were easier to reach than some members of the clergy. These role models believe their faith is an integral part of their success. Their way of giving thanks to God often revolves around speaking to many groups at a fraction of the pay they once earned. Unlike many contemporary athletes who aren't particularly religious, these men and women want to tell all about the greatness of the Catholic faith whether or not the audience has any interest in athletics. This is their new field of competition, and they are showing themselves to be winners by helping others become closer to Jesus Christ and His Church.

DAVID J. HARTLINE

- CHAPTER 12 -

MEGACHURCHES, SALVATION, AND OTHER DEBATED ISSUES

It started in earnest during the 1980s and seemed to take the Protestant world by storm. The incredibly large non-denominational church,[ii] soon to be called the megachurch, seemed an answer to the prayers of many conservative Protestants. They felt at odds with the growing tendency of many mainline Protestant churches to introduce unwanted liberal theology and social policy to their congregations.

Some Catholics (especially those in the South and Midwest) felt challenged by the growth of these churches as some of their fellows in the faith Catholics left for the local megachurch. The recruiting efforts conducted by many of these places were extremely successful. However, as we shall see, a longing for Catholic traditions coupled with the events of September 11, 2001, have demonstrated why these places will not likely last.

The most famous of the megachurches is Joel Osteen's Lakewood Church, located in the former Houston Rockets basketball arena. It employs 300 people and holds four weekend services, including one in Spanish. Between 40,000 and 60,000 people attend each weekend. On average $1 million ends up in the collection basket on any given Sunday.[1] On top of that they have the best lighting and sound system money can buy. Osteen, son of Claude Osteen (a former pastor and an early figure in the Evangelical television revolution), is the megachurch movement's shining star. His down to earth way of preaching and soothing voice is very comforting, and

---

[ii] As its name implies, a non-denominational church is not affiliated with any particular denomination (e.g., Presbyterian, Methodist, etc.). However, that doesn't mean that they don't have denomination-like beliefs on doctrines such as baptism. They do. While they, like all Protestant bodies, have the Bible as their sole foundation, interpretation of that Bible is by and large up to the church's pastor.

he offers a believable approach with his everyday stories about the life and struggles of an average believer.

Another megachurch big name is Rick Warren, author of *The Purpose Driven Life*. This man may be one of history's keenest observers of what does and does not work in Protestant churches. He spent years traveling across the country studying the operations of various congregations, noting what type of preaching was effective. He also observed how successful a church's musical selections were. In addition, he took into account adult faith formation, youth ministry, and Bible study. He literally wrote the book on what constitutes a successful church and turned that into a 20,000 member congregation sitting on 120 acres. Many are unaware that *The Purpose Driven Church* was the forerunner of *The Purpose Drive Life*.[2]

The late 1980s and much of the 1990s saw a perfect storm of bad news complete with sex, drugs, and alcohol scandals hitting not only some of America's churches but also its leadership. For instance, the scandals involving Pentecostal ministers Jimmy Swaggart and Jim and Tammy Faye Bakker soured many Evangelicals. It was enough to make a fire and brimstone preacher wear out his preaching voice. This sort of bad behavior became very conducive to the growth of non-denominational megachurches.

However, it was the events of the social and political worlds that greatly assisted in the megachurches' growth. A growing culture of sexual openness (including legitimization of the gay lifestyle coupled with President Clinton having a sexual relationship with an intern almost as young as his daughter) disgusted many Evangelicals and drove them into the megachurches. Many adults felt these had the programs and personnel capable of helping them and their children navigate our confusing times.

These places of worship offered a wide array of men's and women's groups as well as Bible study and classes of all kinds to assist adults and their children with their spiritual growth. Large non-denominational churches popped up across the country like Wal-Marts or Costcos. Helping the growth of these places of worship were the bad catechetics and abuse scandal in the Catholic Church and problems in the mainline Protestant churches, such as the battles over theological issues and homosexuality.

Along with more people came bigger budgets, and the Sunday service became a grand production, with many churches paying sound and lighting personnel to put the perfect touch on these. Often these same congregations produced plays and concerts, and these served as something of a marketing tool for the good things the churches wanted to highlight. This served to bring in even more people. In addition to Catholics being bewildered about these developments, many small Protestant churches must have felt as if they were the small town mom and pop stores competing against Wal-Mart. It just seemed like there was no end in sight to the growth of the megachurch.

However, a surprising thing happened. Many began to ask the same question Clara Peller did on those famous Wendy's commercials in the 1980s: "Where the beef?"

The people at the megachurches may have felt largely happy with their membership at these places, but starting with the events of September 11, 2001, and culminating with the death of Pope John Paul II, many began to wonder if there wasn't something more to a life in Christ than what such houses of worship were offering them. In addition, some churches didn't even have a service for Christmas 2005 (more on that later). These events caused some to wonder about whether the traditions they left behind in their Catholic or mainline Protestant churches weren't better.

After the terrorist attacks of 9/11, many Catholics could be seen praying in public with rosary beads in hand. This and the many other unique Catholic traditions brought to light not only the purpose of such rituals, but also their power to console in times of crisis. The events following the death of John Paul II brought this power even more clearly to light. Catholics converged by the millions onto St. Peter's Square in Vatican City to pray before and after the Pope's death.

In April 2005, the world saw the signs, symbols, and rituals of the Catholic Church. The breaking of Pope John Paul II's fisherman's ring (which signified that death had ended his pontificate) was just the start of the many age-old traditions the world would see. The beautiful ceremony of transferring his body across St. Peter's Square to lie in state while choristers chanted the Litany of the Saints was mesmerizing. The funeral itself was something to behold. Something else to behold were all who were gripped by the events in Vatican City. A few columnists and more than a few Internet bloggers noted the attention they paid to the events in St. Peter's Square, even if they had not practiced their faith in a while or were not even Catholic.

As if this were not enough, John Paul II's funeral was attended by a who's who of religious, political, and social leaders. The rituals, the incense, the chants, and most importantly the Mass were something people wouldn't have seen even if someone such as the revered Rev. Billy Graham had died. Indeed, the Mass and the Real Presence of Christ are something so awe inspiring that mere words could hardly describe what was occurring. Yet while watching the Pope's funeral, one was able to get a sense of a key difference between Catholicism and Protestantism, since Protestantism was partly born out of a desire to rid Christianity of rituals and symbols.

The Catholic world paused from its mourning in April 2005 while the Conclave of Cardinals convened to elect a new Pope. The pageantry, signs, symbols, and great works of art present in the Sistine Chapel that greeted the electors were an awe-inspiring sight. As noted several times previously, for the first time in history, television viewers followed the cardinals into the chapel as the conclave began. Certainly the Sistine Chapel was a far cry from the look of the new megachurches, which are festooned with little more than theater seats and cup holders.

As the world digested the historic events of April 2005, many former Catholics and high Church Protestants became somewhat nostalgic for the signs and symbols of faith often missing from their large non-denominational churches. Indeed some of these institutions actually have no visible cross on display. This was in part due to research compiled by some megachurches that many parents viewed crosses and other religious symbols with a degree of alarm.

In turn, this helps explain why many non-denominational churches look as religious as a banquet center or concert hall, and why, in the apse of Joel Osteen's church, there is a globe instead of a cross.

Discussing the problems encountered by many churches after someone attends a peppy megachurch service, retiring president of the Methodist Theological Seminary of Ohio Norman Dewire told me, "Sometimes, our church pastors have to deal with those in the congregation that come up to them after services and say, 'We should be more like the megachurch down the street. This is boring. We are just being dragged through the rituals here. It's more exciting at the megachurch.'"

President Dewire went on to talk about who runs the show at the megachurch. "You know, I have been personally told of instances when the music minister at a megachurch didn't get his way and threatened the pastor by saying, 'They are coming here for me not you,'" President Dewire said. "You know what? The music minister was right! They were coming because of him. He puts on a good show, and preaching and the scriptures are far down the list. As far as I am concerned, a lot of those megachurches don't offer much. What's going to happen when someone in those churches needs some spiritual guidance or a personal crisis comes up in their lives? The pastor probably doesn't have the spiritual or psychological training necessary to help them. Often in those megachurches, there isn't a whole of lot of depth in their liturgy or their pastor. It's just cheap grace as far as I am concerned."[3]

Financially speaking, Catholics had always been taught that to serve God meant to live simply. This simple life has been highlighted in the lives of various saints. In contrast, stories began to circulate that some of the more famous megachurch pastors were living in large palatial multi-million dollar homes. Indeed many of the bigger names of Evangelicalism subscribe to the "Prosperity Gospel," the belief some say emanated from John Calvin that God blesses certain people with wealth. Joel Osteen, TD Jakes, Benny Hinn, Creflo Dollar, and Joyce Meyer all subscribe to this school of thought.[ii]

If the funeral of Pope John Paul II and the subsequent election of Pope Benedict XVI unraveled the first chink in the armor of the megachurches, then the bad publicity surrounding the fact that many of these places would be closed for Christmas would begin to unravel the second. Shortly after Thanksgiving 2005, word began to circulate that some of the major American megachurches would be closed for Christmas. At first it seemed to be a hoax or perhaps an urban legend, especially to many Catholics, mainline Protestants, and even members of the secular media.

It was no hoax or urban legend: A number of megachurches did close on one of Christianity's holiest days, and Christmas that year fell on a Sunday! "Why?" many asked. "What could cause a church to close for Christmas?"

[ii] This lifestyle is in sharp contrast to fellow evangelical Rick Warren, pastor of Saddleback Church in Lake Forest, CA. Warren told Larry King in March 2005 that he still drives a four-year-old Ford, doesn't own a yacht, and did not build a bigger house once the millions from sales of his books came rolling his way. According to Wikipedia, "Rick and [his wife] Kay Warren have donated 90% of their income through three foundations: Acts of Mercy (which serves those infected and affected by AIDS), Equipping the Church (which trains church leaders in developing countries), and The Global PEACE Fund, which fights poverty, disease, and illiteracy. Warren no longer takes a salary from Saddleback and repaid all of his salary from the last 25 years back to the church, due to the success of his book sales." Warren also reverse-tithes, a practice of giving away 90 percent of one's earnings.[4]

The answer seemed twofold. Many pastors at these megachurches stressed that worship services can be a big production. There are lighting and sound crews who, along with musicians and ushers, work very hard. As such, these churches' pastors said these employees needed to be with their families on Christmas.

The second reason for canceling Christmas came down to theology and history. Catholics have celebrated Christ's birth since the early days of the Church. Most mainline Protestant communions acknowledge Christmas, although not to the same degree as Catholics. However, some of the early Protestant leaders did not acknowledge Christmas.

As late as the twentieth century, many Calvinist churches didn't have church services on Christmas, unless it fell on a Sunday. John Calvin, Ulrich Zwingli, and John Knox did not believe in celebrating Christmas. Some of the large Evangelical churches are very Calvinist in nature. Megachurches may be non-denominational, but that doesn't mean they are not subject to the influences brought in by those who grew up in a denominational confession.

Senior Minister Jon Weece of Southland Christian Church in Lexington, Kentucky, lashed out at those who second-guessed his decision to not have Christmas Sunday services. "Christmas began as a pagan holiday to the Roman gods," he exclaimed. "If we were really to celebrate the historical birth of Jesus, it would be in January or mid-April."[5]

Fair enough. There is some scintilla of historical truth to that, but Christmas has been celebrated on this date since the earliest days of Christianity. Why do some of these religious leaders now feel the need to close for Christmas, which in 2005 happened to fall on a Sunday? Pastor Weece went on to tell his congregation and the *Lexington Herald-Leader* that Jesus was also criticized for breaking tradition, and he mentioned that in the early Church, there were people who "emphasized religion over relationship."

David Wells, professor of Theology at the Protestant-run Gordon-Conwell Theological Seminary, said, "I think what this does is feed into the individualism that is found throughout American culture, where everyone does their own thing. This is a consumer mentality at work: 'Let's not impose the church on people. Let's not make church in any way inconvenient.'"[6]

While there may be no clear way to discern if the megachurches have peaked, the less than flattering news that has hit them of late cannot have been beneficial.

What the megachurches are like

The Hartford Institute of Religion has been studying megachurches, and their latest 2005 survey found some interesting data. The style of worship is quite different than what Catholics are used to in their churches. Consider, for instance, Warren's Saddleback Church. Among the worship styles offered there are "OverDrive ... for those who like their worship loud," "Ohana" where you can "learn to worship through signing or hula," or "Country," where "country music, boots, and buckles are all part of this worship experience." Then there is the hands in air charismatic style of worship practiced by only a relative few Catholics but which has become increasingly popular in evangelical Protestantism in recent years. This is typically accompanied by so-called "praise and worship" contemporary Christian music.

Their structure is also very different. In 2005, the average megachurch had 20 paid leadership staff positions compared to 13 in 2000. In 2000, the average megachurch received $4.8 million in income; by 2005, that number had risen to $6 million.

The Hartford study also showed that 49 percent of the megachurches were in the South, 25 percent in the West, 20 percent in the Mid-Atlantic region, and 6 percent in the Northeast. Denominationally, 34 percent of the megachurches were non-denominational, 16 percent were Southern Baptist, 10 percent were Baptist and 6 percent were Assemblies of God with the rest being a variety of smaller denominations. Most megachurches had congregations smaller than 5,000 people but 16 percent had congregations larger than 5,000 people.

There were also some other interesting findings in the Hartford study. While megachurches with the least amount of conflict grew the most, these places also had pastors with the least amount of education.[7] Joel Osteen never graduated from the seminary, and yet he is so popular that his new church seats almost 20,000 people at his two Sunday services.

Like many National Basketball Association arenas and movie theaters, Hartford learned the newly built megachurches are made for comfort. Plush, theater-style seats replete with cup holders may remind folks of going to see a movie, but then again comfort and the entertainment-tinged worship are a big part of what draws people to the megachurch. After the powerful praise and worship hymn is over, you can hear the Bible preached while sipping your caramel mocha from Starbucks. Not surprisingly, the Hartford survey also noted that over 90 percent of these congregations use their audiovisual equipment weekly.

Now of course, if they have such equipment, they will use it. After all, that is why they bought it, right? But it begs the question: Why is it necessary? What does any of this – the seats, the sound systems, whatever – have to do with life-transforming, soul-saving *faith*? Do these places really need to give their congregants a huge helping of entertainment alongside their spirituality in order to keep them in the seats?

Perhaps I'm missing something, but it appears that the faith in these places seems to be more about marketing than it is about a deep, profound, and abiding relationship with our savior Jesus Christ, and that is something that needs no special marketing plan.

Please do not misunderstand me. I believe the overwhelming majority of Evangelicals are good people. Their hearts absolutely are in the right place and they have a zeal for Jesus Christ that I frankly wish more Catholics displayed.

But I just don't understand the appeal of the hoopla and sound effects these megachurches offer. To me – and I think most faithful Catholics – Sunday worship is about entering into a deeper relationship with Christ through the graces offered by the Eucharist and the working of the liturgical rituals on body and soul that lift one's heart to God. Think of what we say just before the Preface: "Lift up your hearts." "We lift them up to the Lord." A/V systems, theater seats, and the rest don't just seem extraneous to such true worship, they strike me as being antithetical to them.

I don't see how the megachurch movement can last. Because of this, I have no doubt that here in 2006 we are in a similar place to where we were in the summer of 1989. At that time, I was in Germany visiting relatives. I observed to them that I believed the Berlin Wall would come down by the year 2000. My relations scoffed at me, and yet three months later, on November 9, 1989, that wall was turned into rubble and souvenirs. One day soon people will remember megachurches and the nascent "Emerging Church" movement in the same way, and those who now sit in those theater seats will walk the path in the Catholic Church their forefathers did.

Are Catholics Saved?

Walk into Pentecostal or non-denominational megachurches on any given Sunday, and you will find that many of the congregants – even a majority – are fallen away Catholics.

Why would these people – good souls who thirst to serve the Lord – leave His Real Presence, which only the Catholics and Orthodox have? Why would someone trade the Body and Blood, Soul and Divinity of our Savior Jesus Christ for a mere sermon, no matter how theologically rich or compellingly delivered?

The reason is that most of these former Catholics don't know what they have left. They think they do, but if you ask them the most basic questions about the Faith (several of which we will soon address), it becomes evident that their catechetical formation is not what it could have been.

Frankly, I don't blame on them. It is not totally their fault that they have been impoverished in this way. To some extent, we all have been in the last few decades. My heart breaks for these people with charity and compassion. The urge is to blame them for not seeing the signs warning them that they're leaving a sumptuous banquet and heading for something kept warm under a heat lamp at a convenience store. But is it their fault that the sign posts have been knocked down? How would they know what to even look for?

So very often, these people are leaving that which they don't know. Again, it is heartbreaking and absolutely tragic.

Interestingly, however, this very phenomenon has produced a desire – indeed, a burning hunger – amongst many Catholics who have stayed in the Church to learn their faith better. The good news, therefore, is that after four decades of increasing ignorance about what the Faith teaches, many Catholics are often better catechized today than they have been in generations. Through books such as *Surprised by Truth* (Basilica Press) and Jeff Cavins' *The Great Adventure Bible Timeline* (Ascension Press), Catholics are getting excited about apologetics and Scripture studies. Parishes across the country are holding standing room-only *Great Adventure* study sessions, and the result is that an increasing number people in the Church know the Bible better than ever.

What are some of the questions that lead Catholics out of the Church? Well, think of your own experience. Have you ever opened your front door only to be greeted with, "Are you saved? If the Rapture happened today would you be delivered from the judgment?" "Where is Confession in the Bible? Where does it say you need to tell your sins to a mere *man*?" Some Catholics might shut the door, others might mutter some profanity under their breath, and a small few might argue against these commonly asked questions.

Most Catholics probably won't know what to say, however. They might make a snide comment or chide themselves that they should know their Bible better in order to better engage in a conversation about these topics.

As Patrick Madrid aptly notes, however, most Catholics aren't sure what to do when approached by a fundamentalist toting Bible verses like a gunslinger does a loaded Colt six shooter. This person will often show the Catholic a passage he or she claims speaks about being saved or portends to point to the coming Rapture. In this situation, Catholics are often at a loss about what to do. They either feel they aren't proficient enough in their faith or believe the Church has let them down by not teaching them these supposed basics.

With that understood, what is a Catholic to do, and what do we believe?[8]

First, for the benefit of our separated brethren (and contrary to popular belief), we believe knowing the Bible is absolutely, positively essential to being a follower of Jesus. Catholics were never told they couldn't read the Bible or that it had to be properly interpreted by a priest (although if you are uncertain about a particular passage, asking your parish priest about it is typically a good idea, assuming he thinks with the mind of the Church). St. Pius X told Catholics to read the Gospels "every day." In 1920, Pope Benedict XV said Catholic families needed to own and read a Catholic Bible.[9] Pius XII issued a whole encyclical on the necessity of knowing Sacred

Scripture (*Divino Afflante Spiritu*).

More recently, Vatican II repeated St. Jerome's observation that, "Ignorance of Scripture is ignorance of Christ."[9] In 1979's *Catechesi Tradendae*, John Paul II wrote that "catechesis must be impregnated and penetrated by the thought, the spirit and the outlook of the Bible and the Gospels through assiduous contact with the texts themselves." In the same document, he also encouraged Catholics to memorize scriptural passages and to engage in Bible studies, not merely to learn the scriptures better but to "lead [each other] to live by the Word of God."

Furthermore, the Church has often done what it could to help Catholics know Scripture. In ages past this was quite difficult because most of the faithful were uneducated and thus illiterate. These persons depended on those who were educated to help them grow in their faith.[kk] Stained glass windows and frescoes depicting biblical stories were often the best way for many Catholics to learn the scriptures and the Church's teachings. This is why they were called "the poor man's Bible."

In the late 1800s, the American bishops realized what a problem it was for their flocks to be theologically illiterate in a society that was openly hostile to their faith. As a result, they created a systematic, question and answer way for Catholics to learn their faith, and this proved very effective. This system was called the *Baltimore Catechism*, and for most Catholics who grew up in the United States before Vatican II, it was their introduction to Church teaching and the Bible. Ask people raised in that era "Why did God make you?" and the correct response will probably still roll off their tongue as if

---

[kk] Although Catholics became increasingly better educated over the years, this phenomenon undoubtedly was bequeathed as a mindset from one generation to the next. This probably explains why many Protestants think Catholics have to ask their parish priest how to interpret a particular passage of Scripture. For many years, that was absolutely the case, but strictly because of necessity born of illiteracy at first and then out of habit. And to be fair, it is not as if Protestants do not go to their own pastors for help in interpreting the Bible.

they had learned it yesterday. It may have been rote memorization (deplored by many on the liberal side and even some conservatives), but it was effective in passing on a basic knowledge of the faith.

Despite this and the papal encouragement and exhortations, however, it is true that the Bible was not learned well by most of the faithful.

On the contrary, many Evangelical churches have historically done an excellent job in teaching Scripture to their congregations despite the fact that in the past they, like Catholics, were often quite uneducated. Many Protestant and especially Evangelical churches to this day have weekly Wednesday night Bible studies, and these last from one to three hours (that bespeaks a real and admirable dedication to getting people to know God's word). Some denominations such as the Jehovah's Witnesses spend countless hours teaching their flock how to go door to door talking and debating with others about their interpretation of the Bible.

So it is not hard to see why, when they are confronted with such well-taught individuals, today's Catholics are left speechless. Unlike their grandparents (who at least had learned our faith from the *Baltimore Catechism*), younger Catholics can't give a snap answer to questions, much less quote a passage of Scripture, and so to this extent, the Evangelicals and JWs put Catholics to shame. Most Catholic young people have to study their faith on their own if they want to know what the Church does and does not believe (because they probably did not adequately learn this during CCD, confirmation classes, or parochial school religion courses).[11]

Therefore, how *should* Catholics answer when someone asks them if they are "saved?" Is there a Bible verse that would be helpful?

Catholics should first inform their inquisitors that the Church teaches no one can save himself or herself. Rather the grace for salvation comes as a completely free gift from God that we can do nothing to earn. No good that we do, no act of service we perform, no love that we show is sufficient for salvation absent the free gift of a saving faith in Jesus.^{mm}

Then refer them to 2 Tim. 2:11-13, Rom. 11:17-22 and Heb. 10: 26-31. These verses simply state that we can lose salvation once we have been saved, that a professed faith cannot save someone who lives unfaithfully. If these verses state the truth, then what about that old Protestant hymn, "Once Saved, Always Saved"? How could they sing that song since it isn't true? They still sing that song, but the three aforementioned scripture verses make it abundantly clear that each and every person is capable of rejecting God's love. God will never turn his back on us and throw us into hell for no reason. By rejecting God's love, we risk paying the eternal penalty for our rejection of God's ways.[10]

The proper response to the "Rapture" question might be something like, "The 'Rapture' is nowhere to be found in the Bible, and none of the original men involved in the Protestant Reformation mentioned the Rapture. The Rapture first made it into Christian thought around the same time that the term 'saved' came into the vernacular somewhere around 1800."

I would strongly recommend that everyone who wants to know more about these topics buy *Where's That In The Bible?* by Patrick Madrid. This book does an excellent job of giving short, concise answers to questions Catholics are often asked about their faith. In addition, I also strongly recommend Michael Dubruiel's book, *The*

---

^{ll} Fortunately, through parish-level Bible studies using materials produced by people such as Jeff Cavins, this is slowly changing, another sign of the tide turning. But by and large, Catholics must still search out materials by people such as Patrick Madrid, Scott and Kimberly Hahn, Rosalyn Moss, Steve Kellmeyer, Tim Staples, and Mark Shea if they want to better know their faith and its biblical foundations.

^{mm} It is as Canon 1 from the Council of Trent states: "If anyone says that man can be justified [i.e., saved] before God by his own works, whether done by his own natural powers or through the teaching of the law, without divine grace through Jesus Christ, let him be anathema."

How To Book of the Mass: Everything You Need to Know but No One Ever Taught You. It will help people understand the Mass better and assist them in explaining to others what Catholics believe about our liturgy.

But let's look at the question of how and when the concept of "being saved" *in its current form* came into being.[nn] It originated with the Anabaptists, a German Protestant sect that formed in 1521 and served as the precursor for modern Baptists. However, this belief certainly wasn't the understanding of Martin Luther, who believed in the need for repentance after sin. However, he also believed one could "sin boldly" as long as one "yet more boldly still [believed]."

John Calvin believed that if someone was saved, they were irrevocably saved, but that was only because one could not exercise free will in response to God's grace. According to Calvin, God's grace is simply irresistible grace, and if God doesn't provide it to you, you're eternally lost (so much for a loving God). Still, this wasn't quite the "once saved, always saved" belief system of the Anabaptists. It would take centuries before this concept would be recognizable in today's terms and accepted by the non-denominational Protestants.[oo]

Thus the idea of securing your own salvation simply by proclaiming Jesus as your Lord and Savior was as foreign to most Protestants in colonial America as it is to Catholics today. So how and where did the concept get its start in America?

It got its start in the South, partly due to the influence of Baptist immigrants from Germany, as well as Calvinists from Scotland and the northern part of England.

Many of those from the United Kingdom emigrated not because of desire but because their bad behavior caused their neighbors to put them on the next boat headed for the colonies. These people were incorrigible by and large. After all, why try to be virtuous if you are predestined to heaven or hell? The decision is out of your hands, right?[pp] They also often had a mentality of, "Well, the devil made me do it. It's a good thing Jesus saved me." It was a justification, a way of assuaging guilt over the objective wrong they knew in their heart of hearts that they were committing but couldn't bring themselves to stop. Their attachment to sin was too great, but the thought of enduring hell forever was too much.

So a construct developed and grew over time of "once saved,

---

nn I want to emphasize my recognition that, just as the world has an estimated 30,000-plus Protestant denominations, there are many, many views on justification and salvation within the Protestant world. What follows is not believed by all Protestants, whether mainline or non-denominational. However, the idea of "Just say the 'Sinner's Prayer' once, and you have assurance of eternal salvation" is so prevalent amongst self-proclaimed "Bible-believing" Christians that it bears discussion.

According to even one Protestant source, the major problem with "once saved, always saved" is the "golden ticket into heaven" view of salvation. As noted above, this approach focuses on "the Sinner's Prayer" (or "the Four Spiritual Laws" or "the Romans road") to essentially assure someone that if they pray "to receive Jesus into their heart," then they'll get their golden ticket into heaven for eternity (To be honest, Catholics have their own version of this soft-selling of salvation as well: the "once sacramentized, always saved" mentality that suggests if you have been baptized, catechized, etc., or that you have "been a good person," you'll end up in heaven regardless of whether your life truly reflects a whole-life faith in Christ).

However, everything in the teachings of Jesus and the Apostles makes very clear that we cannot merely say "Lord, Lord" and not do what He says. The man building his house on the rock is not just praying the Sinner's Prayer, but is the one who "listens to these words of Mine and acts on them" (Mt. 7:24).

So while it's true that virtually all Protestants believe salvation comes by grace alone through faith alone, it is also true that most understand that faith is not merely a mental assent but rather a whole-life responsiveness to the invitation of God.

Apparently, the best writer on this subject from a purely Evangelical perspective is Dallas Willard, whose latest book *The Great Omission* is said to expertly deal with this subject. For a Catholic view, check out James Akin's *The Salvation Controversy*. Also recommended is Scott Hahn's audio set "Salvation History."

A good Evangelical debate on "once saved, always saved" took place a few years ago between the rabidly anti-Catholic John MacArthur and Evangelical New Testament scholar Zane Hodges. They discussed "Lordship Salvation," that is, whether Jesus must be Lord to be Savior. MacArthur said yes, Zane said no. Each wrote books, and the books sold like hotcakes.

For a debate between Catholics and Protestants on salvation, check out "The Ultimate Challenge - A Catholic/Protestant Debate."

always saved," which essentially meant that nothing someone did after accepting Jesus as Lord and Savior could cause them to lose their salvation.

As such, African American scholar Dr. Thomas Sowell writes in his book *Black Rednecks and White Liberals* that religious practices of early southern colonial Evangelicals were quite different than those of their northern colonial counterparts or fellow Southerners, who were largely Anglican.[11]

Sowell came across several early documents. One was from a New England man visiting the South who noted, "In some cities, especially if a good number of business men are from the North, the churches are well attended, there being but one sermon for the day. But even here the afternoon and evening are much devoted to amusements."

Another northern observer wrote, "There is no Sabbath ... they work, run, swear and drink here on Sundays just as they do any other day of the week."

Still another observer described a typical southern preacher: "The speaker nearly all the time cried out aloud at the utmost stretch of his voice, as if calling to someone a long distance off. He had the habit of repeating a phrase and exhibited a dramatic habit of leaning over the desk with his arms stretched forward, gesticulating violently, yelling at the highest key and catching his breath with an effort."

Sowell notes that many in the South did not go to church at all

---

[oo] The problem with Catholicism, according to many Evangelicals, is that there appears to be a series of hoops a person has to jump through in order to make it into heaven. However, Catholic theology is a body of rich teachings that goes back 2,000 years. If one is to say that Catholic theology is wrong, then one has to disagree with great minds like St. Augustine, St. Jerome, St. Thomas Aquinas and many others who even Evangelicals and Baptists laud as Christian heroes (e.g., Norman Geisler, etc.). Luther and the other early Protestant leaders accepted the Catholic doctrine on salvation by and large by. One has to go back to the 1800s to find a Protestant scholar who talked about "being saved" as we understand it today and who effectively rejected what the Church and the early Protestant leaders had taught. One therefore has to ask those Protestants who believe in altar calls

and that, subsequently, southern church attendance was lower than in the North. Sowell goes on to say that many people were so drunk on Saturday night that they were in no condition to go to church on Sunday morning.[12]

He also observes that this sort of Jekyll and Hyde lifestyle of drunkenness on Saturday night and fire and brimstone on Sunday morning was widespread in the South among both whites and blacks. Post-World War I migration would bring this lifestyle and faith tradition to the north.[13]

This behavior by folks who claimed they had been saved by Jesus left many Catholics scratching their heads. No one would say most Irish, German, Italian, or other ethnic Catholics did not drink to excess or otherwise sin. Many even sinned on Saturday confident they could get in line for Confession before Mass on Sunday.[rr] But the act of going to Confession involved a recognition that they had sinned and repented for this before the Lord through His instrument, the priest. They did not put on the hypocrisy of drinking and whoring it up in one instance and protesting their salvation in the next with not a shred of worry, remorse, or guilt. In their separated brethren, however, where was the recognition of the character of sin? What happened to putting on the new man in Christ, which is the true mark of salvation?

As noted before, Catholics stand with their Protestant brethren in recognizing that the grace of salvation is wholly a gift and that

---

and being saved, "If the early Protestant leaders never believed this, why do you? Would God have waited 1,800 years to introduce such a teaching? If God had His hand in the Protestant Reformation, wouldn't He have talked about the concept of 'being saved' as you now understand it?"

[rr] This tendency is also called "easy believism," decisional regeneration, and cheap grace (for some context on the notion of cheap grace, see Norman Dewire's comments on megachurches earlier in this chapter). It should be noted that you will rarely note licentiousness among its proponents. They tend to be dogmatic, but not libertines (although there are those who obviously are).

nothing we can do could ever be good enough to earn it. That said, we also realize the Bible clearly shows that salvation can be lost through unrighteous living, a truth that some of our separated brothers and sisters seem to either not know or readily lose sight of.[ss]

This is not to say that this Saturday/Sunday dynamic is the hallmark of all Evangelicals or even Evangelicalism per se. There are many Evangelicals who reject the "once saved, always saved" theology. These people live righteous lives and put many Catholics to shame with the way their actions preach the gospel. Nonetheless, assurance of salvation is something one does not find amongst any other strain of Christianity.

Unfortunately, the consequences of this belief system has found its way into our culture in ways subtle and not. Hank Williams, Hank Williams, Jr., Elvis Presley, and Little Richard could all sing a tear-inducing gospel track while high on drugs or alcohol. Classic rock aficionados can easily understand which state of mind the legendary southern rockers of Lynyrd Skynyrd were in by each song they recorded. "Simple Man" talks of a mother reminding her only son to remember there is "Someone up above." However, "What's Your Name" talks about groupies the band met.[14]

All of this begs the question: "What is the appeal of saying you are saved?" If one had assurance of salvation, why does one need to go to church or assist other Christians? The answer is one doesn't. For a Christian who believes in eternal assurance and who fails to actively pursue holiness or commits acts he or she knows are sinful, his or her salvation is still assured since at one point in their life they accepted Jesus as Lord and Savior. One might still participate in acts as heinous as murder or rape and still be assured of getting into Heaven (according to some Evangelicals).[rr]

"When I hear someone proclaim themselves 'saved' it seems too

---

[rr] Before Vatican II, most parishes offered Confession before each Mass. Sadly, this custom has died out in all but a few places around the country.

[ss] See Mt. 7:21-23; Gal. 5:16-26; Rev. 21:8; 22:15

prideful," said Fr. Bill Hahn. "If you say you are in a relationship with Christ, you can't proclaim it finished. It is dynamic. You wouldn't declare yourself finished with your spouse in your marital relationship on your wedding day. Your marriage is dynamic and growing. When you proclaim yourself 'saved,' it strikes me as a rather self-serving attitude. You wouldn't ever tell your spouse, 'I am finished growing. Our relationship is complete.' Why would you take the same approach with God? As a Catholic, I believe I am in the process of being saved and helping others to be saved, but for me to say I am 'saved' sounds very egotistical and arrogant."[20]

Rapture

Perhaps you have driven down the road and noticed a bumper sticker that said, "In case of the Rapture, this car may be abandoned." You might think, 'What's with the Rapture?' You might have heard it mentioned by some of your friends or heard it mentioned while channel surfing as you passed by an Evangelical religious program. You might wonder, 'Do we Catholics believe in the Rapture (or should we)?' Well, rest assured, the Catholic Church does not believe in the Rapture, and once you find out the rest of the story, as Paul Harvey would say, you will wonder how anyone could ever believe in such an unbiblical teaching.

As noted above, the concept of the Rapture is another puzzling notion that took root in America. This belief, popular among the many non-denominational and Baptist churches, asserts that before the Final Judgment, God will lift all those who are saved into Heaven in order to spare them the grueling End Times. In his book

---

[rr] Of course, Catholics believe you can do all these things and get to heaven, too. The difference is that after doing them, you have to ask the Lord for forgiveness and receive absolution through Confession. This involves admitting you were wrong and a firm resolution that you will amend your life. Each sin must be followed by conversion. A great many Evangelicals and fundamentalists, on the other hand, believe all your sins (past, present, and future) were taken care of the moment you made the decision for Christ. That is the only conversion that matters to them.

Will Catholics Be Left Behind: A Critique of the Rapture and Today's Prophecy Preachers, convert Carl Olson notes the Rapture's roots only go back to the early 1800s, something about which Catholics should remind their Evangelical friends of when these people mention this supposedly "*sola scriptura*" belief.[uu]

John Nelson Darby, an ex-Anglican priest who died in 1882, was the first person to mention the word "Rapture," which he did in 1832. He spent a good deal of time traveling throughout Europe and America pushing this notion. Unfortunately for him, he never knew the fame that eventually was his. His death occurred before his concept became well known.

But then in 1909, Cyrus Scofield published the *Scofield Reference Bible*, which referenced Darby's idea about the Rapture in great detail. The *Scofield Reference Bible* would go on to sell millions. As a result, the idea of the Rapture penetrated the ranks of the Baptist, Methodist, Presbyterian, and Pentecostal confessions. It would later gain favor among the many non-denominational churches.[15]

However, Sarah Lancaster, PhD, professor of Theology at the Methodist Theological Seminary of Ohio, told me, "We are not a 'once saved, always saved' church, and we don't believe in the Rapture. However, that doesn't mean everyone in the pews thinks that. There are a lot of those influences that creep into all churches, including ours."

When prodded as to where the pervasiveness of belief in the Rapture came from, Dr. Lancaster said Hal Lindsey's book *The Late Great Planet Earth* had a lot to do with it. In addition she said, "when someone turns on the television and hears talk of 'once saved, always saved,' they wonder if we in the United Methodist Church believe this as well. They might dig into a book and find that John Wesley had a life changing experience in 1738 at Aldersgate in London. They read into that believing this means he was saved. That's not

---

[uu] Martin Luther coined this phrase (meaning "scripture alone") to describe his belief that the Bible alone is sufficient to determine a Christian's beliefs and is the sole rule of faith. This, of course, leaves no room for Sacred Tradition.

part of our theology. We believe that we are being saved, but we are not already saved."[16]

Anyone familiar with Lindsey's book will recognize that it is chalk full of talk about the Rapture. At last count, Lindsey's book had sold over 30 million copies,[17] so it is not hard to see how this work helped spread belief in this peculiar concept.[w]

The notion of the Rapture perhaps got its biggest boost in 1995, when Tim LaHaye and Jerry B. Jenkins began publishing the *Left Behind* series. Many Catholics don't like the novels because several characters are more than a little anti-Catholic. In fact, the authors bring up historical points that seem to not only attack the Catholic Church but also the core beliefs of Christianity.

For instance, St. Augustine is revered in most Evangelical circles, almost more than he is by some Catholics. Yet LaHaye and Jenkins describe St. Augustine as a "Greek Humanist." They even claim that Constantine's profession of faith was a sham. According to the authors, the man who saw the burning cross aflame with the words, "In this sign, you shall conquer," was a fraud. They go on to claim that it was Constantine who corrupted prayers by having believers pray to the dead, the saints, and Mary. They even bring up tried and true anti-Catholic sayings such as the Catholic Church is "Satan's Babylonian mysticism," and the old canard by Jack Chick (a self professed anti-Catholic) that the Catholic Church is responsible for the deaths of "40 million persons" in the Middle Ages.

This particular fabrication is quite prevalent, as one sees by

---

[w] Which begs the question: Is the esteem in which many hold this belief due solely to the millions books that have been sold, despite the fact that only a few established denominations actually believe in it? The popularity of the Rapture concept is very hard to understand. On the one hand, it is human nature to want to avoid suffering. Yet the Bible (and the Catholic Church) says suffering is part of life. Indeed, it is central to the Christian experience. Fr. Adrian Dionne, OP, former pastor at Holy Trinity Catholic Church, was my boss when I served as principal at Holy Trinity Catholic School. He said he believes the reason some Protestant denominations didn't embrace Good Friday or the crucifix was that it reminded them of the suffering required to bring about Easter Sunday.

looking at various anti-Catholic websites that also ask why Catholics can't be saved and why we don't believe in the Rapture. The interesting thing one should ask anyone who believes such nonsense is, "When did these events happen, and where did they bury all the bodies?" Supposedly they started before the Reformation with attacks on secret groups that yearned for someone like Martin Luther.

Yet, if we take this 40 million figure and spread this out over a 500 year span, it would result in the deaths of tens of thousands of people killed a year by the Church. Well, even if the bulk of the murders happened hundreds of years ago, it would be hard to keep it a secret. The rate of deaths imagined here is greater than the death rate from the Black Plague.

On second thought, had the Church really done this, there would be so few people left in Europe that the plague probably should have wiped us all out. It really is sad to see that someone, *anyone* might actually believe this. While the overwhelming majority of Protestants roll their eyes at such stories and apologize for such craziness, years of anti-Catholic feelings have resulted from these tales, and they do hold sway with many.

If one were to say the *Left Behind* books had been published in someone's basement and sold a few thousand copies at tent revivals, it would be more believable than the reality of the book's 20 million copies sold. It is the best selling Christian fiction book series ever. What is more, Tyndale Publishers estimates that about 11 percent of the books buyers have been Catholic!

Carl Olson says he is stunned when some Catholics write to defend LaHaye and Jenkins' books, noting that a pope in the series is raptured, proving the novels are not anti-Catholic. Olson points out that if these readers had read the text more carefully, they would have seen this pope was raptured *because he rejected the Catholic Church.* Examples like this one are almost mind boggling.[18]

In an article published for Catholic Answers, Catholic author and blogger Jimmy Akin wrote that in the *Left Behind* series, LaHaye gives a passing slap to Pope John Paul II. The fictional Pope Paul II is leading Christians astray in the book. He is praying with people of other religions at the fictional "Iccesse," which sounds a lot like Assisi. The real Pope John Paul II held ecumenical prayer services to pray for peace in Assisi, Italy, with leaders of other religions.[19]

Purgatory

The topic of Purgatory is bound to get a hot debate going between orthodox Catholics and many Protestant groups. In many ways, Protestants think this is amongst the least biblically supported of the Catholic beliefs, and many believe this is where Catholics are most vulnerable.

Many Protestants – particularly Evangelicals who believe in "once saved, always saved" – cannot accept the concept of Purgatory. Purgatory, of course, is the place where souls of the saved go if they need a period of cleansing from the temporal effects of sin before entering Heaven (cf., 1 Cor. 3:15; Rev. 21:27). The Catholic Church teaches that no one knows how many souls go directly to Heaven verses how many spend some time in Purgatory. It should be clearly understood that the only place a soul from Purgatory can go is to Heaven. You cannot go to hell from there. It is not a second chance for those who did not accept salvation before earthly death. *Again, the souls that are there are saved.*

Purgatory has always been a teaching of the Catholic Church.[ww] Jewish scholars of Jesus' time talked of Purgatory. Rabbi Shammai, a well-known rabbi during the time of Jesus, talked of Purgatory.[xx] In 211, Tertullian wrote of Purgatory, while St. John Chrysostom did so in 392, followed by St. Augustine in 419 (to name just a few of the Church Fathers who put pen to paper on this subject).

The majority of Protestants ignore the historical, biblical, and patristic evidence for Purgatory. They try to convince people – especially Catholics – that there is no Purgatory. In one of his "In Touch" programs, Charles Stanley (one of my favorite Evangelicals) tried to reason with Catholics that Purgatory was a cruel teaching. To paraphrase what he said, he told his audience, "How does a church explain to the parents of a 16-year-old girl who's lying dead in a casket after an automobile accident that she might not be in Heaven but in Purgatory?"

Since I have personal experience in this matter, I will answer that question. My sister Renate died in an automobile accident when she was 16-years-old, and while I believe she is in Heaven, she may have spent some cleansing time in Purgatory. God knows that if she has spent any time in Purgatory, my stay there will be infinitely longer. Nevertheless, if a person does make a temporary stop in Purgatory, we know he or she will eventually make it to Heaven. If I cut my hand on a sharp object, I might have to get stitches in order for it to heal. Since it will only be a temporary situation, I don't mind the stitches. They are only designed to help me. Why do some people have to have such a hallmark view of religion?

Confession

Another teaching of the Church that is sure to illicit strong opinions depending on the person is the Sacrament of Reconciliation, or Confession.

Catholics often feel as if they are on the defensive about Confession. When they finally explore this subject in greater depth,

---

ww The San Diego-based apologetic apostolate Catholic Answers is a good source for those wanting to learn more about this subject. They can be found on the Internet at www.catholic.com.

xx Orthodox Jews believe in the concept to this day.

they come to find out that the arguments against it by Protestants are highly tendentious and thus grossly inaccurate. A group of very skilled Protestant clergy and writers have somehow made the Christian world (including many Catholics) believe Confession really is not only unnecessary, it has no biblical or apostolic basis. Nothing could be further from the truth. There is a whole host of evidence from the Bible and early Church to support this sacrament.

Perhaps the most famous verse uttered by Jesus about Confession happened after His resurrection when He met the Apostles and breathed on them saying, "Receive the Holy Spirit. Whose sins you forgive are forgiven them, and whose sins you retain are retained" (Jn. 20:22-23). More biblical evidence can be found in Jas. 5:13-16 and 2 Cor. 5:17-20. An interesting passage is found in Mk. 2:5-11. This contains the familiar story of Jesus telling the paralyzed man that his sins were forgiven and to pick up his and walk. Jesus was illustrating that He as the "Son of man" had the power to forgive sins, and He would later pass that power down through the priesthood as He did in Jn. 20:22-23.

If these examples aren't convincing enough, then look at the writings of the early Church Fathers. St. Barnabas wrote in 74 AD, "You should confess your sins. You should not go to prayer with an evil conscience. This is the way of the light." In 203, Tertullian pleaded with Christians not to be bashful about going to Confession. He told them if they did not confess their sins because they were bashful, that they would perish along with their bashfulness.[21]

After a consistent drop-off in the decades following the Second Vatican Council, Catholics slowly seem to have started embracing the Sacrament of Penance again in recent years. As with many traditions and teachings of the Church, it is the young who appear to be leading the way.

Perhaps the first evidence of this development was in 1993 at World Youth Day in Denver. Priests were hearing confessions for hours on end and some nearly collapsed from exhaustion. At Franciscan University of Steubenville's summer youth conferences, teens stand in the hot Ohio Valley sun for hours waiting in lines that are two city blocks long, patiently waiting for an opportunity to tell a priest their sins. Mark Butler, director of Youth and Young Adult Ministry for the Diocese of Columbus, told me he has seen youth come to Confession on many occasions. Mark said, "Whenever you have large youth gatherings, you are going to need many priests for Confession. The young really embrace this sacrament. I have seen it locally at youth rallies and at various World Youth Days."

When I prompted Butler on why the young seem to embrace this sacrament so much compared to adults, he replied, "Young people are idealistic. They see this as something that is unique to the Catholic faith. They love the sacrament's direct connection to Jesus. You know this is very similar to the devotion shown towards the Eucharist in the Church before the Protestant Reformation. The young believe their lives can be transformed by the Sacrament of Reconciliation."

Conclusion

As we have seen, the Church's teachings of dogmas such as Confession and Purgatory began at the dawn of the Church. Christians who met Jesus and lived in His lifetime acknowledged these teachings. One cannot say the same for "being saved" and the Rapture. Indeed, contrary to common wisdom (and as noted previously), Martin Luther, the architect of the Reformation, never talked about "being saved." He talked about salvation, obviously, but he never used *this* phrase, and he would not have agreed with the current concept behind it.

Furthermore, remember that it wasn't until 1832 that anyone mentioned the word "Rapture," and this concept wasn't even widely known until it was published in the *Scofield Reference Bible* in 1909. Surely if these were the teachings of Christ, we would have had them as long as Confession and Purgatory. One might understand their significance for Protestants if Martin / Luther or John Calvin had taught them as we know them, but they did not. This evidence leads one to ask those churches who teach these concepts that if they were so crucial to being counted amongst the righteous, why didn't God reveal them in the early days of Christianity?

Norman Dewire thinks much of this talk about the Rapture and the *Left Behind* series is just a trend or fad. "It will come and go, just like the megachurches," he said. "People want some substance to their faith. They will come back to the heart of Christianity. It may take a while, but they will come back and leave all of this hype behind."

If God meant for it to be so easy to enter His kingdom by declaring that we were once saved, always saved, why did He make it so difficult to understand this? Surely God would have intervened if it were His intention for us to adopt the idea of "being saved" and for us to believe in the Rapture. God appeared to Peter in a dream and gave His blessing for us to eat pork and certain types of seafood that had been forbidden by Jewish law (cf., Acts 10: 9-16). Surely if God went to the effort to come back to tell us it was okay to eat ribs, crab cakes, and shrimp, why didn't He mention anything about the Rapture or "being saved"? God would not have waited 1,600 years to reveal a different theology of salvation than that held by the Church or 1,800-1,900 years to reveal the Rapture.

To refute such errors (well-intentioned, certainly, but errors nonetheless), the Catholic belief in Scripture and Tradition rises to the occasion time and time again. In the 2,000 year history of the Christianity, there have been many ebbs and flows, and a variety of theological viewpoints. However, the foundation of the Catholic Church remains unchanged through all of these winds of change. It is apt that Jesus said Peter was the rock on which He would build His Church, (Matthew 16:18-19) for a foundation made of rock best stands the test of time.

- CHAPTER 13 -

THE DECLINE OF THE LIBERAL CHURCH

The numbers are astounding. As attendance at Evangelical and Catholic churches continues to grow, the mainline Protestant denominations are seeing an alarming decline in attendance. The declining numbers in liberal denominations are causing the remaining orthodox faithful of these bodies to ask whether this is the direction they believe their denomination should be headed. Many are leaving their churches and heading for something that seems anchored to a more genuine tradition than the denomination they left. The Catholic Church is often the recipient of these people.

As noted previously, consider that from 1990 to 2000, the Presbyterian Communion lost nearly 12 percent of its members, and the Episcopalians lost more than 5 percent. Many believe the numbers have furthered bottomed out in the years since 2000. Dave Shiflett, author of *Exodus: Why Americans Are Fleeing Liberal Churches for Conservative Christianity*, says Methodists have lost 1,000 members a week for the past 30 years.

By contrast, during those past 30 years, the Catholic population has increased by 15 million. As of 2003, there were 63.4 million Catholics in the US. In the previous five years some 85,000-95,000 Catholic converts a year were added to the rolls. Infant baptisms average around one million a year for the same period.[1]

Conservative Evangelical churches have also increased. Assemblies of God (i.e., Pentecostal) churches saw almost a 19 percent increase in membership from 1990 to 2000. The Church of God saw a 40 percent increase during that same period. Southern Baptists also gained during this time, about 750 members per week. Many traditional Protestants have left their mainline Protestant churches for the non-denominational megachurch. About 34 percent of the nation's megachurches are non-denominational and their growth continues for the moment.

This wasn't the first time that traditional Protestantism have been shaken to its core. As Thomas C. Reeves notes in his book *The Empty Church*, the phenomena first occurred in the 1740s when these communions "drank deeply of the Enlightenment." It took the Great Awakening to turn things around, and the changes mostly took place in the Anglican Communion.[2] It doesn't appear that there is a similar phenomenon occurring in our time. If there is, it is leading people into Catholicism and Evangelicalism.

Episcopalians were once the personification of economic success in America. If any church was blue blooded, it was the Episcopalians, with many of its members' bloodlines going back to British royalty. Starting in the 1950s, many in this Communion's leadership started shying away from traditional Christian orthodoxy and began to embrace social activism.

Bishop John Pike was the first in a string of Episcopalian bishops to stray off the reservation. At the height of his renown, Bishop Pike graced the cover of *Time* magazine. He openly expressed doubt about the Trinity, the Virgin Birth, and the Bible's inerrancy. He called upon believers to demythologize the church. After his Communion censured him, he resigned. However, he continued to make the news for his actions, which didn't help him or the Episcopal denomination. After three marriages, a few affairs, bouts with alcoholism (including public drunkenness and even séance participation), Bishop Pike and his wife died in a tragic fall into a gorge in Israel.[3]

Currently, both the Episcopal Communion in the United States and the Anglican Communion worldwide are embroiled in controversies that range from the validity of the openly gay Bishop Gene Robinson's consecration to questions related to women's ordination and the role of the scriptures.

Recall how we previously noted the heterodox views of John Spong, Episcopal bishop emeritus of New Jersey, how he didn't believe Jesus was literally raised from the dead, in the Virgin Birth, or even that God is a supernatural being. His views are sadly illustrative of many in Episcopalian congregations these days (although by no means all).

Perhaps it might have been easier for the former Episcopal ordinary to list what it was he actually did believe. If Bishop Spong were in any other profession, I believe a wise career counselor would have told him to consider another path in life if he was that unhappy with his business or its corporate mission.

I had an Internet encounter with Bishop Spong (or at least with his blog). When I released my article, "The Tide is Turning Towards Catholicism," someone on his website made a passing reference that he or she couldn't believe there were still people who believed in the traditional forms of faith. It might have not occurred to this person to wonder why his or her church was empty and the Catholic and Evangelical churches were full.

The Episcopal and Anglican Communions' politics are also causing a fuss. In early 2006, the Anglican Communion said it would divest itself from companies that do business with Israel. While the Anglicans said they were not taking sides in the Israeli-Palestinian dispute, it certainly seemed like Israel was taking the brunt of the Anglican Church's political actions. The whole affair prompted former Archbishop of Canterbury George Carey to say he was ashamed to be Anglican. Especially irksome to many was the fact that the current Archbishop of Canterbury Rowan Williams voted in favor of the measure.

Church attendance is abysmal at Anglican churches in England. The last year comprehensive data was gathered regarding church attendance was 1999. It showed that Anglicanism had experienced a 23 percent loss of parishioners from the time of the most previous study in 1989, and it had already declined 13 percent from 1979-1989. Less than 5 percent of Britons in their twenties attend church regularly.[4] In 2004, a study showed that, in an average week, more Muslims attend a mosque than Anglicans attend their church. Anglicanism in England dwarfs the other religions in baptized members. Charles Flagherty a London-area Catholic wrote, "The UK bears witness to the liberal elite promulgating an insipid hatred of the holy, of the sacred and of the soul. Now that Anglicanism has given up their hostility to Catholicism, the duty falls to their successors in secularism."[5]

When my "Tide Is Turning ..." article originally came out, a traditional Anglican website in the United Kingdom provided a link to my story. They lamented that unless Anglicans return to their traditions, they would never see the tide turn their way since so many people were leaving for the Catholic Church.

Queen Elizabeth II possesses a title given to King Henry VIII by Pope Leo X before the Reformation. "Defender of the Faith" (*Fidei Defensor*) is a title that British monarchs have proudly used ever since. By the time Prince Charles or perhaps one of his sons takes possession of the title, the Church of England quite possibly could be nothing more than a quaint social club.

Perhaps because of the problems in the Anglican Communion, Anglican British Prime Minister Tony Blair has often attended Catholic Mass with his wife and children. The Prime Minister, unlike his wife Cherie Blair, always worshipped on Sundays. Cherie Blair was raised Catholic and fell away during her college years. After the birth of her children, Mrs. Blair felt the call to return to her Catholic roots and began to attend Mass again. Her husband began to regularly accompany her to Mass. This led to speculation that he would convert to Catholicism after he left office, which is planned for July 2007.[6]

A conversion while in office could spark a thorny legal issue for Blair and Queen Elizabeth II. Catholics are prohibited by law from conferring with the Queen on state matters since she is the head of the Church of England, and the Prime Minister is by law called upon to assist the monarch in the selection of bishops for the Anglican Church. The antiquated anti-Catholic law seems to be the least of Queen Elizabeth's worries. A possible conversion to Catholicism by Britain's highest elected official could present a problem for the Anglican Communion. A high level defection to Catholicism would not only be an embarrassment, but might be seen as the irony it truly is.

Nearly 500 years ago, King Henry VIII left the Catholic Church and formed the Anglican Communion because Pope Clement VII would not annul His Majesty's marriage to Catherine of Aragon so that he might marry Anne Boleyn. What if today's most powerful man in Britain simply said, "I am coming home to the One, Holy, Catholic, and Apostolic Church"?

Unfortunately, the best thing we can learn from our mainline Protestant friends is to avoid their mistakes of indifference to church dissenters and unorthodox ideas. After the Episcopal Communion's hierarchy did little to stop or reprimand Bishops Pike and Spong, many left Episcopalianism for the Catholic Church or Evangelical congregations.

The reason is simple. The faithful want to believe, but if church leaders project a feeling of doubt about the beliefs they preach, so too will members of that church and any prospective converts. If, on the other hand, people see their leaders project confidence that taking a certain path is absolutely the right thing to do, that it is the true thing to do, they will follow, even though they may not fully understand the reasons why or have certain qualms.[yy]

In his song "Reason to Believe," Bruce Springsteen sings of having hope against hope, of believing and trusting despite all the odds. This is what average men and women do in all sorts of situations every day, especially believers. It is what motivates them to keep going notwithstanding the obstacles. If this rock-n-roller of uncertain theological formation can understand what motivates the average believer, can't those in the declining mainline Protestant communions? People want something to believe in. If the mainline congregations want to go back to their activist 1960s period of influence, if they think that is the way to arrest their steady (and seemingly inexorable decline), then perhaps they need to listen to the words of Bob Dylan. In the song, "When You Gonna Wake Up," from his Christian-influenced *Slow Train Coming* album, where he sang about a type of religious belief that seems to place activism over spirituality.

One of the more humorous portions of Shifflet's *Exodus* book involves a description of two men, David Burton and Dean Fisher, who tried to reintroduce God back into the Unitarian Communion. By their own estimates, half of their denomination was now atheist! This reminds me of studies that show about the same percentage of atheists and agnostics teach in many of the Ivy League's Theology departments as believers.

Shiflett tells of a divinity student at San Francisco's Church Divinity School of the Pacific, which is Episcopalian. One day after a furious debate about the divinity of Jesus, with the professor arguing the pro-divinity side, a student approached the academic and observed that it must be tough for him to fit in there because, unlike the others, he actually believed in God. The professor came to the conclusion that his student was right, so he left the school and

---

yy Witness two theological leaders, former Archbishop of Canterbury George Carey (and even more so his successor Rowan Williams) and John Paul II. One witnessed the continual erosion of his Communion's membership, even while he struggled to bend with the day's cultural currents. The other swam against those currents and found millions following him. The world lauded the former and lambasted the latter, and yet the one failed and the other succeeded. Benedict XVI is experiencing something similar.

became Catholic. Some churches just want to make people feel good, but to this man and many like him, the Catholic Church says what it means and means what it says, and that is very attractive.

The Catholic Church also has the ability to silence its members who act in an official capacity and disagree with her teachings. As Norman Dewire put it, "Catholics can take action against a dissenter. If a pastor in our church is preaching what the local bishop thinks might be heresy, there's nothing [the bishop] can do. He doesn't own the building like the Catholic bishop does. We have a General Conference held every four years. We have 1,000 delegates, 500 lay people, and 500 church people. [They are the ones who] have to take action against someone who's brought up on heresy charges."

He added, "We had a bishop, Joe Spragg, a graduate of this school who was brought up on heresy charges in Chicago, where he was bishop. He was eventually cleared, but it took a while and really upset a great many United Methodists. It sounded to me like he wanted to be the John Spong of the United Methodists. We have a Book of Resolutions. There are 368 topics covered. However, some topics and controversies are not [covered], and we don't have a Magisterium like your Church does. You have an advantage [of being able to make] faster decisions that can avoid long drawn-out battles."[7]

I can't help but recall President Dewire's comments when considering those who attack the Church for being too authoritarian. Is the alternative to have a church plagued by inaction? Indeed, it seems from my meeting with President Dewire and from reading Shiflett's book[8] that many mainline Protestant congregations face a growing crisis because of the increasing numbers of activists who have entered them. These people appear more intent on temporal salvation than saving eternal souls. It seems the Catholic Church has had it right all along. There is a reason it has survived 2,000 years.

I predict that as more of the mainline churches lose their congregations, much of their membership will increasingly come toward and into the Church. The people who leave liberal churches often like the liturgy they left behind, especially the Episcopalians, whose liturgy has much in common with the Catholic Mass. There is often no liturgy in a megachurch, so the Catholic Church is a natural alternative for those who want a more structured worship. In a sense, many mainline Protestants are coming full circle some five centuries after their ancestors left the Church. They will find that their return is welcomed with open arms.

One such person is David Bennett, who co-founded the Per Christum blog with his brother Jonathan.

"I became Catholic in August 2004 after struggling with the possibility of becoming Catholic for seven years," he said. "As a student of history, I couldn't accept the concept that Christian truth wasn't made known by God until the sixteenth century. The sacraments, especially the Eucharist, had a strong pull on me."

Bennett said that what finally caused him to become Catholic was that, "In 2003, when I was still an Episcopalian, I became upset when the Anglican Communion had no way of dealing with the election of an openly gay bishop, Gene Robinson. This made me realize that Anglicanism lacked apostolic authority and was just another mainline Protestant body. I just can't imagine St. Paul or St. Athanasius forming committees and commissions to 'study' an issue like a practicing gay bishop. From what I understand, many traditional-minded Christians are seeing what I am seeing and are also 'crossing the Tiber' and becoming Catholic."[8]

In June 2006, I attended the General Episcopal Convention, which took place in Columbus. It was an historic conference, bringing together a very diverse group of believers. Many wondered if the Episcopal Communion would even survive since the greater Anglican Communion was asking its American brethren to apologize for consecrating an openly homosexual bishop and blessing same sex unions.

To my surprise, many Episcopal and Anglican websites linked to my two reports from my CatholicReport.org website. I was edified by the warm and generous comments that many moderate and traditional believers posted on those websites, my website, or to my personal e-mail.

My two posts reported on my strolls around the convention floor and asking questions of a broad range of attendees. Here are some excerpts:

"As I walked through the convention hall, I was struck by the number of attendees wearing the gay flag insignia on their nametag or the button of Integrity, the gay and lesbian rights lobbying group. I estimated that about one quarter of those at the convention were wearing one or both. I asked a delegate whether this meant that all of these people were homosexual. He said he was not a homosexual but rather supported their agenda. I asked him if he thought it would seem odd to those Episcopalians in the pews that this was occurring. He hesitated and stated he thought that while those in the pews probably wouldn't understand this, it was the direction he thought the Episcopal Communion should go. When I asked him to clarify, he just smiled and said, 'Openness.'"

I then spoke with Reverend Susan Russell, who is the president of Integrity.

Dave Hartline: Could you tell me if my assessment is correct or incorrect? It is my observation that Bishop Robinson may get the most press from the liberal or progressive side. However, it is you that seems to be most highly regarded by the liberal faction. To quote one person who said she was very liberal, "Susan won't back down one inch to the fringe on the right and those who have a literal interpretation of all things."

Rev. Susan Russell: Hmmm, that's an interesting assessment you have. I don't know if I am the one to judge that, but I will say this. Gene is a bishop, and his job is to be a conciliator. I am the president of Integrity and I have to fight for the rights of gays and lesbians.

Hartline: When you say the rights of gays and lesbians, what do you mean? I know a lot of traditional [i.e., orthodox] Catholics, Episcopalians, etc., who would say they don't discriminate against anyone, but that gay marriage, civil unions; openly gay clergy has nothing to do with discrimination. It is scriptural.

Russell: Let me tell you something, if someone says they don't discriminate and is still against gay marriage, civil unions, and an openly gay clergy, they discriminate.

Hartline: What about 2,000 years of Christian tradition?

Russell: I find it odd that the people in the Episcopal Church would talk about Scripture as if they were some fringe element fundamentalists. One of the reasons our church broke with Rome was because of issues like the Magisterium. Now they want one? I am a cradle Episcopalian. I still believe in the one, holy, catholic, apostolic Church. I grew up saying that. I don't know if you are aware of it, but that's what we said. I want to have unity with your Church, but we aren't going back to being second-class citizens. You know, we have a level of support in all of the churches, including yours and among some important people too. Just not important enough.

Hartline: What about the Third World's view on the Episcopal Church?

Russell: David, let me stop you right there. We live in the Third World. If you are referring to Africa, Asia, or Latin America, that is the Two-Thirds World. I know that may come across as being politically correct, but that's the way I feel.

Hartline: OK, what about the two-thirds world's view on the Episcopal Church? They seem to be far more conservative than the US and Europe, especially since (at least in Africa's case) they are dealing with Islam. Gay inclusion is not something they want to promote.

Russell: That may be, but we aren't going back, I can tell you that. I certainly believe in dialogue, but I won't give away our rights.

Hartline: Statistically, the liberal or progressive wing of the Episcopal Communion – or of the Catholic Church, for that matter – isn't growing. Why?

Russell: It is growing. I am sure you have been told it is not, but I can tell you it is. I am from Los Angeles, and in West Hollywood and Pasadena our churches are doing very well.

I also was able to speak with the openly gay ordinary of New Hampshire, Bishop Gene Robinson. It was his consecration that touched off the whole debate that was the focus of this convention. We spoke two or three times at the convention, and he was one of the most gracious persons I encountered. And though many of his beliefs are very liberal, there were far more liberal elements at the convention. Here are some of his comments.

Dave Hartline: Would you please tell me if my assessment of you is correct? I have written on my website that you are a liberal (or progressive) but more moderate than some elements here. The reason I ask is that many traditional folks I know don't discriminate against homosexuals, but feel it is not the type of lifestyle God would permit. So they may have no trouble with you as a person but do have trouble with you as an openly gay person, especially a bishop. Susan Russell said that anyone who doesn't accept gay unions, openly gay bishops, etc., is really no different than those who are openly anti-gay. What's your opinion?

Bishop Robinson: Well, first of all, I think you are exactly right.

I am a progressive who is more moderate than some here. To be honest, I have spent more time at this convention talking with conservative people than liberals. I know there are many who don't accept me as a bishop. I have no trouble sitting with them. That's what the word Communion, as in Anglican Communion, is all about. You know, I was denied [the Eucharist] in a conservative diocese. Now that, I thought, was beyond the pale.

Hartline: What are your views on abortion? The reason I ask is I have worked with people in the Catholic Church who I knew to be homosexual, and as liberal or progressive as some were, many seemed to be pro-life. They seemed to equate the unborn with their situation. I don't see that here. How do you feel?

Robinson: Well, I can certainly understand those you spoke of equating their situation with those in the womb. However, I believe in the Episcopal Church's teachings. I believe in viability. I don't counsel women to have an abortion past the first trimester. My advice has always been if you are going to get an abortion, do it quick.

Hartline: When is viability? I just put a story on my website about a baby who survived an abortion years ago, and she just sang in the Colorado General Assembly. What if a woman came to you and said she's getting an abortion in her second or third trimester?

Robinson: Well it's her right to choose so, though I would be personally against it. That's her decision. The young woman you mentioned, well, that's why I believe in getting abortions as early as possible.

Hartline: What about the decline of the mainstream Protestant churches that have embraced a more liberal theology?

Robinson: I think the Bush Administration has a way of scaring Americans about minorities and other religions. They scared us into war, as well. People go with what they are familiar with in times of trouble. However, I want to be clear. I call myself an Evangelical. We need to talk more talk about the Living God and less about church. People's eyes glaze over when they hear the word "church."

After speaking with Bishop Robinson, I spoke with Greg Griffith. He runs the "Standing Firm in the Faith" website. It supports the traditional or conservative side of his denomination. His website was one of a number of Episcopal or Anglican websites that linked to my convention reports.

Dave Hartline: How do you sum up this week? I know it may be difficult, since you have been working day and night for a week and been away from your family. What can you tell us?
Greg Griffith: I will say this: Evil hides, whereas the truth comes out in clarity and honesty. We are upholding the traditions of our church. We are not aggressors. Some would say we are aggressors, but that is ridiculous. We are upholding our faith. The dishonesty of the left was clear to see at this convention.
Hartline: Bishop Robinson told me that he is trying to heal your church, but Susan Russell told me that the progressive side is helping the church. They are growing and have a great potential for growth.
Griffith: Conservative Episcopalians may not like the fact that he is a bishop or his views for that matter. However, he is trying to find a way forward, and he will at least sit and talk with conservatives. Susan Russell is a bomb thrower. She makes outrageous statements and then is surprised or angered when they are questioned. There is no way liberal churches are growing. As far as the potential to grow, yeah, you could say that because right now there's practically no one in them.

One of the main voices of the traditional side is the Reverend Canon Kendall Harmon. He runs the very influential Titusonenine. com website. He is Oxford educated and hails from South Carolina. The following is his assessment of the Episcopal Convention.

Dave Hartline: Where is the Episcopal Church right now?

Canon Harmon: We are in unprecedented territory. The greatest amount of pressure right now is on the Episcopal Church and how it reacts to this convention and to the greater Anglican Communion. Bishop [Katharine Jefferts] Shorri is second on the list, because as the new presiding bishop, many will immediately look to her comments and decisions. There is also a great deal of pressure on Archbishop of Canterbury Rowan Williams. He is going to face tremendous pressure from Anglicans in Africa if they deem the Episcopal Church has brushed off the Windsor Report.

Hartline: How did the Episcopal Church get here? My impression is the folks in the pews are nowhere near this liberal. How did this happen?

Harmon: Societal pressure from the intellectual elites and the willingness of certain bishops during the last three decades to employ and cater to a very different mindset that is often very different from a traditional scriptural mindset. Those on the liberal or progressive side worked very hard to push an agenda and it has worked well for them. They know how to use the appropriate language. My belief is if you are going to use descriptions like "the Spirit is with us," you better be right. I don't believe their agenda is right. Because of their agenda, more and more Episcopalians will leave for the Catholic Church, the Orthodox Church, or Evangelical churches.

Hartline: In your opinion, are there forces at work that could make what is happening in the Episcopal Church happen in the Catholic Church?

Harmon: There are forces at work in the Catholic Church trying to make this happen, but it will never happen in the Catholic Church because you have "clear doctrine," something we haven't had in a long time. Many of your bishops, archbishops, and cardinals have the unique ability of showing themselves to be orthodox and compassionate. It has served the American Catholic Church very well. We do not have a Magisterium as you do.

These individuals, who all have large levels of support in their communion, each had so many interesting things to say. They all lament the division in their church. I think it would be beneficial for every Catholic to read the comments of the four people whose comments are above. I really felt for the Episcopalians who wanted to keep to their church's orthodoxy. When I came home from reporting at that convention, I felt profoundly sad for those people. However my sadness paled in comparison to that of Canon Harmon and Greg Griffith. Fortunately, because of the reasons Canon Harmon outlined, Catholics will not face the same predicament facing the Episcopalians and many other denominations. The clear doctrine he described as being present in the Catholic Church has saved the day for Catholicism.[9]

DAVID J. HARTLINE

- CHAPTER 14 -

THE CRUSADES – MEAN OLD CATHOLIC BULLIES OR DEFENDERS OF THE FAITH?

Ever since the terrorist attacks of September 11, 2001, interest has grown in the Crusades, those much maligned and generally misunderstood medieval wars fought by Christians against the Muslims in the Middle East.

The Crusades were a series of conflicts fought by Christians against Muslims from 1095 to 1270 (with excursions taking place as late as 1669) in order to reclaim and then protect the Holy Land. A secondary purpose was to defend Europe from further Islamic expansion into the continent, yet for years Catholics have felt the need to apologize for this. At a Georgetown University address on November 7, 2001, former President Bill Clinton voiced his belief that the Crusades were awful events perpetrated by so-called Christians. Al Qaeda leader Osama Bin Laden and his chief deputy Dr. Ayman al Zawahiri can rattle off names and dates of the various Crusades and their battles like it was yesterday.[1] Bin Laden even calls those in the West who oppose him "Crusaders."

While many have accepted this conventional wisdom (it confirms what they were taught in school and learned through the media, after all), there are some who have begun to ask what really happened during the Crusades. Were Pope Urban II (who called the first Crusade) and Christians of that age mean old bullies, or might there have actually been some legitimate justification for the Crusades?[zz]

The first signs of recognition that the Crusades were more than just Catholic Christians run amok occurred several days after 9/11 when the eminent professor Dr. Thomas Madden, chairman of Saint

Louis University's History Department, was asked about the Crusades. When he gave a sympathetic view of the Crusades, the reporter was mystified. Was this expert a fraud? Had *anyone* ever defended the Crusades? If there were some justification for the Crusades, what would that mean for the Church today? Would taking away the Crusades mean Islamic extremists forgoing any justification for their actions (since they claim the Crusades were the start of the West's war on Islam)?[2]

My former diocesan colleague Mark Butler is fond of saying, "Mohammad is in many ways the prophet our ancestors were expecting, but Jesus came instead." Islam's prophet Mohammad was able to unite the tribes of the Arabian Peninsula under the banner of belief in one God. Before this, these tribes believed in various pagan deities (there were also many Christians and Jews there). Changing this was not easy for Mohammad. It took the force of arms to achieve unity, which was not uncommon in that age.

However, it was a vastly different approach than that of Jesus of Nazareth. Jesus urged His followers to spread the gospel peacefully and suffer if necessary. Mohammad, on the other hand, told his followers to spread the message peacefully, but if that didn't work, then they were to use the sword.[aaa] By the end of his life, Islam had spread throughout the Arabian Peninsula.

Three centuries after his death, Muslim armies had pushed into southern France after taking Spain. By the year 900 much of North Africa had been conquered, as had the Middle East. It looked as if Europe would soon be next. However, Charlemagne would make his

---

[z] Now, maybe you are wondering what the Crusades have to do with how the tide is turning toward Catholicism. We shall see that the Crusades were largely a defensive action called for by our Orthodox brothers to defend what they felt was an ongoing attack against the faith, especially in the Holy Land where the battle began. By reevaluating the Crusades we may well see that only through Church orthodoxy can we stand firm against those who proclaimed a holy war against us both now and then. As we have seen, that orthodoxy is increasing and is a sign that the tide is turning.

stand near the present holy site of Lourdes as his grandfather Charles Martel had before him at Tours. As a result of these valiant efforts, France remained Christian.

I won't go into great depth about the Crusades but the following brief description of the events is necessary in order to understand the modern-day historical gulf that separates Islam and Christianity, especially Catholicism.[bbb]

In 1095, Pope Urban II received a desperate plea for help from Byzantine Emperor Alexius I Komnenos. His Majesty argued Islam must be stopped (Muslims forces had already taken much of Byzantium's former empire, and their lust for conquest showed no signs of abating).

Urban decided he would raise an army to protect pilgrims journeying to the Holy Land. Men from around Europe, especially France, England, and Germany, volunteered to fight in this holy army. Some brought their wives and families, while others, especially those who were not the first-born sons, saw this fight as a way to escape the drudgery of their lives. However, many were earnest, sincere Catholics who viewed the Crusade as their duty to protect their Christian brothers and sisters in Judea and the holy sites associated with their Savior, Jesus Christ.

The Crusades would last on and off for over 200 years, and the latter ones were initiated by secular rulers such as Holy Roman Emperor Frederick II, not by popes. In 1212, a large force of

---

[aaa] I am often amazed by the ignorance of these basic data that I encounter. Frequently, I have to actually show someone the facts to get them to believe that not all faiths are spread in the same way. For its first three centuries, Islam spread by means of the sword. For its first three centuries, Christianity had no resources to spread its message other than by love of neighbor and word of mouth. In fact, it was subject to violent, indeed deadly persecutions. It is not for nothing that the old Christian maxim says, "The blood of martyrs is the seed of the Church." Many Muslims would agree with this, but to them, it would mean those who die in battle. The Christian means that where there is a great witness (i.e., martyrdom) through persecution, there typically is a directly proportional increase in the number of converts.

children even decided to join the effort (although many were sold into slavery, and few if any made it to the Holy Land). Furthermore, the initial engagements succeeded in the Crusaders' original intent of securing the Holy Land. The Europeans established the Kingdom of Jerusalem, the Counties of Tripoli and Edessa, and the Principality of Antioch.

Eventually, however, believers in Islam regained the land they originally held. Islamic armies were almost always much larger than the Christians and had shorter supply lines than their foes. After the conflict, trade routes were established, and even though the Crusades had been violent and acrimonious, with blood curdling atrocities on either side, each of the warring parties gradually got on with the business of doing business, as was the custom back then. It was only centuries afterwards that the Crusades became stigmatized the way they are today.

But why *did* the Crusades become stigmatized? Remember that the Islamic world was at its peak during the Crusades. They led the world in math, science, and exploration. However, that would soon change, as a series of events both internal and external to the Muslim world would negatively impact the fortunes of Islam. Genghis Khan attacked from the north and the east. The plague, although never effecting the Islamic world, slowed trade with the West. Occasional infighting between Shiites and Sunnis weakened Islam's strength.

It is true that the Ottoman Empire, based in Istanbul (the former Constantinople), achieved great power, and Islam still appeared ascendant for several centuries. However, the final expulsion of the Moors from Spain in 1492 was followed by the breaking of the Saracen navy at Lepanto (aka, Naupactos, Greece) in 1571, which in turn was followed by the crushing of the Ottoman army by Polish King John Sobieski outside Vienna on September 11, 1683. Then on September 11, 1697, Prince Eugene of Savoy and his troops killed 20,000 Turkish soldiers, after which the Ottomans were forced to

---

[bbb] For a more in-depth treatment of this subject, purchase Hilaire Belloc's *The Crusades*, available from TAN Books.

cede much of the Balkans to Austria. All this began the slow but inexorable decline of the Muslim world. Some would say it continues to this day, while others would argue the slide was at least halted with the discovery of oil.

In an October 2001, *Washington Post* story, Professor Mary-Jane Deeb stated, "The Islamic world has a very fluid sense of time. For them events like the Crusades, a thousand years ago, are as immediate as yesterday. And they are very, very, powerful events in the Arab mind. A lot of Islamic rhetoric revolves around the Crusades."[3]

This is especially true for adherents of an obscure sect of Islam, Wahhabism, which sprouted from the poor, barren land of the Arabian Peninsula in the eighteenth century. Wahhabism's founder Muhammad ibn Abd al Wahab lived his life tucked away in the then-poor Arabia. He believed Islam had become too "watered down," and he wanted to return it to what he saw as its original purity.[4] If you wonder what kind of a regime Wahab would have liked, consider Afghanistan under the Taliban. The way Afghanistan was ruled prior to September 11 is a perfect example of the ideal under Wahhabism, which has strict rules along with a powerful military arm, Al Qaeda.

World religions occasionally have radical or militant offshoots that claim to be the true, pure form of the faith itself. When these radical offshoots spring up in poor and remote areas, they may be of interest to sociologists, but not the world in general because they have no impact beyond the area in which they germinate. In the case of Wahhabism, however, nothing could be further from the truth.

For instance, had Wahhabism sprung up in Bangladesh, it probably would have meant nothing to the rest of world except the Bangladeshis. However, when oil was discovered in the Arabian Peninsula, Wahhabism was well positioned to expand its influence. The Saud family would rule the Arabian Peninsula as a royal family with absolute power, while the Wahhabis controlled the moral and religious laws and enforced the separation of the sexes in all things.[ccc]

Due to the wealth it accumulated through its privileged place in Saudi society, Wahhabism has spread throughout the Islamic world and even into Western Europe and America through immigration to these areas. Most mosques have seen some form of this unwelcome influence. Wahhabi money enables a mosque to offer its congregants enhanced programs, but it also brings militant speakers who urge those attending to become "real" Muslims.

During the boom decade of the 1990s, Wahhabi control was allowed to envelop many mosques in the West because, like the planning for the 9/11 attacks, many refused to believe there was trouble happening right under their noses. Even when a Muslim imam was shot for opposing such militancy, few were aware of the danger Wahhabism posed.

Enter September 11, 2001, when the world began to see what the militants want. However, aren't they just opposed to western values and influence? Why should Christians (specifically the Church) worry?

To see what Wahhabism and Al Qaeda have in store for the West one must understand the godfather of Al Qaeda, Abdullah Yusuf Azzam. He was a Palestinian who became a legend after fighting against the Soviet Union in the mountains of Afghanistan. He mentored Osama Bin Laden and had a vision of a totally united global Islam. This vision kept his relentless energy going as he first fought the Soviets and then planned to fight the "Christian West."

Ironically, he restated his intent as he traveled across the United States raising money during speaking events extolling the resurgence of the Caliphate.[5] The idea of the Caliphate (laws not made by governments but by Islam) has been around since Islam's beginnings. Recently, there were some hints of this notion of the Caliphate for the Christian West, mainly before September 11, 2001. Occasionally

---

ccc Saudi Arabia is not like the West. Men and women rarely go out together, even husbands and wives. Women are not permitted to drive and are often confined to their homes. If they want to go to the mall or get groceries, they need a close male relative to accompany them.

demonstrators could be seen in New York and Washington, DC, with signs that read, "Voting Is Sin," or "Only Allah Rules and Governs," but they were more prevalent in London.

The man who influenced all in the modern jihadist movement, including Azzam, was Sayyid Qutb. He had great influence on many in the world of radical Islam. The peculiar thing about Qutb was his American education. In the early 1950s, he received a Master's degree from Colorado State College of Education (today called University of Northern Colorado), but he became outraged at American culture. Couples going out in public, sock hops, and Christian denominations not conducting investigations to see if there were adulterers or homosexuals in their midst caused Qutb to believe Islam must become more radicalized. He believed Christianity had failed. Qutb's brother, Muhammad, later became a professor of Islamic Studies in Saudi Arabia, and Dr. al Zawahiri was one of his students.[6]

Against this growing militant sentiment, Pope John Paul II tried everything in his power to reach out to Islam throughout his papacy. Similarly, Pope Benedict XVI has tried to maintain a respectful and open dialogue. However, the approach taken by Benedict is much different than what we saw under John Paul II.[ddd] For most of the late Pope's pontificate, militant Islam was not seen as a threat, and he continually reached out to Islam (as he had done with all religions). John Paul apologized for some of the actions of the Crusades, specifically the actions of some of the Crusaders.

Indeed, Pope John Paul II's reaching out to Islam once got him into trouble with some Catholics. Conservative Catholics and Islamic critics often note his infamous Koran kissing episode of May 14, 1999. At best, it put the Pope in a difficult position. It was never really confirmed whether Pope John Paul II actually kissed

---

[ddd] Witness Benedict's talk at the University of Regensburg (Germany), where he boldly quoted the Byzantine Emperor Manual II Paleologos, who said, "Show me just what Muhammad brought that was new and there you will find things only evil and inhuman, such as his command to spread by the sword the faith he preached."

the Koran or some other Islamic Holy Book, but all reports said it was the Koran. Defenders said the pontiff was merely showing his appreciation for a series of gifts he received.[7] Some will defend the incident by pointing out that Europeans are more demonstrative with emotions when greeting people. For example, on October 3, 2003, John Paul II received the Archbishop of Canterbury Rowan Williams. Archbishop Williams got on his knees and kissed Pope John Paul II's ring. This wasn't the archbishop abdicating his primacy but a gesture of kindness.

John Paul was merely continuing a long tradition of the Church reaching out to Islam. It wasn't until the end of his pontificate, for instance, that the Church officially recognized Israel's borders. The feeling was that while recognizing Israel was important, the Church felt a special obligation to look after Christians living in Muslim lands. This was important because of *dhimmitude*.

An Egyptian Jewish scholar named Bat Ye'or was the first to give the word a definition, although the assassinated Lebanese Christian leader Bashir Gemayel is officially credited with coining the term during a September 14, 1982, speech.[8]

Ye'or wanted to understand the persecution she felt growing up in Egypt. She found that while Muslims always boasted they were respectful of other faiths, under Islamic rule Christians and Jews had to pay for centuries a special *jizya* tax[eee] and were not allowed to rise in society the way they could have if they had been Muslims.

[eee] Christians see the jizya as a humiliating imposition of second-class status in Muslim societies. In the Koran 9:29, it reads, "Fight those who believe not in Allah nor the Last Day, nor hold forbidden that which hath been forbidden by Allah and His Messenger, nor acknowledge the religion of Truth, (even if they are) of the People of the Book, until they pay the jizya with willing submission, and feel themselves subdued." Also, according to Wikipedia.org, Al-Zamakhshari, a commentator on the Koran, said that "the Jizyah shall be taken from them with belittlement and humiliation. The dhimmi shall come in person, walking not riding. When he pays, he shall stand, while the tax collector sits. The collector shall seize him by the scruff of the neck, shake him, and say 'Pay the Jizyah!' and when he pays it he shall be slapped on the nape of the neck."

Ye'or and others contended that while Christians in Arab countries did have some prominent families and were a sizable lot in the early 1900s, representing around 10 percent of the region's population, Christians on the whole were a beaten down group.[fff]

As further evidence of his solicitude toward Muslims, John Paul II received Palestinian Liberation Organization Chairman Yasser Arafat several times. Arafat often said the pontiff was very favorable to the Palestinian cause and had sympathies for the Intifada (the Palestinian Uprising). In 2000, an aging and trembling Pope John Paul II visited the Holy Land. He made stops in Israel, Egypt, Jordan, and Syria. He became the first Pope to pray in a mosque. No Christian religious leader had ever reached out more to Islam than Pope John Paul II. Yet to radical Islam, the only true way for an infidel (i.e., non-Muslim) to reach out is to convert. To them, Rome was (is) in apostasy. Christianity would have to be dealt with, and soon the Vatican (and the world) would find out what that meant.

After the events of September 11, 2001, anti-terrorism officials would come across many plots to attack Rome. There would be still other plots hatched to attack the Church, but the most spectacular was to have actually occurred before 9/11, and involved destroying the famous Strasbourg Cathedral in France. Al Qaeda wanted to blow up the cathedral in 2000 when it was filled with worshippers.

Muslims, however, consider the jizya entirely just. They say it pays for protection via the military for Christians, Jews, and other non-Muslims in Islamic societies. As Wikipedia puts it, "The Shia jurist, Grand Ayatollah Makarem Shirazi states in *Tafsir Nemooneh* that the main philosophy of jizya is that it is only a financial aid to those Muslims who are in the charge of safeguarding the security of the state and dhimmi's lives and properties on their behalf." However, Al-Mawardi (the famous Shafi'i jurist of Baghdad), stated in *al-Ahkam as-Sultaniyyah* (The Laws of Islamic Governance) that jizya is paid by the enemy in return for peace, and if the payment of jizya ceases, then jihad is resumed.

[fff] For more on this subject, see Bat Ye'or's *Islam and Dhimmitude: Where Civilizations Collide*, Madison/Teaneck, NJ, Fairleigh Dickinson University Press/ Associated University Presses, 2003

Perhaps Osama Bin Laden wasn't aware of the decline in church attendance in the West, especially in France. Thus even if the plot had been successful, it would not have had the intended effect.

Perhaps Rome became more of a target after Italian Prime Minster Silvio Berlusconi said what many in the West also thought, that the West (i.e., Christianity) was superior to Islam. "We should be conscious of the superiority of our civilization," he told journalists, "which consists of a value system that has given people widespread prosperity in those countries that embrace it, and guarantees respect for human rights and religion. This respect certainly does not exist in Islamic countries."[9]

The tide began to turn on September 11, 2001, because much of the world – secular and religious – could now see radical Islam for what it was. For years Christians, especially Pope John Paul II, had tried to resolve the differences with Islam, even to the point of the Pope receiving criticism from many faithful for being too apologetic for past Catholic transgressions, both real and perceived.

But radical Islam was not to be assuaged. It always fed on the burning bitterness that was the realization of what could have been had their ancestors achieved victory in Europe. It wasn't like there weren't enough opportunities.

For instance, many radical Islamists mention Andalusia as if it were a popular vacation destination. Andalusia was the name Muslims gave to conquered Spain, but Andalusia failed to exist after the late 1400s because of successive victories by Christians over Moorish forces there.[10] Vienna was literally in the sights of the Ottoman armies when a hailstorm gave the western forces enough time to fortify their positions and prevent the taking of the city.

As noted previously, one of the greatest naval battles ever fought was the Battle of Lepanto. A superior Turkish Muslim naval force was not only defeated but also thousands of Christian slaves held on the Turkish vessels were freed. For Catholics of the era, it wasn't just a victory, it was a miracle, because some saw an apparition of the Virgin Mary. Many Europeans truly believed this victory was a sign of the Blessed Mother's protection, so much so that Catholics still remember the victory at Lepanto, not only in words when we say, "Our Lady of Victory, pray for us,"[11] but also the day, October 7, which the Church marks as the Feast of Our Lady of the Rosary (previously known as the Feast of Our Lady of Victory). St. Pius V instituted the feast to commemorate how he was given a vision of the battle scene through a window while praying the rosary. Combatants confirmed that the moment the Pope had his vision was the same at which the tide of the battle turned in favor of the Christians.

If ideas of Jihad are coming from militants in the Islamic world, one might ask if people are talking about a small handful of renegades. I wish we were. In survey after survey done in the Islamic world, however, Osama Bin Laden gets higher ratings than every Middle Eastern Muslim leader. The government of Saudi Arabia has a great deal of trouble with the clerics who believe Saudi Arabia, a country which still has public beheadings and will not allow women to drive (let alone vote), is becoming too liberal. Egyptian leader Hosni Mubarak's government pleaded with the Bush Administration not to force them to have the free and open elections that gave Hamas an electoral victory in Palestinian areas. Mubarak feared a free election would bring another radical Islamic political group such as the Muslim Brotherhood into power.

Patrick Egbuchunam, a Catholic writer from predominantly Muslim Nigeria, voiced his frustration with Islam's lack of constructive dialogue with Christianity.

"Muslims must learn from the success of Malaysia and know that you can remain true to your faith and still embrace liberty and freedom," said Egbuchunam. "This involves criticism in good faith. Why are most Islamic countries ruled by despots? Despite oil most Arab nations are still under-developed. Saudi Arabia uses its wealth to sponsor the construction of mosques in Europe and America, yet will not allow churches in its own land. Christians in Muslim lands are deprived of their freedoms. We should not be shy to tell Muslims the truth. Dialogue is a two-way process. So far it has been a monologue."[12]

When Catholics try to sound a clarion call about these frightening conditions in the Muslim world, they are often attacked as bigots. Robert Spencer, the Catholic writer and founder of the "Jihad Watch" website, is one such person.[13] Spencer has written several books about Islam, the Crusades, and Catholicism. His *The Politically Incorrect Guide to Islam (and the Crusades)* and *Inside Islam* (which Spencer co-wrote with Muslim convert Daniel Ali) are two very well researched works.[ggg]

Even though Spencer's heritage is Middle Eastern, and despite his great familiarity with that part of the world, many Catholic groups and the media were afraid of the potential wrath associating with him might bring. Spencer simply points out that when Abu Musab al Zarqawi (before his 2006 death in a coalition bombing) gruesomely beheaded someone on videotape, he read a section of the Koran he believes justified his actions. Can any Christian actually take some part of the words of Jesus to justify violent actions?

Spencer's national television appearances have helped change naive perceptions about radical Islam. Perceptions changed even more following the uproar that surrounded a cartoon of Islam's prophet Mohammad in early 2006. Possibly no event showed the divide between Islam and the West as much as this episode.

A Danish cartoonist trying to write children's books was unaware that Islamic law prohibits one from making an image of Mohammad.[hhh] He innocently decided to create a cartoon image of the Prophet with a turban that looked like a bomb.[iii] After its appearance in a Danish newspaper, that country's Muslims alerted their counterparts in the Middle East, and the whole episode exploded on the world

---

[ggg] Indeed, Fr. Mitch Pacwa who is well respected in orthodox Catholic circles, enthusiastically endorsed *Inside Islam* by Ascension Press.[13]

stage several months later in February 2006. To say the Danes are not a very religious people would be an understatement. Only 3.2 percent of Danes attend church on a regular basis compared to the United States, where over 50 percent of the populace does.

The Islamic world erupted and took out its revenge not only on Danish products like Danish pastries but also on the Christian world in general. Pope Benedict XVI, President Bush, and many other world leaders condemned the cartoons as being offensive to Muslims. Yet in several countries in the Middle East and North Africa, protestors attacked Western embassies and burned Catholic churches to the ground. In Turkey, a priest was shot in the back while saying Mass.[14] In Nigeria, a priest was beaten to death and dozens of Christians were burned and beaten to death by Muslim mobs. The same mobs set fire to churches, as well. In Libya, home of the theological giant St. Augustine, churches were burned, some of which contained ancient relics and documents.[15] Al Qaeda in Iraq claimed credit for a string of attacks against churches, including the Holy See's nunciature in Baghdad. After these events, the Vatican issued a stern address, stronger than any it had ever given.

Increasingly Pope Benedict has taken a stronger stance against Islamic extremism. In Spring 2006, a conference on the Crusades took place at a seminary in Rome. In the past this conference might have never been allowed (it probably would have been deemed too provocative to Muslim sensibilities). However, in a world where Pope Benedict had said many times that Muslims must condemn those who attack in the name of God, the climate is now different. Additionally,

---

[hhh] A very small minority of Muslim scholars disagrees.

[iii] As one online commentator put it, "But which is the greater insult? A Danish artist indicating a connection between Islam and terrorism? Or those terrorists, who have killed thousands of civilians in New York, London, Bali, Madrid, Casablanca and Istanbul - and have done their dirty deeds in the name of Allah the Merciful? If terrorism is an insult against Islam, why don't you fight terrorism instead of getting mad with a Danish artist, whose only crime is that he's pointing out your ostrich-like denial. Don't kill the messenger."

in a May 2006 speech in Florida, George Cardinal Pell of Australia gave perhaps the bluntest assessment of Islam ever given by such a high-ranking Church official. Pell spoke of the centuries of persecution Christians have suffered while living in Islamic ruled areas.[16]

Later the cartoon unrest spread to the West, not in the form of violence but in the form of demonstrations where some of the demonstrators held graphic posters that said "Behead those who dishonor the Prophet." Another poster showed Buckingham Palace and the White House flying under an Islamic flag.[17] The *New York Times* refused to print the cartoons of Mohammad. However, on the same day it printed a story about the controversy regarding whether or not pictures of Mohammad should be shown, the newspaper ran a photograph of an infamous art display that was shown in New York some years earlier. The work was a collage of the Virgin Mary covered in elephant dung and cut up pornographic photos.

The irony could not have been more striking. Yet it didn't end there. Some years earlier the artist Juan Serrano displayed the infamous *Piss Christ* work, which was a photo of a crucifix immersed in a beaker of the creator's urine. Understandably, this caused a great deal of outrage in the Christian community. The *New York Times* and most of the media establishment had no qualms about showing that "work of art." Why was this cartoon of Mohammad different? It was different because the *Times* knew it was inconceivable that Christians would kill the editors or blow up the Old Grey Lady's headquarters. The same could not be said of the Prophet's followers.

On September 12, 2006, Pope Benedict spoke to an academic gathering in Regensburg, Germany. The Holy Father quoted a 14th century text written by besieged Byzantine Emperor Manuel II Paleologos. The text made some unflattering references to Muhammad and the spreading of Islam by the sword.

While it was clearly understood that Pope Benedict was only making a passing reference to the text, riots broke out in the Muslim world. An Italian nun working in Somalia was killed, several churches of various denominations were attacked and burned in the Palestinian West Bank. In the following days, on several occasions, Pope Benedict made it clear that those were not his words. Yet, the Holy Father was taken to task by many Muslim political and religious leaders.

Even in the West Muslim protestors were visible. Catholic worshippers at Westminster Cathedral in London were greeted with chilling signs warning of Pope Benedict and Rome's demise. To add insult to injury, some Christians said that Pope Benedict had blundered. If ever *dhimmitude* could be seen on the evening news, it was evident for all to see in September 2006. Have those Christians who said the Pope blundered ever asked those in the Saudi government why no churches are allowed there? Only Islam is permitted in Saudi Arabia. While millions of Christians toil in Saudi Arabia working the menial jobs no Saudi will do, the Saudi government will not allow one church to be built in the kingdom for those who serve the Saudis (before the Islamic era there were churches in Saudi Arabia). Yet, the Saudis have funded the construction of a $50 million mosque in Rome within view of the Vatican, the largest in Europe, where death to infidels has been preached.

In any event, the Christian particularly Catholic "Pajamas Media" (as Dan Rather infamously dubbed the blogosphere) showed its fury.

Oddly enough, this series of events was indeed one of the Catholic Church's finest hours. The Church reacted with charity and outstretched arms rather than with violence in the face of attack. She never wavered from her message or condoned those who would perpetrate violence in her defense. The Bride of Christ lived out her message of love, hope, and peace. With a quiet dignity that spoke volumes, the ancient Catholic remnant in the Middle East and North Africa showed the Islamic populations of those areas what might have been had there been no invasions, forced conversions, *dhimmitude*, and beheadings.

While many of the Church's critics have attacked the hierarchy, including the papacy, it would seem many moderate Muslims would love to have such a hierarchy and the voice of a leader such as the Pope. Had the string of violent events that occurred in Islam occurred in the Catholic Church, a multitude of papal announcements would have been released. The Pope would have used every opportunity to denounce the violent events. His cardinals and bishops around the world would have joined him, too.

Fortunately, the Church enjoys the luxury of not having to explain what Jesus meant. His words were (and are) clear to this day. The Church does not have to explain that the Messiah did not carry a sword into battle. The Church does not have to explain away beheadings and harems. With all its faults, the Church does not have to explain away any such events because they never happened for her as they did for Islam. Instead, the Church, like Jesus who established it, is still reaching out trying to help all around it. Jesus said there might come a time when a believer would have to leave a location and shake the dust off their feet. That time has not yet come. Even in the midst of being attacked, the Church still reaches out to all.

As a sidebar, I confess to always having had an interest in Islam. I grew up with Muslim neighbors. We played football and basketball in the winter and golf in the summer every day I can remember. I wondered what made their faith different. I also studied the Koran. I had several Middle Eastern students who were my friends in college. One year I had a Palestinian Muslim, Palestinian Christian, Lebanese Christian, and Lebanese Muslim all on the same floor of my dorm. The Muslim students I knew embraced modernity and had no use for radicals, but they told me about their fear of the extremists and of Osama Bin Laden years before I had ever heard of suicide bombings and Al Qaeda.

We do see hope against this backdrop of world terror. Walid Shoebat was a terrorist who, while debating his future wife and using her Catholic Bible to prove her wrong, found he could not. He became a Christian and wrote the book *Why I Left Jihad: The Root of Terrorism and the Return of Radical Islam.* Today he travels and speaks to audiences about his violent past and gives them hope for a Christ-filled future.

The Crusades were an attempt to protect the faithful against ruthless and intolerant violence in the land where the faith began. It would behoove us to remember that Islamic radicals are still operating under the same paradigm they were centuries ago. These radicals are not only endangering Christians but also moderates of their own faith. Because of 9/11, suicide bombers in the Middle East, terrorist attacks around the world, the Danish cartoon crisis, an Afghan man almost being beheaded for converting to Christianity, and the violent reaction to Pope Benedict's speech in Regensburg, the world is wiser to Islamic radicals.[iii]

As a result of this, we can hope that, finally, the Crusaders will be seen for what they were ... simple, faithful people who felt a call to sacrifice all they had for the faith and their brothers and sisters in Christ. Catholics have reached out to Islam since the beginning and that continues today. Pope John Paul II bent over backwards for Islam, yet the jihadists still plotted against him. Surely, in light of the horrific events of the last few years, we can now understand what the Crusaders were up against, for it is what Catholics are still up against from the forces of radical Islam.

[iii] Indonesia recently executed three Catholic Christians and denied them access to the sacraments before their deaths.

DAVID J. HARTLINE

- CHAPTER 15 -

THE CATHOLIC VOTE

Is there a Catholic vote, and if so, what does the future hold for it?

Certainly, Catholics vote, but they no longer vote in the same en masse block as they once did. For most of the time since pollsters started doing exit polls, the Democrats have typically held the Catholic vote.[kkk] Not surprisingly in 1960, John F. Kennedy received about 80 percent of the Catholic vote, but the number of Catholics voting for Democrats has gone downhill ever since. Nonetheless, the percentage of Catholics voting for Democrats in national elections has remained strong. Even with Ronald Reagan's 1984 landslide reelection victory against Democrat Walter Mondale, in which President Reagan won 49 states, Mondale still received 45 percent of the Catholic vote. How could Senator John Kerry, a Catholic who often talked of his faith, lose the Catholic vote to President George W. Bush, a Methodist who was mired in a series of negative stories and events as Election Day rolled around?

Before answering this question, let's look at what constitutes the Catholic vote. In his book, Shiflett tells of Al Regnery, the famed conservative media mogul and book publisher who left the Episcopal Communion because of its increasingly liberal leanings and became Catholic. Regnery notes that when it was revealed during the 2000 presidential campaign that then-Governor George W. Bush had been arrested some 25 years previous for drunk driving, some Evangelicals stayed home on Election Day, even though Bush was a changed man

---

[kkk] Richard Nixon was the first Republican to win the Catholic vote, which he did in his 1972 contest against George McGovern. That year also marked the beginning of the Catholic exodus out of the Democratic Party. Ronald Reagan and George H.W. Bush won the Catholic vote between 1980-88.

and had given up alcohol. Their staying at home almost cost Bush the election. Regnery said Catholics are firm in their beliefs but are also ready to forgive once the person had mended their ways, a belief Regnery admires.[1]

That aside, I contend there are three voting groups within Catholicism: liberal Catholics, middle of the road Catholics, and conservative Catholics, the latter of which I call the "pray, pay, and obey Catholics." According to George Marlin's book, *The American Catholic Voter: Two Hundred Years of Political Impact*, 17 percent of Catholic in 1994 voters dubbed themselves liberal, 39 percent moderate and 40 percent conservative. I would contend that these numbers have changed. A strictly hypothetical guess would place the numbers today at 15 percent for liberal Catholics, 37 percent for moderate Catholics and 45 percent of Catholics calling themselves conservative, the rest being undecided.[2]

By and large, liberal Catholic voters are concentrated in the Northeast and West and pockets of the Midwest, mostly in university towns. They may or may not go to Mass regularly, but they are often outspoken in their views that the Church needs to move to the left on issues of war and peace, abortion, homosexuality, and women's ordination. They believe they are championing the values of the Second Vatican Council, held between 1962 and 1965, which they believed was meant to adapt the Church to the values of the modern secular world. Among their heroes are Bl. John XXIII, retired Auxiliary Bishop of Detroit Thomas Gumbleton, and Sr. Joan Chittister, OSB.

Moderate Catholics reside in all areas of the United States. Their heroes are easy going clergy like Msgr. Thomas Hartman of the God Squad, who often appears on television with his friend Rabbi Marc Gellman to talk of unity and shared experiences.

This demographic's political and theological views are open to debate. Typically, they are against abortion but may not be adamantly so. They often disagree with the Church's stand on birth control and a celibate priesthood. This group can be persuaded to vote for almost any candidate except for one who is considered to be an avowed liberal Democrat or a very conservative Republican. There are more individuals in this group who lean conservative than liberal.

"Pray, pay, and obey Catholics" have seen their size and strength increase. They are located throughout the country but are strongest in the Midwest and South, and their numbers are noticeably growing in areas that have conservative bishops. Their heroes are figures such as John Paul II, Benedict XVI, and Mother Angelica. This group is comprised of people from all economic and ethnic backgrounds. While they often serve their parish in many ways, they are still not in as many powerful positions in diocesan offices as their liberal counterparts (who have been entrenched in Church positions of power and influence since the 1960s and 1970s).

This is perhaps the most important group to understand because is the one that is so often missed by pundits. These are those Catholics who actually go to Mass, contribute to their parish, and vote in large numbers. The 2004 presidential election was one of the first during which most pollsters asked respondents if they went to Mass regularly or were practicing Catholics. Even with those questions one might imagine the numbers being skewed because some folks might be a little reticent to admit they don't go to Mass regularly. This all goes to the heart of the matter: What is a Catholic? What makes one more likely to say one is a Catholic despite not having been inside a Catholic church in years?

For many, Catholicism is nothing more than an ethnic identity. Think of the Irish, Germans, Italians, Polish, and Latin Americans. It is often harder for people in these ethnic groups to say they are not Catholic (despite not having been to Mass since the Johnson Administration) than it is for a non-practicing Methodist to say they do not belong to that denomination. I am sure I am not alone in knowing people who haven't been inside a Catholic church in years but who nonetheless *insist* they are Catholic.

So when pollsters try to determine what constitutes the "Catholic vote," these cultural Catholics place them in a difficult position. Some may argue that Judaism also has a similar dynamic because many of those claiming to be such are simply cultural Jews; they are in no way religiously observant. However, cultural Judaism has become accepted and even expected. This is not the case with Catholics. If you tell someone, "I'm a Catholic," the expectation in that person's head is that you obviously go to Mass, Confession, and eat fish on Fridays during Lent. And yet there is this host of quasi-Catholics out there whose faith informs their political decisions not one scintilla but who nonetheless are counted as part of the "Catholic" vote.

Against this backdrop one can predict with a great deal of reliability the Catholic vote based on which "Catholic" voters attend Mass regularly or not, although some clarification is necessary.

There are 63.4 million Catholics in America.[3] If the subset that attends Mass on a weekly basis comprises between one-third and one-half of Catholics, that number is still at least 20 million people. This group is not getting any smaller. Indeed, we can expect it to grow, especially where there are conservative bishops and archbishops.

The Election of 2004

Let us examine the election of 2004. President George W. Bush, an occasionally inarticulate but steadfast Methodist, beat the verbose Catholic Senator John Kerry. More importantly, he captured the Catholic vote, becoming the first Republican to do so since his father had won the presidency in 1988. Was it because Americans felt safer with President Bush, given that Osama Bin Laden released one of his famous videotapes on the eve of the election? Was it because Senator

Kerry had acquired the tag of a flip flopper due to his many missteps, especially the infamous, "I actually did vote for the $87 billion before I voted against it"? Perhaps it might have had something to do with the fact that several bishops refused to permit Senator Kerry to receive Communion in their diocese or archdiocese due to his unwavering and staunch support for legalized abortion.

Many political analysts will argue that since Catholics have made it to the top of the ladder, they really are just like other Americans. While true on the surface, Catholics are not just like everyone else. By and large, they bring a religious dimension to their involvement in the public square that many people of other religions do not. They care deeply about issues such as workers rights, the homeless, the defenseless, and the poor. Political observers love to show how some Catholics disagree with the Church on issues like abortion, the death penalty, contraception, and gay marriage. These same people, however, ignore how many agree with the Church's stands of these issues relative to others with the same socioeconomic status.

Consequently, the most underreported dimension of the 2004 presidential election was the impact on the Catholic vote of those bishops and archbishops who refused Senator Kerry communion because of his abortion stance. The mainstream media gave people the impression that Catholics felt outrage because some bishops did this. While these bishops' actions did outrage liberal Catholics (and led to a document I will discuss in a few paragraphs), it also generated debate.

The debate centered around the Church's teachings on life. It seemed to give the upper hand to those bishops and archbishops who would have denied Senator Kerry the Eucharist because it enabled them to repeatedly explain and defend the Church's position on abortion, the right to life, euthanasia, stem cell research, homosexual marriage, and other non-negotiable positions.

When the issue of abortion and partial birth abortion are framed and debated in light of recent technology that makes it possible to see an unborn child, the pro-life side wins. When the abortion debate is framed around a women's right to choose being taken away by an institution, such as the Church or State, the pro-abortion side wins. Increasingly, Catholic pro-life leaders were getting their message out by using 4-D ultrasound images of an unborn child, which allow the public to understand what is really at stake when buzz phrases such as "ending a pregnancy" are discussed. Pictures and personal stories have been very successful when compared to the often impersonal arguments of the rights of an individual to do what he or she wants.

Even in areas of the country that did not fall under bishops who are perceived as conservative (such as Ohio and western Pennsylvania), Catholics voted for President Bush in surprising numbers. The Democrat Mayor of Youngstown, Ohio, George McKelvey even endorsed President Bush. Catholics Against Kerry, a pro-life group, organized a strong movement against him in northeast Ohio and western Pennsylvania. Time and time again, Senator Kerry had to visit these economically depressed, historically pro-Democratic areas that should have been a sure thing for him, even resorting to goose hunting to shore up his support. While Kerry won Pennsylvania by a surprisingly low 2 percent, and while he eked out a win in heavily industrialized northeastern Ohio, his efforts weren't enough for victory in the rest of the Buckeye state. Senator Kerry was hoping to build up huge margins in northeast Ohio to counter Bush's strong support in the western and southwestern parts of the state. He didn't, which meant he lost Ohio and effectively the presidential race. The reason? Many of the ethnic Catholics he hoped would be his base would not vote for him.

Anyone who does not believe a "Catholic vote" exists needs to digest the following statistics. Catholics who say they went to weekly Mass helped President Bush turn the corner in many crucial states, and they certainly kept it close in other states. In the crucial state of

Ohio, self-identified Catholics made up 26 percent of the voters, and they voted for President Bush 55 percent to 44 percent. However, Catholics who say they went to Mass weekly, voted for President Bush 65 percent to 35 percent over Senator Kerry. President Bush won the Catholic vote by 156,000 votes in Ohio. He won the entire state by 136,000 votes. Obviously, if Senator Kerry could have appealed more to those of his own faith, he would have won Ohio and the presidential election.

In the crucial state of Florida, which had the dubious distinction of deciding the 2000 presidential election, the results among Catholics were 57 percent to 42 percent for President Bush. Catholic Floridians who attend Mass weekly voted for President Bush almost 2-to-1 (or 66 percent to 34 percent).

In the liberal Northeastern states where Senator Kerry won, Catholics kept President Bush in the race. Few know of the following statistics:

- Senator Kerry won the Catholic vote in his home state of Massachusetts by just 50 percent to 49 percent.
- He lost the Catholic vote in New York 51 percent to 48 percent.
- President Bush might have won the Empire State if not for the fact that the atheists and agnostics who make up 12 percent of the New York City electorate pulled the lever for his opponent 78 percent to 19 percent.
- Kerry won New Hampshire but lost that state's Catholic vote to President Bush 63 percent to 35 percent.[4]

The aforementioned data came from CNN exit polls and have been consistent with other election data. However, it should be noted that the data from these exit polls might actually under-represent the Catholic voter who goes to Mass weekly. One can assume that some

"Catholic guilt" may come into play with those who say they go to Mass weekly but really don't. It might be easier for them to say they do. They won't fib about the candidate for whom they are voting, but they might not be totally forthright about their frequency of Mass attendance.

As for the degree of accuracy provided by exit polls, I can speak from personal experience. Some years ago, I worked for a polling company, and we were always warned about the fact that the exit data doesn't always represent the true vote. The skewed data usually involved voters saying they voted for school levies when they may not have or against candidates who were deemed outside the mainstream when they did. Therefore, one could conclude that the percentage of Catholics who attend Mass weekly and who voted against Senator Kerry was actually higher since some of those who do not regularly attend Mass might have not been totally honest, thereby skewing the data.

A skeptic could counter that the high percentage of Catholic votes for President Bush was a fluke brought on by Senator Kerry's poor campaign strategy, which snapped defeat out of the jaws of victory. A videotape released by Al Qaeda leader Osama Bin Laden the weekend before the election also helped President Bush's reelection.

However, that analysis is faulty in several ways. First, Senator Kerry was deemed to have won all three presidential debates. He was a war hero and won several medals in Vietnam (although the Swift Vets and POWs for Truth obviously did some damage to his war hero image). President Bush acknowledged Senator Kerry's honorable military service. If voters were so taken with Senator Kerry as a leader, wouldn't they have thought he was more capable of seeing to it that Osama Bin Laden was caught? If it is true that the Osama Bin Laden tape hurt him, as Senator Kerry conjectures, it was only because the voters didn't trust that he could do any better than President Bush. With all his medals and military experience, the electorate and especially the Catholic electorate still trusted and felt more comfortable with the values of the Methodist President Bush to get the job done.[5]

The fact is that faithful Catholics are growing in numbers, and they will not vote for candidates who approve of abortion or other liberal social issues (e.g., same sex marriage). Unless Democratic candidates realize this, they are going to find themselves with similar election results. In his updated, *The American Catholic Voter*, Marlin cites a University of Akron study that shows that 72 percent of faithful Catholics voted for President Bush in 2004. This is up 16 percent from the previous election, a swing that is almost unheard of in modern American politics.[6]

It does seem the Democratic Party is realizing the strength of the traditional values oriented Catholic voter. However, the Party is beholden to its increasingly radicalized liberal wing, and this fealty often comes at the expense of its traditional blue-collar base, which is socially moderate-to-conservative. The "Hollywood" wing of the Democratic Party sees abortion as being closer to a birth right or a sacrament than what many working class Democrats might see it as, which is either a tough moral decision or something akin to murder.

The Hollywood wing has pushed for the party to include a link to the radicalized pro-abortion group Catholics for a Free Choice on the Party's website. For many faithful Catholics, this group is akin to the puppet Vichy government being considered the legitimate government of France during the Nazi occupation. It was a non-starter for most Frenchman just as Catholics for a Free Choice is a non-starter for most Catholics.

While the Democratic Party's website includes a Catholics for a Free Choice link, it does not include a link to Democrats for Life. One might have expected more from the Party's then-Chairman Terry McAuliffe, who graduated from Catholic University of America. These website shenanigans and outright hypocrisy not only upset

Catholic League President William Donohue, but also Democrats for Life Executive Director Kristen Day. "Because we want to protect the rights of the unborn, our own Party says we're automatically Republicans?" she asked incredulously. "This has to be the reason that our Party is having trouble appealing to many people in churches."

Ray Flynn, who was a longtime Democratic Party stalwart, the former mayor of Boston, and an ambassador to the Vatican under President Clinton, expressed his frustration in the following statement: "So, where are we supposed to go? We still think we're old-line progressive Democrats. We're right where we always have been. We didn't move. The Democratic Party moved. It left us."[7]

All this data hasn't been lost on Democratic strategists who don't care so much about what Hollywood thinks but rather what it will take to win. The results of the 2004 election led Senator Chuck Schumer (D-NY) to recruit Pennsylvania Treasurer Robert Casey, Jr., to run against US Senator Rick Santorum (R-PA). The 2004 election results also lead Democratic Senator Harry Reid of Nevada to endorse pro-life former Indiana Congressman Tim Roemer for chairman of the Democratic National Committee. Roemer lost to Howard Dean, but many in the Democratic Party started to get the message that they needed to shift back to the middle, and this made some on the far left nervous.

Stan Greenberg, former pollster for President Clinton, drew up a memo in 2005 called "Reclaiming the White Catholic Vote." Greenberg noted that President Clinton won the white Catholic vote by 7 percent in 1996, Vice President Al Gore lost it by 7 percent in 2000 (although he won the overall Catholic vote that year), and Senator Kerry lost it by 13 percent in 2004.

After his objective factual statements, however, Greenberg's 17-page memo makes faulty assertions about Catholics.[8] For instance, Greenberg claims Catholics are only concerned about abortion and really are ambivalent about homosexuality claiming "homosexuality should be accepted rather than discouraged." Perhaps Greenburg is unaware of theological distinction between Catholics and Evangelicals on the issue of homosexuality. Unlike most Evangelical churches, who say most homosexuals choose to feel they way they do, Catholic teaching has always stated that while some individuals have an attraction towards the same sex, that behavior is "disordered" and should not be acted upon.

Greenberg goes on to say, Catholics feel "very uncomfortable with Christian evangelical groups." In this Greenberg is mistaken. As early as 1984, John Cardinal O'Connor of New York and Reverend Jerry Falwell, founder of the Moral Majority, formed a partnership for like-minded political and social goals. In 1994, Fr. Richard John Neuhaus and a host of prominent Evangelicals including Chuck Colson, the repentant Watergate burglar and founder of Prison Ministries, formed a group called "Evangelicals and Catholics Together." While Greenberg's assertion may be true for liberal Catholics, it certainly is not true for faithful Catholics, who may have theological disagreements with Evangelicals, but who often find more agreement than disagreement with them in the political realm. Election results and a variety of social issues and movements prove the validity of this assertion.

The genesis of abortion as a major campaign factor in American politics occurred during the 1984 presidential race. Cardinal O'Connor of New York was outraged over then-Democratic Governor Mario Cuomo's belief that political support for abortion was compatible with his Catholic faith. For the same reason, Cardinal O'Connor also directed his anger at the Democratic Party's vice presidential nominee Geraldine Ferraro. This delighted the "Reagan Democrats," who were largely Catholic and blue collar. Their political beliefs were moderate, even liberal on economic issues, but staunchly conservative on social issues such as abortion. They began to leave the Democratic Party after George McGovern won the Democrats' nomination for President in 1972. For this constituency, deciding whether to vote their pocketbooks or for traditional values was never a question. Thus, as a result of their concern over the nation's moral direction, many Catholic union members have supported not only GOP presidential candidates but nominally Republican Pat Buchanan's maverick presidential candidacies in the 1990s. Indeed, to the extent his bids for the White House were successful, it was in large part due to this support.

In any event, Cardinal O' Connor's admonition was one of those rare times when Catholic politicians were strongly taken to task by a member of the Church's hierarchy. While the tiff made news, little if anything happened because of it. However, the effort to get Catholic pro-choice politicians to live their lives with "integrity," as the Church put it, had begun.

The next major battle in the Catholic abortion wars came in 1992 when Pennsylvania Governor Robert Casey was denied an opportunity to speak at the Democratic Party's convention because of his pro-life views. Realizing he needed the Catholic vote, the ever-congenial Bill Clinton sent his chief political strategist James "the Ragin' Cajun"[9] to smooth things over. Carville had also managed Casey's successful run for the governor's mansion, so this made sense. Ultimately, however, he was unsuccessful in resolving the Catholic divisions within the Party.

Perhaps a greater understanding of the 1994 document "Evangelicals and Catholics Together" by Fr. Richard John Neuhaus and Charles Colson is needed. For it was after the release of this document that Catholics and Evangelicals (who started coming together under the loose alliance started by Cardinal O'Connor and Reverend Falwell) solidified a political partnership. The document was signed by a host of Catholic and Evangelical leaders. While it rankled each side's fringe elements, this document set the stage for a common front in politics.[10]

The abortion front of the culture wars experienced something of a lull in the 1990s, although there were some small skirmishes. The Monica Lewinsky scandal broke a little over a year after President Clinton had won reelection. Vice President Al Gore, who was first elected to Congress as a pro-life Democrat from Tennessee in 1976, had increasingly become more liberal on not only abortion but a whole host of other social issues. This perceived decline in moral values – along with the President vetoing several partial-birth abortion bans – helped continue the steep decline in Catholics who voted for pro-choice candidates that began under Ronald Reagan in 1980. Whatever his reasons for doing so, Clinton's failure to abolish what even many pro-abortion supporters called a heinous procedure left many Catholic voters permanently disenchanted with the "Man from Hope," as well as with anyone associated with him. This helps explain why Gore lost the white Catholic vote in 2000 (although he won the overall Catholic vote by four points). It also explains why Gore was so reluctant to campaign with his old running mate.

As noted previously, John Kerry had his own Catholic problem during the 2004 campaign. His unflinching support not just for "choice" but for abortion as a good that needed the protection of the law – coupled with many in the hierarchy's increasing refusal to give pro-choice Catholics a pass – led to many unwanted headlines for the Massachusetts blueblood. Plus, the man was simply a poor candidate. Kerry has a speaking style that makes him sound like a stiff Ivy League professor rather than someone who could identify with the average voter. All of this combined to make a nominee with whom many Catholics and other Americans were not comfortable.

Which brings us to the $1,000,000 question: "Where does the Catholic vote go in 2008?" Will the Democrats change their perspective and open themselves up to pro-life candidates? What about the Republicans? Will they stay the same conservative course? To answer these questions, let us look at some recent developments.

Many political junkies became enthralled by the successful candidacy of Tim Kaine, a pro-life and anti-death penalty Catholic who was elected governor of Virginia. Some political analysts are wondering if the Democratic Party will use examples such as Tim Kaine's pro-life candidacy to bolster their attempts at gaining the White House in 2008.

I have no doubt that many Democratic political strategists such as Stan Greenberg and James Carville would feel very comfortable nominating someone with pro-life views for the second spot on a national ticket. However, the Party's growing extremist liberal base would see this as unforgivable heresy.

These people are typically upper income and live in the urbane areas of American cities. Their affluence is often the result of jobs in the technology or creative fields like the arts. While the old left is entrenched in government jobs, their children – who largely share their parents' beliefs – now work in the private sector.

Democrats must also pay close attention to homosexual voters who, while they can be conservative, are usually more liberal than most Americans. What is more, these voters have become very politically active. They often have a good deal of disposable income since most don't have children. As a result, advertisers increasingly seek their economic power, and Democrat candidates want their votes (not to mention their campaign contributions).

As a result of this growing affluence, the left is raising a great deal of money for Democratic candidates. In 2004, Senator Kerry's campaign spending was on par with President Bush's. But the left is not going to raise money for candidates who don't tow the pro-abortion line. They have already made this abundantly clear.

In early 2005, after Democrats began doing some soul searching about the so-called "God gap" that had cost them the previous fall's election, many suggested that the Party needed to choose pro-life former Indiana Congressman Tim Roemer as its next Party chairman as a way of reaching out to socially conservative voters. In an effort to relate to this increasingly crucial part of the electorate, even Senator Hillary Clinton chimed in, saying, "We should be able to agree that we want every child born in this country to be wanted, cherished and loved."

Apparently, these warm sentiments of love for children were too much for some in the abortion crowd. The liberal magazine *American Prospect Online* reported the reaction to Senator Clinton's statement was swift. "My head nearly lifted off my shoulders and spun around, I was so mad," said one pro-choice Democrat describing her reaction to the speech given by Senator Clinton.[11]

Karen Pearl, interim president of Planned Parenthood, told the *New York Times* that if Democrats move away from their pro-abortion plank, "that could be the real birth of a third-party movement." Karen White, political director of EMILY's List, a group that raises money for female pro-abortion candidates, stated the following on the organization's website: "We fought like mad to beat back the Republicans. Little did we know that we would have just as much to fear from some within the Democratic Party."

Perhaps the best reason why Democrats will never nominate a pro-life candidate for President came from the mouths of two pro-abortion backers, one Republican and one Democrat. Republicans for Choice President Ann Stone said, "The pro-choice donors in each party tend to be the more wealthy." Finally, Planned Parenthood's Karen Pearl added, "When the day is done, I don't believe they will backslide, in part because of the importance of abortion to the Party's base of activists and contributors." In other words, it's about the money, baby.

Lest anyone think that the abortion issue scares only Democrats, one need only look at the campaign of former GOP Congressman Pat Toomey of Pennsylvania. This unknown backbencher decided to challenge Republican US Senator Arlen Specter in their Party's primary. Having already spent 24 years in the Senate, the liberal Specter had amassed a sizable war chest, and he outspent relative neophyte Toomey five-to-one. In addition, President Bush and US Senator Rick Santorum both campaigned heavily for Specter. Yet Toomey and his army of pro-life, door-knocking volunteers managed to come within a few thousand votes of defeating the pro-choice incumbent. As Marlin put it in his book, *The American Catholic Voter*, "Toomey sent shock waves through the liberal pro-abortion establishment."[12]

What does all of this mean for the 2008 presidential race? Will the pro-life debate be an issue for the Democrats? Will there be any pro-life Democratic candidates? What about the Republicans? Will there be any pro-abortion Republicans in the 2008 Presidential race? Could a pro-abortion Republican nominee ever win the Republican nomination? The answer is very simple for both parties. As mentioned before, the Democrats will never nominate a pro-life candidate for President, and the Republicans will never nominate a pro-abortion candidate for President.

Some people think former New York City Mayor Rudy Giuliani would make a good President. Certainly the nation was impressed with his leadership during the dark days following 9/11, when he helped lead his city through a crisis the likes of which few have ever seen. But if one is looking for the former mayor to change his position on abortion, that probably will never happen (although stranger things have). However, even if Giuliani was pro-life, there is the messy matter of his marriages and the public demise of his last marriage (where he had informed the public about its end and of his new relationship before he told his wife). The more the faithful Catholic finds out about this type of thing, the less chance there is for Giuliani to win the Republican nomination for President.

How about US Senator John McCain (R-AZ)? Possibly the biggest thing going against him is that he has rankled traditional Republicans with his maverick stances. Could he win the Catholic vote? Well, he is not Catholic, but he is pro-life, his wife is Catholic, and their children are receiving a parochial education. Senator McCain even opened his house to hold a fundraiser for his child's Catholic school. The senator's heroic exploits from his days in Vietnam and the injuries he still carries from that are a constant reminder of his grace and toughness under the most harrowing of circumstances.

In so many ways, the Catholic vote has come down to an individual's stance on abortion. The issue should have been the cause of a Democrat civil war, only it was never fought because so many combatants left to join the Republican side. Unlike the American Civil War, there was never a "bloody Kansas." The electorate simply chose their sides and slowly but surely, the clarion call of faith pushed more to decide to move abortion up on their list of important issues. Perhaps the Revolutionary War would be a better analogy for the abortion debate and the Catholic vote, as it was a long drawn-out affair that resulted in tremendous change, the repercussions of which are still reverberating.

Moral values as an election issue are not strictly an American phenomenon, either. Canadians also weighed in on them during their own election in January 2006.

Canada and America have seemingly gone in opposite directions as the new millennium has progressed. As with Western Europe, Canada has moved in a more liberal direction. More emphasis on social spending and the greater availability of abortion during anytime in the pregnancy has become the norm across Canada. In addition, same sex marriage was legalized within the last few years.

So it came as a surprise to many observers when Canadians elected the conservative Stephen Harper as their prime minister. Why did Canadians put Harper's Conservative Alliance into power? The war on terrorism was not an issue, as they were not attacked on 9/11 (indeed the country seems to be very much against their southern neighbor's war in Iraq).

Some say the Canadian election was all about a scandal involving the then-ruling Liberal Party. Also, during its nearly 15 years in power, they had developed a tin ear on a number of issues (not the least of which was homosexual marriage).

But voters (at least those who are Catholic) had traditionally supported the Liberals through thick and thin based on that Party's legacy of support of "social justice" and immigrant issues.

However, Catholic support began to evaporate during the 2006 election. The reason can be seen in data compiled by the Canadian polling firm Ipsos Reid. While 11 percent of Canadians as a whole felt that abortion and same sex marriage were issues that mattered, 22 percent of Catholics who attend Mass weekly believed the same. The percentage was even higher for Canadian Protestants who attended church services weekly. The data showed that even north of the border Catholics were forging alliances with like-minded Protestants.[13]

Regardless of where they live, traditional Catholic values are working their way into the electoral process. Some skeptics will argue that there really isn't a "Catholic vote," since Catholics tend to vote the same way as their upper-middle class peers. However, if yet another sign is needed that the tide is turning, practicing Catholics are voting with the Church on many social issues, regardless of their socioeconomic status. As a result, the political parties have had to adjust their messages on issues such as abortion and same sex marriage. The Catholic vote is growing stronger.

- CHAPTER 16 -

CATHOLIC SOCIAL ISSUES, SOCIAL ACTION AND GOOD WORKS

Catholics have always placed a high value on the so-called social Gospel, which is the belief that Christ's words must be put into action. Though mentioning works and salvation in the same sentence may be a no-no for many Evangelicals, it never has been for Catholics. Furthermore, while Catholicism teaches one cannot attain salvation solely by doing good works, "Faith without works is dead" (Jas. 2:17).

Because of this, Catholics have always felt that participation in the political process and helping the needy are essential (cf., *Gaudium et Spes* 75). As a matter of fact, in a 1947 address to the Congress of the International Union of Catholic Women's Leagues, Pius XII even said that to not vote *in certain circumstances* (such as "when the interests of religion are at stake") constituted "a grave sin, a mortal offense of omission."[1]

Starting in the 1980s, Catholics and Evangelicals forged political alliances around some core issues such as abortion. However, other issues – such as birth control, the death penalty, and (to some degree) homosexuality – have caused a split between Catholics and Evangelicals. While both groups share aspects of unity on these topics, there are some obvious differences.

Abortion has been a hotly debated topic as far back as ancient Greece and Rome. Aristotle thought abortions were permissible for unborn males up to 40 days after conception, while 90 days was permissible for unborn females. (Of course, Aristotle never said how one was supposed to determine the gender of a child in the womb.) With such views widely accepted during classical times, Roman prostitutes and others created a booming business for ancient abortionists.

In the face of this, the Catholic Church tried to persuade pregnant women to drop off unwanted children at places of refuge that were set up in cities throughout the Roman Empire. Indeed, the early Christians were completely against abortion. The *Didache*, the oldest non-scriptural piece of Christian writing, declared, "Thou shall not murder a child by abortion." Saints such as Clement of Alexandria, Jerome, Basil and Ambrose, to name a few, all wrote in opposition to the practice. Shortly after the year 200 AD, the Church Father Tertullian said the following concerning abortion in his letter to non-Christians: "To hinder a birth is merely a speedier man-killing, nor does it matter you take away a life that is born, or destroy one that is coming to birth. That is a man which is going to be one; you have the fruit already in the seed."

All the early Protestant Reformation leaders, including Martin Luther and John Calvin, roundly condemned abortion. The condemnation of abortion continued until very recently. Dietrich Bonhoeffer, who was a hero to many Christians for defying Adolf Hitler and to many liberal Christians for his views on war, also strongly condemned abortion.[2]

The number of women having abortions has risen and fallen throughout history. There was a sharp increase in abortions in America during the 1840s, partially due to abortionists placing newspaper advertisements. The American Medical Association was formed in 1847, and it immediately took strong action against those having abortions and abortion practitioners, strongly condemning both of them.

And while the abortion crowd has always talked about the huge toll that back alley abortions can have, even as late as the 1960s, *The Kinsey Report* stated that in 1967, doctors performed 85 percent of all abortions. Furthermore, roughly 3,000 women died from botched abortions in the years before *Roe v. Wade*, not the tens of thousands that abortion supporters claim. The number of abortion-related deaths had dropped below 100 in each of the two years preceding the Supreme Court's decision, and had been steadily dropping since 1958. Even today women die in medically supervised abortion clinics but the actual number of deaths is not known (it is probably around 100). None of this is to minimize the tragedy that occurs when a woman loses her life in this way. It is simply to say that the other side is not always accurate with its statistics, and that one should take them with a grain of salt.

In any event, prior to the 1960s, all religious denominations opposed abortion, but that decade saw the first cracks appearing in this opposition for many mainline churches. By the early 1970s, only the Roman Catholic Church was still firmly against abortion. In 1970, the Presbyterian Church stated women should have free and open access to abortions without restrictions. In that same year, the United Methodists, United Church of Christ, and the Evangelical Lutheran Church of America all declared themselves open to abortion as an option for women (although their statements' wording was not as open-ended as the Presbyterians' position). Even the Southern Baptist Convention, the most conservative Protestant denomination, said abortion could be an option for women who might suffer from the psychological distress of a child.

Christianity Today magazine (*CT*) noted that 1971 was the last year they would refer to "therapeutic abortions." As late as 1968, 25 Evangelical theologians said the following: "Whether or not the performance of induced abortion is sinful we are not agreed, but the necessity of it and the permissibility of it under certain circumstances we are in accord." None other than the revered Southern Baptist leader W.A. Criswell, an early friend to Catholics, African Americans, and other minorities said, "I have always felt that it was only after a child was born and had life separate from its mother that it became an individual person, and it has always therefore, seemed to me that what was best for the mother and for the future should be allowed."[3] *CT* said of this comment, "It would be years before such a statement from an Evangelical leader would be unthinkable." Thankfully, Pastor Criswell later repudiated his remarks and became a staunch pro-lifer.

Dr. R. Albert Mohler, Jr., president of the Southern Baptist Theological Seminary in Louisville, KY, noted this about abortion in the *Christian Post*: "The early Evangelical response to legalized abortion was woefully inadequate. Some of the largest Evangelical denominations approved at first some version of abortion on demand."

The reason, according to *CP*, was that "evangelicals simply could not imagine themselves lining up with Roman Catholics, nor could they imagine that the Supreme Court of their beloved nation (which they thought of as Protestant) would support a cause directly opposed to Christian values."

Consequently when the US Supreme Court legalized most abortions in its infamous January 1973 *Roe v. Wade* decision, the Catholic Church was the only major denomination to take political and social action against it. The Southern Baptist Convention actually passed a resolution in favor of the decision. And while many Evangelical pastors thundered about the Court's verdict from their pulpits, most Evangelicals at that time didn't believe in political or social involvement. The idea of Evangelical social action would not enter the political world until Jerry Falwell started the Moral Majority in 1980.

As pointed out in a retrospective on abortion in *Christianity Today*, when the Supreme Court issued its ruling, "few in the media realized the impact it would have on the Christian world. *Time* magazine gave the *Roe v. Wade* decision two pages in the back of its edition, while *Newsweek* gave it one. An editorial in the *Christian*

Century magazine stated, 'This is a beautifully accurate balance of individual vs. social rights. It is a decision both pro-abortionists and anti-abortionists can live with.'"[4]

When the Moral Majority was started and began interacting with Catholic groups of similar thought, the political left thundered that this portended an intrusion by the Church into the lives of individuals. The political left had no problem with the Catholic Church becoming politically active to help Dr. Martin Luther King, Jr., during the civil rights movement. When the Catholic Church stood up for the civil rights of the unborn, however, the political left was appalled.

A surprising turn of events occurred in the late 1990s. The pro-life movement and the Catholic Church in general received a surprising convert. The famous "Jane Roe" of *Roe v. Wade* fame, Norma McCorvey, left the abortion movement in part because she felt like it had used her. She was initially brought to Christ and out of the culture of death through the efforts of Evangelical minister Flip Benham, although she refused to say which denomination she had chosen. McCorvey stated she was still discerning her Christian identity. In 1998, she came into the Catholic Church. She currently heads Crossing Over Ministries in Texas, which does outreach to all those affected by abortion. She has assisted Priests for Life Director Fr. Frank Pavone (and continues to do so).

The pro-life issue is a difficult one to measure through polling data. Polls seem to shift wildly, and the wording used in framing the questions is often crucial. Ramesh Ponnuru's book *The Party of Death* outlines this and the general political trends taking place vis-à-vis abortion. Through books like Ponnuru's, the defensive posture of pro-abortion Catholic politicians, and the recent appointments to the Supreme Court of Justice Samuel Alito and Chief Justice John Roberts, it is clear that the pro-life side is on the offensive. The tide is turning toward life.

The death penalty also is an important issue for many Catholics. Yet other Christian denominations do not share the Catholic Church's general opposition to it. Many Evangelicals were elated when the Supreme Court ruled that the death penalty was a legal form of punishment in 1976. Evangelicals (as well as many Americans) felt that the death penalty might deter violent acts and was a just punishment for crimes such as murder.[III] Thirty years later, we are still not any less violent or safer than we were in 1976. Although it once allowed capital punishment (and still does to some extent), why does the Church today not support the death penalty? Also, has the Church swayed anyone who did believe in it?

The Church has said that one of the overriding reasons for its opposition to the death penalty is the fact that crime is not stopped because an individual believes he or she might be executed. Most crimes are spontaneous acts committed by individuals who have little or no guidance in their lives. They are selfish people acting out of a sense of "me" and not "we." Thus the fear of execution does not factor in when they are making a decision (to the extent that their crime *is* a decision).

More importantly than the possibility that it may have no deterrent effect, however, the Church feels that executing the guilty person takes away their chance for repentance as well as their opportunity to witness to those in prison and on the outside. Perhaps no other example is a better illustration of this than what occurred with a Texas inmate in 1999.

Carla Faye Tucker participated in a gruesome, drug-induced murder in 1975. Her mother used drugs, and Carla fell into that lifestyle as well. After her incarceration, Carla changed her life and became a born again Christian. By all accounts, her conversion was real and spectacular. As the date came for her execution in 1999, many activists, including conservative religious commentator Rev. Pat Robertson, lobbied then-Texas Governor George W. Bush to

---

[III] Of course, so do many Catholics, as this is a subject on which faithful Catholics may disagree.

commute her sentence to life in prison.

All attempts to commute Tucker's sentence ended in her 1999 execution. The story resurfaced again in the 2000 presidential race. Conservative columnist Tucker Carlson left an interview with Bush shocked at what he sensed was the governor's callous mocking of Tucker. Carlson said he mocked her pleas for her life.[5] The Bush camp hurriedly released a statement saying Carlson misunderstood what the governor had said. The statement went on to say he was happy that she had turned her life around, but he could not commute the sentence handed down by a Texas judge.

Therein the whole "eye for an eye" theology was laid bare and empty. Here was a woman who was genuinely repentant, and whose life could have been used as a powerful witness to other incarcerated individuals, but who now would be simply a memory. The Catholic Church's reminder of Jesus' admonishing those who live by the philosophy of an "eye for an eye" (cf. Mt. 5:38-39) may have fallen on deaf ears at the time. However, as with many of the teachings of the Catholic Church that were initially misunderstood, the Church was supported by the unlikeliest of allies (i.e., death penalty supporter Pat Robertson).

As for George W. Bush, many Catholics would go on to greatly respect his leadership as he guided the country through the post September 11, 2001, crisis, the Iraq War and many other crises. However, for many Catholics, the Carla Faye Tucker incident would be Bush's low point and one many would never quite understand.

A cynic might wonder how the tide could be turning if a majority of Americans support the death penalty. While this is true, clearly inroads have been made. As previously noted, Virginia Gov. Tim Kaine won election in the conservative state of Virginia despite his anti-death penalty stance. In Maryland, conservative and death penalty opponent Lt. Governor Michael Steele was the Republican nominee to be that state's US Senator. Although Catholic, both men come from different backgrounds: Kaine is white and from a conservative southern state, Steele is black and hails from a liberal state, yet each opposes capital punishment. The death penalty's popularity has been slipping in recent years, and it is in part because of the courageous stands taken by men such as Kaine and Steele.[mmm]

Birth Control

Many people, including most Catholics, do not understand the Church's teachings on birth control. Surely they will say there is no way the tide is turning towards the Church's position on this. However, recent developments are showing even on this contentious issue Catholics and Evangelicals are increasingly coming to see the wisdom of the Church's position. In the post-nuclear family age, the Church's teachings on this subject that may seem to be out of an ancient era. However, the Church's teachings on contraception were agreed upon by every Christian denomination until 1930, when the Anglican/Episcopal Church became the first to allow birth control.

The Church recognizes there are certainly many days in the month when sexual relations cannot lead to pregnancy, and it condones sexual activity during these times for those who have a compelling reason to avoid conception (e.g., legitimate poverty, etc.). Indeed, pregnancy is always a long shot to begin with. Even when couples in their 20s and 30s try to time sexual relations in a way that will lead to conception, they achieve success just 25 percent of the time. Regardless, the Church teaches that every sexual act *must* be open to the transmission of life.

When people ignore this age-old wisdom, negative consequences arise. Perhaps the most illustrative example of this can be seen in the dangerously low childbirth rates in Western Europe that are threatening civilization there.[nnn] Several European powerhouse

---

[mmm] Furthermore, according to the Death Penalty Information Center, "A 1995 Hart Research Poll of police chiefs in the U.S. found that the majority of the chiefs do not believe that the death penalty is an effective law enforcement tool."

economies, especially those of Great Britain and Germany, face a ticking time bomb as the numbers of those still working cannot support those who will soon retire. Demographers say that for a nation to replenish its population, the average woman must have 2.1 children over the course of her life. No nation in western Europe, however, is at that level. Ireland comes the closest at 1.9 births per woman. Italy is 1.24 births per woman. Indeed, the only country in all of Europe that has a near-replacement level fertility rate is predominantly Muslim Albania.

Partly as a result of such factors, even Protestant commentators have begun questioning their once rock solid support for birth control.

Agnieszka Tennant, senior associate editor of *Christianity Today*, surprised many in Evangelical circles when she wrote a tell-all article about her experience with birth control and later her rejection of it.

"[The oral contraceptive] Mircette and I became one shortly before my wedding day. In a way, my union with the wallet-sized green box of 28 pills was more complete than the bond I had with my husband."

Tennant went on to note that Dr. Walter Larimore, who is often heard on Dr. James Dobson's "Focus On the Family" radio show, is concerned that the Pill may cause spontaneous abortions. Tennant concludes her article by stating, "I want my faith to be ... imaginative. When Jesus appears on my doorstep – disguised as a cluster of 128 cells or a single mother who could use some free baby-sitting – He'd better find an open door."[6]

Evangelical leaders such as Charles Colson have pointed out the dangers brought to bear when a society has low birth rates and high rates of sexual activity outside of marriage. However, the Catholic Church's teaching on birth control may have had its unlikeliest supporter in Dr. Mohler. He has often debated Catholic leaders

---

[nnn] Compare this to the booming fertility rates amongst Muslims, both in the countries in which they are indigenous and in those where they have migrated.

on topics ranging from salvation to papal authority. However, his comments on birth control raised a few eyebrows across the country.

"A growing number of Evangelical Christians are rethinking the issue of birth control and facing the hard questions posed by reproductive technologies," he wrote in *The Christian Post*. He went on to talk about, of all things, *Humanae Vitae*, Paul VI's encyclical on birth control. "We should look closely at the Catholic moral argument as found in *Humanae Vitae*," he said. "Evangelicals will find themselves in surprising agreement with much of the encyclical's argument. As the Pope warned, widespread use of the Pill has led to serious consequences including marital infidelity and rampant sexual immorality. In reality, the Pill allowed a near-total abandonment of Christian sexual morality in the larger culture. Once the sex act was severed from the likelihood of childbearing, the traditional structure of sexual morality collapsed."[7]

These are strong words of support coming from someone who has often questioned the papacy's very legitimacy.

Like-minded people and those who disagreed with Mohler immediately commented on his argument. Evangelicals such as Charles Colson saw the ills that have been created by a society that revels in programs such as hit HBO program "Sex and the City," whose whole premise would not be possible without the Pill. Another hit is the show "Desperate Housewives," which shows sexually active women doing what sexually active men on television did for years. Somehow the television audience is supposed to think this portrays equality. Many Christians have found it to simply demonstrates the sadness of modern mores and serves as yet another message from the media that premarital and extramarital sex are fine as along as one uses birth control.

But while society seems to be undermining Christian ethics at break-neck speed, there are signs that tide is beginning to turn. The fact that these signs come from Evangelicals such as Dr. Mohler, Charles Colson, and prominent writer Agnieszka Tennant makes it all the more special that Christian unity is starting to be achieved on this front. Perhaps the battle will soon be joined in full and then taken to the general society.

Disaster Relief

The world has seen a number of terrible disasters in the last few years, and when it comes to relief efforts, no groups have been as visible as Catholic Charities and Catholic Relief Services (CC deals with all emergencies and cases of need in the United States, while CRS handles these situations outside the United States). Whether it was the south Asian tsunami of late 2004, the Pakistani earthquake of 2005, Hurricane Wilma's pummeling of Mexico in 2005, or the worst natural disaster to hit America in decades, Hurricane Katrina, CRS and CC were there to assist those in need. The work of CC and CRS often goes unseen or unreported, but with the spate of natural disasters that have hit the globe, this is less and less the case; their work has been seen and noticed. Indeed, outside of the Red Cross, these two organizations are perhaps the world's best-known relief agencies. They provide a helping hand and a true witness of faith in action no matter the faith of the victim.

Evangelicals started getting involved en masse with relief help in the 1980s. Reverend Pat Robinson's "700 Club" television program organized food drives across the United States. In addition, Robinson's group sent physicians to Latin America to treat and provide various forms of care to those suffering. In the aftermath of Hurricane Katrina, Evangelical church groups poured into the affected regions of Louisiana, Mississippi, and Alabama.

While Evangelical groups have been assisting the needy of the areas devastated by Hurricane Katrina in great numbers, it has been the organization, know-how, and resources of the CC that have brought hope to the needy for decades. As governments on the local, state and national levels, failed to cope with the aftermath of the hurricane, Catholic Charities was there doing its best to help millions in perhaps the most trying situation they have ever faced on US soil.

On the heels of Hurricane Katrina came Hurricane Rita. Although it did substantial damage, it was not as bad Katrina, praise God. In any other year, Hurricane Rita would have seemed a disaster of epic proportions were it not for the millions of people who left the Houston and Galveston areas prior to Rita's making landfall. Hurricane Wilma, the last major hurricane of the season, caused severe damage to Mexico's Yucatan Peninsula and then slammed west to east across southern Florida. Again, were it not for the extraordinary destruction wrought by Katrina, Wilma would have been the worst hurricane of the season.

All told Catholic Charities collected $154 million dollars for relief efforts, and the St. Vincent DePaul Society collected $1.6 million more and provided assistance for individuals to obtain millions in grants. In addition, the Knights of Columbus collected $4.2 million, and Catholic school children even got into the act, collecting a little over $1 million for Hurricane Katrina victims.[8]

Catholics also filled up their parishes' collection plates and showed their generosity in ways large and small. For instance, Pat Schmitz, a Grand Knight for the Knights of Columbus Council in Powell, Ohio, felt moved by his pastor's plea to assist the needy in the hurricane-ravaged areas on the Gulf Coast. He and many others plan to continue their assistance to the needy of the Gulf Coast long after its effects leave the collective memory.

Because of the efforts of so many large-hearted Catholics, some in the Gulf Coast are beginning to see signs of hope. Fr. Steve Bruno, a parish priest at St. Elizabeth Ann Seton in Kenner, Louisiana, said, "I have witnessed a resurgence of faith, a realization of how life is, and an appreciation of the 'important things' in life." While Fr. Bruno noted that tensions can be high because of two or more families living under one roof, he also noted signs of hope with the young and their tremendous ability to bounce back.

I noted this myself while attending the 2005 National Catholic Youth Convention in Atlanta a few months after Katrina struck. A large of group of young people from the areas effected by the hurricane attended the convention. The fact that some even made it to Atlanta was a story in and of itself. These young people wanted to tell all who would listen about the many spiritual lessons they had learned. They also thanked all who were in attendance for their generosity. Their witness was a powerful show of faith for the rest of the attendees.

Of course, the call to serve hits some people differently than it does others. Joel Torczon of Bakersfield, California envisioned retiring in 15-20 years and playing endless rounds of golf. "I wanted to catch up on all those years that I couldn't get on the course enough to satisfy my golfing hunger," he said.

However, a funny thing happened: Torczon realized God wanted him to serve.

"When I look to retirement now, I envision helping the poor either in this country or in some remote part of the world," Torczon told me. "I want to serve their material needs, but most importantly I want to aid them in their spiritual needs."[9]

Catholicism has always been about putting faith into action. It is not enough to simply be faithful; rather, faith must be exercised like a muscle or it will grow flaccid, weak, and eventually atrophy. Unfortunately, Catholics have often been alone in their efforts to help the poor downtrodden and disposed (witness the Church being the only Christian religious body to have always opposed abortion). The growing number of *mea culpa* remarks by some of the Protestant world's leading spokesmen stand as testimony to this. But they also show a growing awareness by many that this is an area where the Church has really gotten it right. As such, it is another sign that the tide is turning.

- CHAPTER 17 -

NOW YOU SEE ... THE TIDE IS TURNING

It is clear from all we have seen in the first years of this new millennium that the tide is turning towards Catholicism. While in a broader sense it is turning towards traditional Christianity, in its most specific sense it is turning towards the Church. We see the broader sense in the various alliances between the Catholic Church and other churches and communions that respect Christian orthodoxy. Since Christians are turning towards the traditional, Catholics should be excited about the fact that our Church will grow because of this. Why will the megachurches soon peak? Considering their acceptance of any and all beliefs and lifestyles, why haven't the liberal churches been more successful in attracting more members? Faithful Catholics understand that being orthodox is the only way the Church has ever grown. Experiments to the contrary have been a disaster.

Sometimes when I hear those who question, attack, or belittle the Catholic Church, I cannot help but think of the voice of God answering Job after that man questioned God and His ways (cf., Job 38-40). Do those who belittle the Mass not understand the significance of the bodily presence of Jesus in the Eucharist or the beauty of chant or the singing of the Schubert's "Ave Maria"? Do they not fathom the simple beauty of sharing morning Mass with just a few dozen others? What about the beauty of the sacraments and their communal nature that bind together the various passages of life from baptism through communion and confirmation, then to marriage, and culminating in death? How could one not be in awe of the presence of God in a child's baptism or first Holy Communion? What about Confirmation and a child becoming an adult in the eyes of the Church? What about a Catholic wedding? Haven't you felt more spiritually connected after leaving a Catholic wedding Mass than after having left a simple 20-minute Protestant ceremony? Why would anyone reject the family bond of these sacraments and passages of life?

Perhaps Bishop Campbell of Columbus (who earned his doctorate in History) said it best when referring to the peaks and valleys of the Church's history.

"If anyone is under the illusion that we have been through a rough stretch with scandals or with the decline in vocations we witnessed in the '70s and '80s, they have no idea of Church history," he said. "We have seen far worse, and now, with the worst of the abuse scandal behind us and with vocations on the rise, we are moving in the right direction. Somehow we have managed to get through all of that in 2,000 years, and I think that speaks volumes about who we are and what we are about."[1]

In Catholicism's darkest days untold suffering has been both self-inflicted and inflicted upon us by others. No exact records exist for the thousands of martyrs who died for the Catholic faith before Constantine legalized Christianity in 325 AD. Yet the Faith persevered and ultimately became the official religion of the Roman Empire. While this was happening, the Church had to combat Arianism (this was the movement started by Arius ca. 320 AD who questioned the divinity of Christ by equating Him more with a social activist than a messiah).[2]

Later in Rome, just as Christianity was beginning to ascend, the Roman Empire collapsed. The Church became the unofficial educator and de facto government in Europe when all civil institutions ceased to exist. It kept society from disintegrating. The collapse of the Roman Empire coupled with barbarian invasions from the north made for a tough go in Europe. However, with the help of Irish priests and missionaries, along with St. Benedict, who shaped the monastic movement, Europe began to blossom again and grow.

Still, all of this turmoil made Europe an easy target for invasion. Islamic warriors first invaded the Middle East and southern Europe in the eighth and ninth centuries. Successive waves of invading Muslims committed countless atrocities, leaving thousands dead in their wake. Today, against almost insurmountable odds, Catholic communities continue to exist throughout the Middle East. They are small and getting smaller, yet they remain. Spain was almost completely conquered by Muslim armies, but Christian forces ultimately persevered and, as a result, Spain is a Catholic country.[3]

What about the Church's self-inflicted problems during the Middle Ages and beyond? Some contend there were even popes who secretly married, cavorted with mistresses (Popes John XII and Alexander VI are examples of this) or engaged in violent acts. Despite occasionally being led by bad men, the Church still survives. How many other institutions would have crumbled under the weight of all this sin and decadence? Yet God saw fit for the Church to find the right people to save it, just like He did for His chosen people, Israel.

More than a few skeptics, both Protestant and Catholic, have raised an eyebrow when I have put forward my thesis that the tide is turning towards Catholicism. Some are polite and say, "Oh, you think the tide is turning towards Catholicism? I thought it was turning away from Catholicism." Others can hardly contain their skepticism: "What about the abuse scandal? How can the tide possibly be turning with that still over our heads?" Some have accused me of being my usual hopeful self, but I think our faith is about hope. Anyway, I believe I have outlined all the reasons in the previous chapters but some probably are still not satisfied. They will say to me, "Dave, you have no idea the damage the abuse scandal has caused the Church. Look at the late night comedians. It has been open season since the abuse scandal broke out. Everything –

DAVID J. HARTLINE

from the priesthood to the Eucharist – has been lampooned. So how can you say the tide be turning?!" Often they end their criticism by saying, "You have no idea what some of these people, parishes, and dioceses went through, so it's really hard for you to make this judgment." That's where they're wrong.

My childhood parish went through one of the worst abuse scandals in the region. My diocese reportedly paid out more to the victims in my parish than it did in any other case of abuse. The worst of the guilty priest's abuses occurred when I was in the seventh and eighth grade, and I remember that time well. Let me first say that I was not abused as I understand it, but certainly my friends and I experienced many unwanted remarks and touches. We all seemed to hope that maybe Father wasn't sure of what he was saying. I was *sure* he didn't understand the sexual innuendos he was making. Time would tell us a different story.

There was the obligatory trip to this priest's lakefront cabin that was often the topic of much conversation and teasing. I was never there, but it was a dreadful experience for those who were, one full of sexual remarks and pranks. This took place in the presence of other priests who delighted in being around adolescent boys. There are other stories far too explicit to mention. I often wonder what toll this behavior took on some I grew up with and knew so well.

It rarely is mentioned these days and for good reason. The priest in question was laicized from priesthood after the events came to light in the late 1980s. He spent time in jail.°°° Thankfully, compared to some dioceses, my diocese was barely touched by the abuse scandal.

°°° Like this priest, it is interesting that, to my knowledge, none of those convicted of sexual abuse were even remotely orthodox. My pastor painted over frescoes in the church and replaced the altar crucifix with an empty, wood cross over a whitewashed wall because a "new Church" was coming. He gave pride of place to the banal, adenoidal, atonal modern liturgical music, and only grudgingly allowed one or two old classics to slip into the repertoire when absolutely necessary. He tried to foist so-called liturgical dance onto an unsuspecting, blue collar parish. I could go and on about him. Read the stories of his partners in crime, and these

Our local bishops seemed to listen to their conscience instead of those in the medical community who said men like this could be "reformed with secular psychiatry."[4]

Those events transformed many of my friends and me. Some chose to leave or have little to do with the Church, but many are still active and trying to do their best with what God gave them in life. There is a school of thought that states that vocations or church involvement can come from parishes that were hit with scandal because some were so incensed by what they saw, they felt they had to take some action.

Perhaps that is why I do what I do. For years I have worked for the Church as a teacher, coach, principal, and as a diocesan administrator. My time is now devoted to writing (my CatholicReport.org blog and, hopefully, more books) as well as speaking. I get particularly upset at groups, organizations, or schools of thought that think the Church must change her doctrines because of these evil men and those that protected them. I take the opposite view: To change the Church would be to go against what God has taught us in the last 2,000 years. When the Church strays from her teachings and morality is blurred, a climate exists for events like the abuse scandal to occur. The Church could not have survived 2,000 years without the guidance of the Holy Spirit, and His truth does not change. There have been mistakes and scandals, but one must stare evil in the eye, not accommodate it. That is the message I take out of all that I saw.

For years men were accepted into the priesthood because most in the Church believed it when these individuals told them that

---

men were indistinguishable in respect to their deconstructionist tendencies (i.e., that they wanted to deconstruct everything that had heretofore made the Church great). The only exception I'm aware of is a priest I was told of from the Diocese of Sacramento. Reportedly, he would quote John Paul II's encyclicals at length, gave great homilies period, and was exceedingly reverent when celebrating the Mass. He was accused of molesting two youths and removed from ministry. Although no determination of guilt or innocence has been made known, one news source says he "no longer serves as [a priest]."

they felt the clerical life is where God wanted them. Only later did we learn that some abusive priests felt the priesthood was a safe place for them to hide sexual feelings they did not understand or want to explain.

Starting in the 1990s (and with even greater vigor after the abuse scandal broke), the Church took a harder look at candidates for the priesthood. In a conversation before the scandal came to light, a vocations director told me, "I have had some men in their 30s and 40s come into my office and say, 'I think I am supposed to be a priest.'" When he asked them what made them think so, some told him, "Well, I haven't had a date in a couple of years, so I think that's a sign." The vocations director went on to say, "Did you ever think that if God wanted you to be a priest, maybe you would have dates every week but still feel unfulfilled?" He told me the candidates are so puzzled when he asks that question, most can't even respond.

The priesthood cannot be a refuge from life's problems, whatever those may be. There are so many who need help, but you can't help them if you are seeking refuge. The vocations director also said, "Now you know why I have to turn down more men than I [accept]. Otherwise, no one would be happy. It would not be a happy place for these men and certainly not for those in their parish."

That vocations director made those comments to me several years ago. However, it is a different story today. In the last few years the quality of candidates studying for the priesthood has greatly increased. Almost gone are the days of lost men thinking the priesthood might be a happy escape from the trials and tribulations of life. The seriousness of the mission and the newfound emphasis on getting the right candidate has steered away many of those men who might have otherwise once been accepted by seminaries.

There can be a further discussion as to when the tide started turning. Some will argue it began in 1978, the year Pope John Paul II was elected pontiff. It could also be argued that the tide started to turn when President Ronald Reagan appointed the first US ambassador to the Vatican in 1981. This initially caused some uproar among Evangelicals, but it eventually resulted in closer working relationships between these people and Catholics.

Some would argue that Denver's 1993 World Youth Day was a turning point because young people overcame many obstacles and showed up in great numbers. Still others might say it was the 1994 "Evangelicals and Catholics Together" document, which created not only a closer working relationship on a host of issues but also resulted in the Catholic Church being further accepted into the mainstream of religious, political, and cultural life. Finally, it could be argued that the tide did not start to turn until the death of Pope John Paul II. With the election of Pope Benedict seemingly cementing the legacy of "John Paul the Great" and the worst of the abuse scandal behind the Church, one could say that the tide really didn't start to turn until all of these factors were in place.

Wherever one believes the tide began turning, there can be no doubt that change is afoot, and its force is being felt in all areas of life. Whether it is more fidelity to the teachings of the Church by Catholics, the growing importance of the faithful Catholic vote, or the cultural influences in film, music, and sports, the tide has turned, and the evidence of it shows in all of these areas.

To some, the Church may have seemed adrift for much of the 1970s, but there can be no doubt that under the leadership of John Paul II and Benedict XVI, the barque of Peter is slowly getting back on course. We also see the effects of strong leadership in dioceses where the priests and bishops adhere to the teachings of the Church. Vocations are up, schools and parishes are becoming more solid, and the faithful have responded by donating their service and gifts.

There was a time when Catholics almost sheepishly took grief from some fundamentalist door knockers about their faith. The new defenders are arming Catholics with answers to the door knockers' questions. To many Catholic defenders or apologists, it almost seemed ludicrous that Catholics would be "called out" for their devotion to Mary, belief in Purgatory, recitation of the rosary, and belief in apostolic succession. Most of these beliefs have been practiced since some of those who knew Christ were still alive.

Knowing this history and the biblical citations for these beliefs, many Catholic "new defenders" are answering back with the Catholic teachings from Scripture and Tradition. The logical question would be if some of these Evangelicals are such sticklers for Scripture, why don't they have the same beliefs we have had since Christianity's infancy, the apostolic era?

Some from the mainline Protestant churches have left these institutions to attend Evangelical churches or even Catholic parishes as a result of not always being guided by a firm hand. This is understandable because Jesus was a forceful leader. Those who listened to Jesus marveled at His directness and lack of the aloofness that was so often a trait of ancient Israel's religious leaders. Jesus recognized that a firm set of rules was necessary for His Church to survive. With that firmness came love and forgiveness. Today the Church reaches out to all, wanting and desiring them to come home. However, it must be on God's terms, not mankind's. This is what often sets the Catholic Church apart from other churches and communions. The Catholic Church has a sacred responsibility to reach out to others while at the same time reminding them they cannot make decisions and laws on their own. One must follow the ways Jesus set for us.

The "Evangelicals and Catholic Together" document was the first sign in the post-Cold War era that separated believers could overcome theological differences. This document was created in order to give orthodox Christians a voice in a society that was increasingly becoming hostile to traditional voices of faith. It was also a reaction to a society where religion is increasingly being relegated to the museum or where religion is seen as just another lifestyle or social service agency as opposed to the nation's foundation. In any event, Catholics and Evangelicals found a way to come together. Let us hope that they continue to do so and in ways that are not just political, but theological, as well.[5]

The Catholic Church has a great deal in common with the Anglican/Episcopal Communion. Even the Lutheran Communion and the Catholic Church share a great deal. While one might not hear a Catholic or Lutheran say such a thing, one would definitely hear it from other churches, especially Evangelicals. Increasingly, both faiths have been reaching out to each other. This openness has led to the creation of several documents that convey the common beliefs of the Lutheran Communion, the Anglican/Communion, and the Catholic Church, and that gives hope for true Christian unity. (The only fly in the ointment is the increasingly liberal direction of the Anglican/Episcopal denomination.)

The hope for unity has led many Catholics, Lutherans, and Episcopalians to envision a day when these churches could become one. Some Lutherans were upset when Richard John Neuhaus became a Catholic priest. However, Fr. Neuhaus has said he could not wait forever. He wanted to see Christian unity in his lifetime, so he joined the Church his Lutheran denomination left some 500 years ago.

The change for Scott Hahn was also deliberate. His conversion to the Catholic Church was not as well noticed as Neuhaus'. However, his prolific writing and his St. Paul Center for Biblical Theology have been responsible for much fruit in the Catholic world.

Perhaps one of the most noteworthy Evangelical conversions to Catholicism in this new millennium came from Alex Jones, an African-American Pentecostal minister in Detroit. He struggled with the haunting question as to why God would permit Catholicism to exist for 1,500 years. He consulted with Steve Ray, another Evangelical convert, and though Jones' wife was somewhat hostile at first, they both eventually came into the Church. Jones is now a Catholic deacon and popular on the speaking circuit.[6]

Recently two conservative Protestant theologians, Craig Blomberg, a Baptist, and Donald Hagner, an Evangelical, have surprised their constituencies with their remarks about St. Peter and his role in the early Church. Blomberg says, "The play on words between Peter's name (*Petros*) and the word rock (*petra*) makes sense only if Peter is the Rock and if Jesus is about to explain the significance of this identification."

Donald Hagner says this about Peter: "The frequent attempts that have been made, largely in the past (that Peter is the rock) in favor of the view that the confession itself is the rock ... seem to be largely motivated by Protestant prejudices against a passage that is used by the Roman Catholics to justify the papacy."[7]

The contention that most Protestant scholars make against the papacy is that Jesus never meant for there to be apostolic succession as understood by Catholics. These solons don't believe Jesus was saying Peter would be the first of 265 popes. Now we see two well-respected Protestant theologians who back up Catholic contentions that Jesus meant exactly what He said regarding Peter being the "rock" on which He would build His Church.[PPP]

Doug Henry, a professor at the Southern Baptist Convention-affiliated Baylor University, took some heat when he visited the Vatican and wrote that Baptists simply can't go it alone forever. He wrote there are some truths in Catholicism. His sympathy for a Baptist Magisterium, however, drew howls of disapproval from tried and true Baptists. They retorted that the Bible is their Magisterium.[8] It was a shame that someone didn't ask these people why they keep putting God in a box. God can't continue working authoritatively through people past the year 100 AD? This was roughly the year the last Book of the New Testament, the Book of Revelation, was written. Why can't God continue to confirm His faithful in the truth

---

[PPP] More on this subject can be found on the Catholic Answers website at www.catholic.com.

through the magisterial combination of Scripture and Tradition, as Catholics believe? As Mark Shea put it, with the arguments made by Blomberg, Hagner, and Henry, perhaps some Evangelicals were starting to look beyond "my personal truth of the moment."

Mark Noll left Wheaton College for Notre Dame so he could pursue his idea of Christian unity. Noll teaches Religion, but he was not just any professor. As a matter of fact, he was considered to be one of Evangelicalism's most distinguished minds. Wheaton Provost Stan Jones said, "I think he helped us break caricatures of Evangelical anti-intellectualism." While Noll wasn't converting like Hahn had, he was making it known that he felt more at home in a Catholic intellectual setting.[9]

Perhaps the biggest surprise to come out of Wheaton College was the firing of Professor Joshua Hochschild, who converted to Catholicism on Easter 2004. Hochschild is a medieval philosophy scholar, and few in that field are anything but Catholic, so the move wasn't a surprise. Some Catholics had no trouble with Wheaton's decision. They actually wished that Catholic colleges were as committed to their beliefs. In any event, this is yet another story of an orthodox Christian pondering how Catholicism could have survived 2,000 years, and over 1,500 years before Luther came on the scene, if it were not on the course that God intended it.[10]

The drive towards unity does not always sit well with the true blue of each faith. One might be surprised to type in "Catholic" or "Evangelical" in an Internet search engine and see how many results are negative, especially among Evangelicals. It may be hard to picture Evangelicals such as Rick Warren, Chuck Colson, or Charles Stanley being called sellouts and liberals, but it does often happen on the worldwide web. Even faithful Catholic sites can be leery of or hostile to talk about Christian unity. Often the most militant talk comes from converts to Catholicism who do not want any part of what they left behind.

Columbus policeman Larry Newman says one of the greatest joys about being Catholic is the world unity. "Being a convert I love the symbols and traditions the Church has," said Newman. "The history of the Church is intellectually appealing to me. I was very active in the church I left, and I had no plans to convert. But as I began to understand my wife's faith, I began to see the beauty of Catholicism. Of all things, it really hit me on a family cruise. We were on the ship with people from all over the United States and the world. While we all couldn't understand each other, we all understood the Mass that was held on board. It was a feeling of great unity and joy."

There have been a number of people who have addressed the topic of being happy about our Catholic faith in light of so much misunderstanding about it. Catholic author Kathy Coffey gave a talk in Texas, and the transcript of the talk was reprinted in *Catholic Update*. In her talk she lists her Top Nine reasons for being Catholic.

Before Kathy gives her Top Nine list, however, she asks a very important question, using an illustration from Jn. 6:67: "Do you also want to leave?" She makes note of how many times Jesus tried to be a balm to sooth the apostles' aches and pains, only for them to engage in incessant quarreling.[11]

I will only relate the first three reasons she mentions:

1. We are community.
2. Catholicism is universal
3. Catholics make bold claims.

We are a community that shares the same liturgy. The Mass is our way of remembering Jesus and re-presenting (as opposed to recreating) His eternal sacrifice. "Do this in remembrance of me," Jesus said. We do as He asked, and that is one reason why the Mass is so important to us. It has been done this way through the centuries. If one were to be transported back in time to the catacombs of Rome, to the days when being a member of the Faith meant death, one would find the Masses back then would have many similarities to the Mass of today.

I hope no one ever has to go to a funeral Mass for a loved one cut down in the prime of his or her life, as I have. For me it was my 16-year-old sister Renate. The Mass rises to a whole new level in that sort of circumstance. It not only makes people remember a loved one, it also offers comfort because the loved one is being comforted by Jesus, Whose Real Presence is at the Mass and Who went through so much for us. The Mass reminds us of Jesus' sacrifice. The mystery of death is laid bare by the mystery of life. The Mass reminds us that in the darkest moments of our despair, new life awaits. It is a powerful experience that brings some consolation in the midst of untold suffering.

God can come into our lives with a powerful experience when we least expect it. The day I finished writing this book, my mom called and said she wanted to tell me she felt a great burden had been lifted from her shoulders. My sister's death, which I mentioned above, occurred 21 years ago. She died in a traffic accident along a rural stretch of highway near my childhood home in north central Ohio. My mother's fear had always been that my sister died alone on the road with no one to comfort her. An Ohio State Highway Patrol officer who treated two of my sister's friends for minor injuries tried to convince my parents that before he arrived, a Good Samaritan husband and wife had pulled over to assist my sister. However, my parents wondered if this was just a nice story he made up to ease their pain.

My mother always visited an elderly woman at a nearby nursing home who had no living relatives. Then this particular weekend, at this woman's funeral, a woman who had worked at the nursing home approached my mom. She asked my mom her name, since there were so few people there, and she recognized my mother from visiting patients. My mother gave this woman her name, and this woman proceeded to tell my mom that she and her husband were the two Good Samaritans who comforted my sister as she lay dying on the road. They prayed for her and waited until the Highway Patrol and the ambulance arrived. A 21-year burden was lifted from my parents' shoulders as they realized that someone actually was there, praying and consoling my sister. The reason my mom went to this nursing home was that my sister, 21 years before, would visit those who had no relatives because she was moved to aid the elderly after seeing a program on television. After my sister's death, my mom went weekly.

The twenty-first anniversary of my sister's death had been especially tough since my mom was regularly seeing my sister's friends' children out and about in the community. Yet in the depths of despair, the Holy Spirit found a way for my mom and this Good Samaritan to meet and thereby eased my parents' pain. My family was helped for many years by a community of believers, many of which represented that spirit of "Catholic community."

Catholicism is universal. Just as someone traveling back in time would find that Mass was celebrated in ages past in much the same way it is today, they would also see how Mass is celebrated the same across the world. The word "Catholic" comes from the Greek word for "universal," and the Church is certainly that. Never was this universality more apparent than at the various World Youth Days when youth from over 100 countries gathered in one spot every two or three years to celebrate and worship together. Many have recognized a religious calling through their experiences at such a unifying and historical event.

Coffey's third point was that Catholics make bold claims about the faith. The more I thought about Coffey's third reason, the more the image of Jesus healing the paralytic man came to mind. The Pharisees tried to stop Jesus, asking how He could say this man's sins were forgiven. They wanted to throw the forgiveness of sins in His face, but Jesus rebuffed them by meeting their question head on. He asked them which would be easier, for Him to tell the man his sins were forgiven, or for the man to pick up his mat and walk away (keep in mind that the popular belief back then was that the man was paralytic precisely because he had sinned)? When the man walked away healed, many became believers (cf. Lk. 8:18-26).

The Church makes bold claims. She claims she is the one, true faith, that she alone has the fullness of truth. She claims that Jesus is truly present in what looks like ordinary bread and wine. She says Mary was immaculately conceived, that she herself conceived and then gave birth while keeping her virginity intact, and that she not only remained ever virgin, but was assumed body and soul into heaven at the end of her life.

These bold claims cause small miracles in that they help hardened sinners to transform their lives, so that those once lost now are found. They help the philanderer become chaste. They cause someone to think, 'The Church gave me help and love when I needed it most. That old lady over there is struggling with her groceries. I'll go help her out as a way of paying God back for all He's done for me.' They prompt a family to give a homebound person a ride to Mass or an elderly couple to sacrifice some of their fixed income for the needs of the parish and or school.

I began the chapter talking about the beauty of the Catholic tradition, a tradition that goes back 2,000 years. Think about where we are now. How many countries across the world have sizeable Catholic populations? How did these populations get so large, and why are some of strongest and most devout Catholic communities also some of the poorest? The love possessed by a Catholic missionary, whether in the fifth century, the fifteenth century or the twentieth century helped these people to see the light of the Church. Unlike some denominations, the Catholic Church is growing wherever you find it. The same can be said for vocations. Only in Europe and North America is there a priest shortage, and in North American that tide seems to be turning. Perhaps the harvest will be late in coming to Europe, but it will come, and when it does, it will be great.

Have you ever been on vacation with a churchgoing non-denominational Protestant family? My experience is that they either don't go to church or they look at the phone book and feel like they are at the craps table in Vegas wondering what their vacation church might have in store for them.

Catholics, though? Sure, they may have to sit through a priest's boring homily or suffer through an inappropriate, even horrifying liturgy when they go to a strange parish. But by and large they know they will get the once for all sacrifice of Calvary on the altar re-presented (however imperfectly).

In fact, Catholics have known for 2,000 years what they are getting. All Catholic churches recite the Nicene Creed, for example, which was established in 325 AD. There will be a crucifix and a tabernacle, and there will be a priest from the priesthood Jesus established. There will also be some form of a confessional, a sacrament that Jesus established (cf., Jn. 20:22-23). There will be the Mass Jesus established at the Last Supper, and there people will find His Real Presence in the Eucharist (cf., Jn. 6:32-71). When people travel and find themselves in need of assistance, the same Catholic Church that has assisted pilgrims for centuries will be there to aid them. If travelers meet with an awful tragedy, or someone close to them is severely ill or injured, a priest will be there to perform last rites or anointing of the sick, something priests have done for ages (cf., Mk. 6:31).

All Christian doctrine is united in teaching that because of Christ's death and resurrection, Satan is finished. We know the ending to this story. However, much like a remnant band of soldiers who would rather kill as many as they can before they are defeated, Satan and his demons continue their attempts to snatch victory out of the jaws of defeat. We know Satan will not win but, like that remnant band of soldiers, he and his minions can bring far too many souls with them. Thus the abuse scandal was another desperate attempt on his part to ruin the institution Christ created with these words: "And I say to you, you are Peter and upon this rock I will build My Church, and the gates of the netherworld shall not prevail against it. I will give you the keys to the kingdom of Heaven. Whatever you bind on earth shall be bound in Heaven: and whatever you loose on earth shall be loosed in Heaven" (Mt. 16:18-19).

With those words, Christ entrusted St. Peter with the authority to lead the Church. St. Peter became the first pope, and every subsequent pope is his successor. The Church believes its teaching authority comes from two sources, Scripture and Tradition, both of which come from Christ. While Martin Luther only believed in *sola scriptura*, the Catholic Church believes in Scripture plus Tradition, as St. Paul explains in 1 Cor. 11:2 and 2 Thes. 2:15. How could it be that we ignore all the wisdom of the great men and women God sent us in the 1,900 years after the apostolic era? Catholics believe God continues to speak His wisdom through the Church to all of His children, and this wisdom is consistent with Scripture and Tradition. God would never go against His own word; it would be impossible for Him to do so.

When we see orthodox Catholicism taught, we see the fruits of 2,000 years of the Holy Spirit's guidance. We also see this in the sacraments and in the witness of love by those around the world. We see it in a reenergized youth at events like World Youth Day, where they embrace sacraments such as Confession so heartily that priests end up hearing Confessions for hours at a time. We see it in the burgeoning crop of vocations, especially in the Third World, where many have responded to the call of Popes John Paul II and Benedict XVI in record numbers. We see it in Catholic Charities and in Catholic Relief Services, where the destitute are being shown love and kindness in the midst of suffering and destruction.

Who couldn't have been moved by the events of April 2005 when millions descended on Vatican City for John Paul's funeral and Benedict's election? The multitudes, coupled with the signs, symbols, and traditions of the Church, were a powerful testament not only to believers but also to non-believers as well.

The Catholic Church is a sleeping giant. In it rests the hopes, dreams, knowledge, and faith of 2,000 years. Sometimes the road may be lonely and frustrating. I can't tell you how many Catholic authors and musicians I have talked to who are sad that Catholic books and music are not being sold or marketed in the way they would like. However, on the other hand, they see all the hopes, dreams, knowledge and faith of that sleeping giant slowly being realized. Much like most Spring dawns, many feel a slight chill, but the old and wise know the day is only beginning, and the warmth and glow of a beautiful sunny day will soon be here.

It is easy to forget that in the dark days of World War II, many had their doubts about the future of all churches, let alone the Catholic Church. Some saw doom and gloom for the world. In their eyes, democracy and faith were out, and totalitarianism, conquest, and death were in. However, World War II's aftermath brought about what some believe was Catholicism's Golden Age.

A few years ago I ask an older priest, Fr. Thomas Shonebarger, why the 1940s and 1950s were Catholicism's Golden Era?[qqq] Fr. Shonebarger actually knew Fr. Thomas Merton, the famous scholarly monk and author of one of the greatest stories of faith in the twentieth century, *The Seven Story Mountain*. They met when he studied at the Abbey of Gethsemani in Kentucky. For a time, he even served as Merton's assistant. Fr. Shonebarger looked at me and smiled, and said, "David, you did not live through World War II. You could

---

[qqq] While many believe this, others have a different take. Fr. John Hardon, SJ, and others say this period is when all the problems began that came to a head at and after Vatican II.

never understand why faith was so important to all, and [why] the seminaries were full in the 1940s and 1950s."

He must have noticed the puzzled look on my face. Then standing in front of me, he put his hand on my shoulder and said, "In the 1940s and 1950s, too many children did not have a living father, too many wives no longer had their husbands, and too many brothers and sisters no longer had a brother. 'How could this all happen, and what did it mean?' many thought. They took their concerns to the only place they could get an answer, their house of worship. I can remember having to go to Mass early on Sundays just so we didn't stand. Morning Mass was also well attended by the young and old. Lancaster [Ohio] was hardly a metropolis, but even Mass in that small town was always well attended. We had to make sense of the horror we just experienced."

Today people of faith, Catholics included, struggle with many problems both in their own lives and a world filled with anxiety, terrorism, disease, etc. In any struggle, one is often comforted by familiarity and the knowledge that others have gone through similar trials and tribulations. The Catholic Church is a 2,000-year-old Church full of stories of men and women experiencing and persevering through many trials and tribulations. Catholic churches are full of symbols representing the 2,000-year-old history of these men and women.

Although we may turn away from it in modern times, struggle has been part of the faith since the beginning. Some Catholics in the world today know about that struggle, but all Catholics know the Church will be there for them as she has been for 2,000 years through the good and the bad. Three centuries after the Roman Empire tried to destroy Christ and His Church, His disciples brought that empire to its knees with their weapons of faith, hope, and love. Then, when it had fallen into ruin, those believers tried to build up the same empire that had tried to destroy them. Something like the scenario that continues in modern times, where faithful are trying to build up the world in the image of Christ, even as some in our world attack the faith He preached.

Today the Catholic Church leads the spiritual traveler through life with seven sacraments and with the love and mercy it has given the world for two millennia. In whichever part of the world the traveler may be, one thing has held true since the days of Christ and His apostles: The journey may be long but its fruits are beyond compare. Travelers have sought these fruits for 2,000 years. Wherever a traveler is in his or her journey, he or she can take solace in the fact that Jesus, His apostles, and their successors will help lead the way.

NOTES:

Chapter 1: Events of April 2005

1. *Pope John Paul II*, CBS Television, originally aired April 2006

2. George Weigel, *God's Choice: Pope Benedict XVI and the Future of the Catholic Church*, p. 65, New York, Harper Collins, 2005

3. MSNBC, "Hardball with Chris Matthews" www.msnbc.com", April 14, 2005

4. Sr. Joan Chittister "He was the Grandfather of Their Souls," *National Catholic Reporter*, www.ncr.com, April 8, 2005

5. "Andrew Sullivan Reflects on the Pontificate of Pope John Paul II," www.andrewsullivan.com, April 7-8, 2005

6. *PJ Kennedy & Sons Catholic Directory*, National Register Publishing, 2005

7. Kathleen Parker, "The World Needs a Father," *USA Today*, April 10, 2005

8. JJ Haynes-Rivas, "Surprised By Grief," *National Catholic Reporter Online*, May 13, 2005 http://ncronline.org

9. "Betting on the Papal Election," CNN, www.cnn.com, April 17-18, 2005

10. Cardinal Ratzinger's homily at the Mass for the opening of the Conclave as seen on coverage by EWTN, April 18, 2005

11. Fr. Richard John Neuhaus, "Libertas Ecclesiae," *First Things*, http://www.firstthings.com/romediary/romediary.htm#041805, April 18, 2005

12. "Scarborough Country," Joe Scarborough, "Mea Culpa On Doubts About the Election of Pope Benedict, MSNBC Television, April 20, 2006

Chapter 2: Defenders of the faith (Laity)

1. Patrick Madrid, *Surprised By Truth*, www.surprisedbytruth.com

2. Catholic Answers, www.catholicanswers.com

3. Amy Welborn, "Open Book Blog," www.amywelborn.typepad.com/openbook

4. Matthew Pinto, Ascension Press, www.ascensionpress.com

5. Arthur Jones, "The Roman Imposition," *National Catholic Reporter*, www.natcath.com, September 9, 2005

6. E-mail correspondence from Ramon Tancinco

7. Dave Hartline, "What If Catholic Remarks Were In The Ohio State House And No One Told You? January 2006, www.catholicreport.org

Chapter 3: Youth Embrace Catholic Tradition

1. CBS Movie, *Pope John Paul II*, April 2006

2. George Weigel, *God's Choice: Pope Benedict XVI and the Future of the Catholic Church*, p. 65, New York, Harper Collins, 2005

3. Tim Drake, *Young and Catholic*, p. 99, Manchester, New Hampshire, Sophia Institute Press, 2004

4. Jim Stingl, "Ratzinger Photo Serves As Memento Of Visit To Rome, Not Hero Worship," *Milwaukee Journal Sentinel*, April 4, 2005

5. Fr. Bill Hahn, Epiphany homily, at St. Joan of Arc Church, Powell, Ohio, January 2006

6. Personal interview with Bishop Robert Carlson, Diocese of Saginaw, Michigan, www.catholicreport.org, May 1, 2005

7. Cardinal Francis George, "One Year After the Death of Pope John Paul II," CNN, April 2006

8. Archbishop Renato Baccardo, "One Year After the Death of Pope Paul II," CNN, April 2006

Chapter 4: Growth of Tradition in the Clergy and Religious Orders

1. Sisters of Mary, Ann Arbor, Michigan, www.sistersofmary.com

2. Personal conversation with Sr. Ave Maria, St. Joan of Arc Church, Powell, Ohio, January 2006

3. Personal conversation with a priest who wishes to remain anonymous, 1999.

4. Tim Drake, *Young and Catholic*, p. 179, Sophia Institute Press, Manchester, New Hampshire, 2004

5. *PJ Kennedy & Sons Catholic Directory*, National Register Publishing, 2005

6. Interview with Bishop Frederick Campbell, Diocese of Columbus, March 24, 2006

7. Conversation with Fr. Bill Hahn, associate pastor, St Joan of Arc, Powell, Ohio, April 27, 2006

8. Jeff Ziegler, "Priestly Vocations In America: A Look At The Numbers," *Catholic World Report*, July 2005

9. Byron Pitts, "The New Faces of Faith," CBS Evening News, April 11, 2005

10. Conversation with Fr. Victor Udechukwu, Nigerian priest currently working in the Wheeling-Charleston Diocese, April 4, 2006

11. "57 Priests Ordained in Hanoi, Vietnam," *Catholic World News*, www.cwnews.com, March 2006

12. Professor Mark Ruff, Saint Louis University, e-mail correspondence, March 2006

13. Interview with Bishop Robert Carlson Diocese of the Saginaw, www.CatholicReport.org, May 1, 2006

14. Interview with FOCUS spokeswoman Nikki Shasserre, www.CatholicReport.org, April 4, 2006

Chapter 5: Defender of the Faith – Clergy and Religious

1. Conversation with a priest who wished not to be identified, 1999.

2. Kathryn Jean Lopez, "The Media Mogul You Never Heard Of," *National Review Online*, www.nationalreview.com/nr_comment/nr_comment081501a.shtml, August 15, 2001

3. Raymond Arroyo, *Mother Angelica: The Remarkable Story of a Nun, Her Nerve, and a Network of Miracles*, New York, Doubleday, 2005

4. Interview with Bishop Frederick Campbell, Diocese Of Columbus, March 24, 2006

5. Interview with Bishop Robert Kurtz, CR, Diocese of Bermuda, www.CatholicReport.org, November 17, 2005

6. Interview with Fr. Jeff Rimmelspach, pastor of St. Joan of Arc Parish, Powell, Ohio, March 30, 2006

7. Interview with Bishop Robert Carlson, Diocese of Saginaw, May 1, 2006

Chapter 6: There's Something About Mary

1. "Mary and the Church," Catholic Answers, www.catholicanswers.com

2. "Marian Apparitions," EWTN, www.ewtn.com/faith/Teachings/Maryd7.htm

3. "Italian Commission Says Bulgarians, KGB Assisted In Papal Assassination Plot," Reuters, March 3, 2006.

4. Lt. Col. John Guilmartin, USAF, "Tactics at the Battle of Lepanto Clarified: The Impact of Social, Economic and Political Factions on 16th Century Galley Warfare," www.angelfire.com/ga4/guilmartin.com/Lepanto.html

5. "Fatima & Guadalupe," Living Miracles, www.livingmiracles.net/Guadalupe

6. "Mary Apparitions," EWTN, www.ewtn/faith/Teachings/Maryd7.htm

7. Zeitoun News, www.zeitoun.org

8. John Ankerberg, "What About Marian Apparitions," www.ankerberg.org/roman-catholicism

9. Dave Hartline, "The Truth About What Happened in Carey," www.CatholicReport.org, August 2005

10. Ian Paisley, Wikipedia Internet Encyclopedia http://enwiki.org/ianpaisley

11. John Leo, "Bush's Appearance At Bob Jones U Will Dog Him All The Way," www.jewishworldnews.com, March 1, 2000

12. Dr. Scott Hahn, *Hail, Holy Queen*, p. 174-75, New York, Doubleday, 2001

13. Dr. Ludwig Ott, *Fundamentals of Catholic Dogma*, book 3, part 3, Ch. 2, §3.1.e

14. http://en.wikipedia.org/wiki/Immaculate_Conception

15. Personal conversation with Notre Dame Football Coach Gerry Faust, October 2005. Referenced story from his book, *The Golden Dream*, Champaign, Illinois, Sports Publishing, LLC, 1997

Chapter 7: Eucharist and the Catholic Embrace of It

1. Bruce Heydt, "Turning Point: Luther's Lost Opportunity," *Christianity Today*, www.christianitytoday.com, January 11, 2004

2. Cardinal Joseph Ratzinger, *Pilgrim Fellowship of Faith*, pp106-107, San Francisco, Ignatius Press, 2005

3. "Pope Benedict Calls Church the Link that Brings True Communion Between God, Mankind," Catholic News Agency, www.catholicnewsagency.com,March 30, 2006

4. "Politically Incorrect," ABC Television, March 5, 2002. Reported in *The Catholic League 2002 Annual Report*, www.catholicleague.org

5. "Justin Martyr First Apology, 151 AD," *Catholic Answers*, www.catholic.com

6. Fr. John A Hardon, SJ, "The History of Eucharistic Adoration," www.cfpeople.org/Apologetics

7. Clare Lazzuri, "Return To The Mysteries of the Eucharist, Says Father Groeschel," www.CatholicHerald.com

8. Ibid

9. Personal interview with Tom Craughwell, April 2006.

10. St. Katherine Drexel, EWTN Library, www.ewtn.com

11. "Atlanta Vocations Boom Attributed To Adoration," www.perpetualadoration.org

12. Ed Wilkinson, "Bishop Calls For Perpetual Adoration of the Eucharist," *The Tablet*, May 2003

13. Personal interview with Bishop Robert Carlson, Diocese of Saginaw, www.CatholicReport.org, May 1, 2006

14. "Ancient Roman Catholic Ritual Makes Comeback," WCCO TV, January 2005

15. "More Parishes in Archdiocese Discovering Benefits of Perpetual Adoration," *The Criterion*, October 28, 2005.

16. Chris Kelly, e-mail correspondence, May 14, 2006

17. Clare Lazzuri, "Return to the Mysteries of the Eucharist, Says Father Groeschel," www.CatholicHerald.com

18. Kathryn Jean Lopez, "The Media Mogul You Never Heard Of," *National Review Online*, http://www.nationalreview.com/nr_comment/nr_comment081501a.shtml, August 15, 2001

19. Karl Keating, "Eucharist," Catholic Answers, www.catholic.com

20. Personal interview with Fr. Bill Hahn, associate pastor of St. Joan of Arc, Powell, Ohio, April 27, 2006

Chapter 8: Catholic Schools

1. Timothy Walch, *Parish School: American Catholic Parochial Education from Colonial Times to the Present*, p 263, New York, Crossroad Herder, 1995

2. Lucia McQuaide, e-mail correspondence, March 14, 2006

3. Sandy Lape, e-mail correspondence, March 21, 2006

4. Kitty Quinn, e-mail correspondence March 21, 2006

5. Dianna Dudzinski, e-mail correspondence, March 14, 2006

6. Susan Shaver, e-mail correspondence March 16, 2006

7. "National Study of Youth and Religion," a research report produced for the National Federation of Catholic Youth Ministry, December 2004

8. Nina Shokraii Rees, "Why Catholic Schools Spell Success For America's Inner-city Children," Heritage Foundation, www.heritage.org/Research/UrbanIssues/BG1128.cfm, June 30, 1997

9.   Jeri Rod, e-mail correspondence, May 16, 2006

10. National Catholic Education Association, www.ncea.org

11. Interview with Bishop Robert Carlson, Diocese of Saginaw, www.CatholicReport.org, May 1, 2006

12. Fr. Tim Hayes, e-mail correspondence, March 30, 2006

13. Joy Patterson, e-mail correspondence, May 15, 2006

14. George Archibald, "Public Schools No Place For Teacher's Kids," *Washington Times*, September 24, 2004

15. Rocco Fumi, e-mail correspondence, March 15, 2006

16. Interview with Mike Winters, principal of Bishop Hartley High School, April 25, 2006

17. Correspondence with Dan Garrick, principal of St Francis DeSales High School, March 16, 2006

18. Fr. Tim Hayes, e-mail correspondence, March 21, 2006

Chapter 9: Catholic Higher Education

1.   Tim Drake, "Some Faculty Offended By Cardinal Arinze's Remarks At Georgetown," *National Catholic Register*, May 2003

2.   Julia Dunn, "Answer To Prayer," *Washington Times*, September 8, 2003

3.   Tamar Lewin, "A Catholic College Will Rise In Florida," *New York Times*, February 10, 2003

4. Tim Drake, *Young and Catholic*, p. 55, Manchester, New Hampshire, Sophia Institute Press, 2004

5. Interview with FOCUS Spokeswoman Nikki Shasserre, www.CatholicReport.org, April 4, 2006

Chapter 10: Catholicism and Popular Culture

1. Emily Fredix, "Catholics Hope to Get in on Religious Radio Boom," *USA Today*, January 1, 2006

2. Julia Dunn "5,000 Pastors Cheer Mel Gibson's Passion," *Washington Times*, January 21, 2004

3. Amy Welborn, *Decoding Da Vinci*, pp. 23-111, Huntington, Indiana, Our Sunday Visitor, 2004

4. "Praise For the "Da Vinci Code," DanBrown.com

5. "God or the Girl," A&E Network, www.A&E.com

6. Interview with Dan DeMatte, www.CatholicReport.org, April 2006

7. Interview with Fr. Jeff Coning, www.CatholicReport.org, April 2006

8. Ryan Hammel, "Tolkien and Led Zeppelin," www.louisville.edu/~rlhammer03/LOTRZeppelin.html

9. Interview with Tony Melendez, www.CatholicReport.org, November 2005

10. Interview with Larry Nolte, May 9, 2006

11. E-mail correspondence with David Wang, May 16, 2006

12. Conversation with Jerry Elliott, May 17, 2006

Chapter 11: Catholic Athletes & Coaches

1. Interview with Lou Holtz, www.CatholicReport.org, October 24, 2005

2. Interview with Gerry Faust, www.CatholicReport.org, October 25, 2005

3. Dave Hartline, "Charlie Weis A Coach Who Leads By Example" www.CatholicReport.org, October 17, 2006

4. Interview with Rudy Ruettiger, www.CatholicReport.org, October 2005

5. Interview with Danny Abramowicz, EWTN, August 5, 2004, excerpted in *Our Sunday Visitor*, www.osv.com/danny

6. Interview with Dick Vitale, May 9, 2006

7. Carol Glatz, "Olympic Biathlete From Minnesota Finds Calm, Strength In Prayer," *Catholic News Service*, February 14, 2006

Chapter 12: Megachurches, Salvation, and Other Debated Issues

1. Ralph Blumenthal, "A Preacher's Credo: Eliminate the Negative, Accentuate Prosperity," *New York Times*, March 30, 2006.

2. Rick Warren, *The Purpose Driven Church*, Grand Rapids, MI, Zondervan, 1995

3. Interview with President Norman Dewire, Methodist Theological Seminary of Ohio, April 2006

4. Rick Warren, interview on "Larry King Live," CNN, March 2005

5. Frank Lockwood, "Defense of Canceling Church on Christmas," *Lexington Herald-Leader*, December 11, 2005

6. "Some Megachurches Closing For Christmas," titusonenine, http://titusonenine.classicalanglican.net

7. "Profile of Total US Megachurches," Hartford Institute of Religious Research. http://hirr.hartsem.edu/org/megastoday2005_profile.html

8. Patrick Madrid, St. Joan of Arc Parish talk, July 2005

9. "Catholics and the Bible," Catholic Answers. http://www.catholicanswers.com

10. Ibid

11. Thomas Sowell, *Black Rednecks and White Liberals*, pgs. 24-27, San Francisco, Encounter Books, 2005

12. Ibid

13. Ibid

14. Lynyrd Skynyrd, "Simple Man," *Pronounced Leh-Nerd Skin-Nerd*, MCA Records, 1973. Lynyrd Skynyrd "What's Your Name," Street Survivors, MCA Records, 1977.

15. Carl Olson, "LeHaying the Rapture on Thick," *Envoy Magazine*, taken from Envoy Online, http://envoymagazine.com

16. Interview with Sarah Lawrence, PhD, professor of Theology, Methodist Theological Seminary of Ohio, April 2006

17. Hal Lindsey, *The Late Great Planet Earth*, Grand Rapids, Michigan, Zondervan Publishing House, 1977

18. Carl Olson, "LeHaying the Rapture on Thick," *Envoy Magazine*, taken from Envoy Online, http://envoymagazine.com

19. Jimmy Akin, "False Prophet," www.catholianswers.com

20. Interview with Fr. Bill Hahn, Associate Pastor of St. Joan of Arc Church, Powell, Ohio

22. "Confession," Catholics Answers, www.catholicanswers.com

Chapter 13: Decline of the Liberal Church

1. Dave Shiflett, Exodus; *Why Americans Are Fleeing Liberal Churches For Conservative Christianity*, p. xiii (Introduction), New York, Sentinel, 2005

2. Ibid.

3. Michael Lampen, "Bishop James Pike: Visionary or Heretic?" www.gracecathedral.org

4. Dave Shiflett, *Exodus; Why Americans Are Fleeing Liberal Churches For Conservative Christianity*, pgs. 48-49, New York, Sentinel, 2005

5. Charles Flagherty, E-mail Correspondence, July 2006.

6. Ruth Gledhill, "Cherie Meets Pope Benedict as Speculation Grows that Blair Will Convert," *London Times*, April 29, 2006

7. Interview with Norman Dewire, president of the Ohio Methodist Theological Seminary

8. E-mail correspondence with David Bennett, May 12, 2006

9. Report From the Episcopal General Convention, June 15 -22, 2006, www.CatholicReport.org

Chapter 14: The Crusades – Mean Old Bullies or Defenders of the Faith?

1. "Messages of Osama Bin Laden & Dr Ayman Al Zawahiri," Intel Center, www.intelcenter.com

2. Thomas Madden, *A Concise History of the Crusades: Critical Issues in History*, Lanham, Maryland, Rowman and Littlefield, Inc., 1999

3. Ken Ringle, "Crusaders' Giant Footprints," *Washington Post*, October 23, 2001

4. "Wahhabism," taken From Wikipedia, http://en.wikipedia.org/wiki/Wahhabism

5. Steve Emerson, "Abdullah Assam: The Man Before Osama Bin Laden," www.iacsp.com

6. "Sayyid Qutb," Wikipedia, http://en.wikipedia.org/wiki/Sayyid-Qutb

7. "Pope John Paul II Kisses Koran," Gregaitis, www.grgaitis.net/articles/scandals.html

8. See http://en.wikipedia.org/wiki/Dhimmitude and http://akouri.blogspot.com/

9.   Don Feder, "Berlusconi backs Western civilization," *World Net Daily*, http://www.worldnetdaily.com/news/article.asp?ARTICLE_ID=24827

10. Robert Spencer, *The Politically Incorrect Guide To Islam (and the Crusades)* p. 113 Washington, DC, Regnery Publishing Inc. 2005

11. "Battle of Lepanto," ETWN Library, www.ewtn.com/library/mary/olislam.htm

12. Patrick Egbuchunam, response to Pope Benedict's Regensburg address, September 18, 2006, www.CatholicReport.org

13. Robert Spencer interview, www.CatholicReport.org, September 2005

14. "Catholic Priest Murdered In Turkey," *Catholic World News*, www.cwnews.com, February 6, 2006

15. "Islamic Protests Against Danish Cartoon Controversy Use Violent Images," *Jihad Watch*, http://www.jihadwacth.org, February 2006

16. Cardinal George Pell, "Islam and Western Democracies," Legatus Summit, Naples, Florida, www.sydney.catholic.org.au, April 2, 2006

17. "Islamic Protests Against Danish Cartoon Controversy Use Violent Images," Jihad Watch, www.jihadwatch.org, February 2006

Chapter 15: Catholic Vote

1.   Dave Shiflett, *Exodus; Why Americans Are Fleeing Liberal Churches For Conservative Christianity*, p. 82, New York, Sentinel, 2005

2.   George Marlin, *The American Catholic Voter: 200 Years of Political Impact,* p 322, South Bend, Indiana, St. Augustine's Press 2004

3. United States Catholic Conference of Catholic Bishops, www.usccb.com

4. CNN exit poll data, www.cnn.com/Election/2004

5. Paul Kengor, "Kerry Loses His Faith," *American Spectator*, www.americanspectator.org

6. George Marlin, *The American Catholic Voter: 200 Years of Political Impact*, South Bend, Indiana, St. Augustine's Press, 2004

7. Terry Mattingly, "Whither the Catholic, Catholic Voters?" www.gospelcom.net

8. Ibid

9. David Kirkpatrick, "For Democrats, Rethinking Abortion Run Risks," New York Times, February 16, 2005

10. "Evangelicals and Catholic Together: The Christian Mission in the New Millennium," Fr. Richard John Neuhaus, Charles Colson, *First Things*, May 1994, www.firstthings.com/ftissues/ft9405/mission.html

11. Terence Samuel, "Battle Born," *American Prospect Online*, January 28, 2005, www.prospect.org

12. George Marlin, *The American Catholic Voter: 200 Years of Political Impact*, p. 335, South Bend, Indiana, St. Augustine's Press, 2004

13. Deborah Gyapong, "Quebec Catholic Desert Liberals in Droves," Western Catholic Reporter, www.wcr.ab.ca

Chapter 16: Catholic Social Issues, Social Action, and Good Works

1. See http://www.rcam.org/library/pastoral_statements/1981-1986/0013.htm

2. R. Albert Mohler, Jr., "Can Christians Use Birth Control?" *Christian Post*, www.christianpost.com December 28, 2005

3. Tim Stafford "Abortion Wars," *Christianity Today*, January 22, 2003

4. Tucker Carlson, "Interview with Governor George W Bush," *Talk Magazine*, September 1999.

5. Agnieszka Tennant, "A Hard Pill to Swallow," *Christianity Today*, www.christianitytoday.com/ct/2005/011/22.70.html, November 8, 2005

6. R. Albert Mohler, Jr., "Can Christians Use Birth Control?" *Christian Post*

7. "2005 Hurricane Relief Facts and Figures," Catholic Charities, www.catholiccharities.usa.org

8. E-mail correspondence from Joel Torczon, March 16, 2006

Chapter 17: Now You See ...The Tide is Turning

1. Interview with Bishop Frederick Campbell, Diocese of Columbus, March 24, 2006

2. "History of the Catholic Church," Catholic Answers, www.catholicanswers.com

3. "Background for the Madrid Bombings," Debka Files, www.debka.com, March 14, 2004

4. Personal reflections of a priest in my parish who was convicted of molestation and various other crimes.

5. "Evangelicals and Catholics Together," *First Things*, (May 1994), pgs 15-22, www.firstthings.com/ftissues/ft9405/mission.html

6. Steve Ray, "My Name is Alex Jones," Ignatius Insight, www.ignatiusinsight.com

7. "Peter is the Rock," *Catholic Answers*, www.catholic.com/thisrock/1998/9801word.asp

8. Ken Camp, "Notre Dame Model for Baylor Generates Debate," *Baptist Standard*, February 17, 2006, www.baptiststandard.com

9. Rob Moll, "Mark Noll Leaving Wheaton for Notre Dame," *Christianity Today*, February 9, 2006, www.christianitytoday.com

10. Amy Welborn, "Evangelicals and Catholics Not Together," www.amywelborn.com, January 7, 2006

11. Kathy Coffey, "Ten Reasons to be Catholic", *Catholic Update*, http://www.americancatholic.org/Newsletters/CU/ac0498.asp

INDEX

Purpose Driven Church, The, 154
Purpose Driven Life, The, 154

Q

Quinn, Kitty, 109
Qutb, Sayyid, 205

R

Rapture, 164, 167, 173-177, 180, 181
Ratzinger, Joseph Cardinal (see also Benedict XVI), 9-13, 24, 26, 39, 92
Reagan, President Ronald Wilson, 36, 72, 217, 229, 257
Reconciliation, Sacrament of (see also Penance, Sacrament of), 33, 38,
    179, 180
Regensburg address of Pope Benedict XVI, 205, 212, 215
Reni, Guido, 137
REO Speedwagon, 130
Rimmelspach, Fr. Jeff, 66-67
Roberts, US Supreme Court Chief Justice John, 241
Robinson, Episcopalian Bishop Gene, 185, 190, 191, 193-195
Rod, Jeri, 111
Roe v. Wade, 238, 240, 241,
Roemer, former Congressman Tim, 226, 231
Rosary, 33, 54, 69, 74, 82-84, 116, 119, 144, 155, 209, 258
Rossetti, Patrick, 114
Ruettiger, Rudy, 144, 146-147
Russell, Episcopalian Reverend Susan, 191-193, 194, 195

S

St. Ambrose, 70, 238
St. Anthony of Padua, 148
St. Athanasius, 70, 190
St. Augustine, 70, 99, 117, 170, 175, 178, 211

DAVID J. HARTLINE

ABOUT THE AUTHOR

David Hartline is a former Catholic school teacher, coach, principal, and diocesan administrator. In addition to his educational experiences, he has also worked for a think tank on Capitol Hill in Washington, DC. Hartline is the founder and editor of the Catholic Report web site (CatholicReport.org). He and his family reside in the Columbus, Ohio, area.

DAVID J. HARTLINE

To get the latest in news about the Church and the world, or to order copies of this book online, go to www.CatholicReport.org.

GIVE A GIFT OF HOPE AND INSPIRATION TO YOUR LOVED ONES.

Ask us about bulk discounts available on orders of 10 or more copies. Contact us at:

Catholic
WORD

W5180 Jefferson St.
Necedah, WI 54646
Phone: 800-932-3826
Fax: 608-565-2025